The INDIA I Know
And of HINDUISM

The INDIA I Know And of HINDUISM

from a south Indian woman writer

Indira G

PARTRIDGE

To order additional copies of this book, contact
Partridge India
000 800 10062 62
orders.india@partridgepublishing.com

www.partridgepublishing.com/india

CONTENTS

I dedicate this book to my mother
Kuchibhotla Durgavathi

ACKNOWLEDGEMENTS

First and foremost, I thank my husband Sri G. K. Rao for all the support given in writing this book and for other pursuits and endeavours that led to my writing. Next, to my two sons, for their keen intent and effort in showing me the Western world (the UK, Europe, and USA) by personally taking me to places to get a perspective. I am also indebted to Sri Arun Shourie, who indirectly helped me to understand India and the world affairs on wide-ranging topics especially, in the 1990s through his knowledgeable columns. I thank Pragna Bharati team for their continual support while I worked and for the consent to publish the reports and articles required. In this regard, I personally owe much to both the organising and joint organising secretaries of the present setup, Sri B. S. Sarma and N. Nagaraja Rao for their help. Last but not least, to Sri Ram Madhav (general secretary-BJP) for his encouragement when he was the organising secretary of Pragna Bharati, Hyderabad.

PREFACE

The narrative of this book is based to an extent on my life journey starting from the year I joined as a teacher of English in a school in old city, Hyderabad in Andhra Pradesh (United) in 1988. After being a homemaker for nearly a decade, bringing up my two children, I joined the service. More than money, I had the urge to contribute something to the society by way of educating schoolchildren and to keep myself a productive citizen, which had driven me to the job. This activity of teaching in a school led me to a different kind of exposure to the outside world.

In this book, I began with Ram Janmabhoomi movement in Hyderabad, how the difficulties were faced by general public on those curfew days. The chaos and turmoil on the streets was agonizing both physically and mentally. In the course of time, how my thoughts and reactions for Ram Janmabhoomi movement emerged and how I got associated to an organisation backed by the RSS, I described in detail in my book. I did not have any Sangh background before being associated with them. I had grown up, basically, with patriotic feelings for the country and to respect all national leaders inculcated at school and home fronts like any ordinary Indian.

The impact of Ayodhya temple movement, here in south, was not as vigorous as in north of India. However, Sri Advani's Rath Yatra highlighted the matter throughout the length and breadth for the Hindu majorities to know that their genuine wishes were not respected by the secular governments. The reason being the appeasement of a section of minorities. The shooting of kar sevaks by the Samajwadi Party Government in Uttar Pradesh and the subsequent statements by all leaders were an eye-opener. The BJP had made a headway because of the Ram Janmabhoomi movement, otherwise a political non-entity in southern states in those days. Basically, the BJP has been stronger in the northern states of India. Hence, whatever I write should be viewed from a person of south, strongly from a Congress-ruled state.

Of course, in AP (United) we were also ruled by the TDP (Telugu Desam Party) for a reasonably long period. Both the Congress and the TDP were on the same page as far as so-called system of secularism practiced by the parties.

I also mentioned about two persons who influenced me tremendously during the course of time. One was Sri Arun Shourie, the renowned journalist and columnist whose writings I was drawn into at the time of Ayodhya movement. Before that, he was unknown to me as I never found time neither to read news nor to know the bigger picture of India (other than the local news) as I was a hands-on mother to my children in '80s. My brief interactions and correspondence with him also I made a mention of in this book.

The other person, besides Sri Arun Shourie, who influenced me was Sri Ram Madhav, the RSS Pracharak, in-charge of the organisation Pragna Bharati. I have had many interactions with him before joining the organisation. And because of the common interest evolved during the discussions, he then invited me into the organisation Pragna Bharati. I deliberated in this book the sequences of events that led me to get associated with the organisation. I elaborated in detail my impressions about Sri Arun Shourie and Sri Ram Madhav on their writings and work, which inspired me.

The affection of Sri Ram Madhav at that point of time made me to be a part of the organisation and to work. My knowledge of the RSS was insignificant initially. Ram Madhav had never told me how the RSS works. However, he occasionally provided much material that had been written by the organisation heads, some of which I have mentioned in my writing. A few thoughts are elicited from them.

As the organising-secretary, Sri Ram Madhav played a pivotal role in co-ordinating work within the organisation with his excellent skills in connecting to people and networking. He being the fountainhead, all of us were mere namesake and titular heads of organising bodies.

In some chapters of this book, I have just touched upon the topics of some important meetings of the organisation and have given important inputs to ponder from all the meetings. However, these meetings were conducted way back. Most of them were in 1995 and early 2000. After the organising secretary, Sri Ram Madhav, shifted to New Delhi in 2002, there was a slowdown in the activities of the organisation Pragna Bharati. And my presence in the organisation was minimal.

I also highlighted in certain chapters about my realisations on media and television debates. They were about the so-called secular-liberal voice of the media, where it went wrong in my opinion. After hearing the debates and opinions on all freedoms, nationalism, and other issues of importance, over a long period on English TV news channels, I have no doubt in my mind that many Indians do not know the language the media speaks or the thought they convey. There is a disconnect between common people and English media. The rights guaranteed and principles adopted in the Constitution, which the media tom-toms are unaware of by most of the Indians. For the common people go by conventions, culture, and traditions of this country. This is handed over to them invariably from their families for generations.

In the whole part of narrating incidents, my stand was more of a conservative Indian, occasionally that of a liberal. Further, writing about ideology does not carry immunity from ideology. However, I always feel that the English media enlightened me of things otherwise obscure to me. In this regard, I treat the celebrated anchors to be my gurus in a small way. They provided the ingredients to make my own recipe with added flavours that I faithfully dished out in the last chapters of the book.

The organisational work had not impaired my main work of teaching in the school. It is not me alone; many in the organisation was holding responsible positions in their offices and yet devoting their personal private time for the cause. Almost all the members in the organisation Pragna Bharati were employees of either state or central government undertakings, public sector banks, or reputed multinationals.

However, in this book, as it became imperative on my part, I bisected people of the country into communities only to show as an evidence, the malice that underlies because of certain policies of the so-called secular governments. My intention was to express perspectives and perceptions without bias and prejudice against any community.

I also have written many personal interactions and correspondence with eminent people, viz. Sri Arun Shourie and Sri Ram Madhav, which I have retrieved from my memory line. While retrieving, there perhaps may have been some short comings here and there, which not necessarily be construed as the deliberate choice of this author.

I want to place on record, whatever aberrations committed on my part were not intentional. I have no hesitation to humbly submit that at no point of time in my writing, I had any intention of hurting anyone's sentiments.

Last but not least, the objective of writing this book is to highlight for the younger generations about some facts that happened in the history and their impact on the present. A kind of a throwback! A kind of letting steam out of me! A kind of venting the agony! A kind of bringing awareness! I am not advocating the younger generation to join the politics, if it is not their priority, but I ask them to pay heed to what the politicians promise and what they deliver. I think they should have some grasp on the history of the country and the society around them. Certainly, that will help to evolve as a person. Today's generation has technology in hand; let that be not used in breach, let that be used as a privilege.

In conclusion, I would like to state that this book contains multi-faceted views, though the basic thread is my perceptions and my opinions.

INTRODUCTION

Life is so fascinating. It takes so many twists and turns. Sometimes, the turns are so unexpected that they change you and your mind-set so completely and so dramatically. You learn from places you go to and people around you. When you are thick in a community other than yours, and if that community behaves differently, there will be some shocks, for sure.

We all think that we are awake when we are not sleeping literally on bed, but that is not true. Sometimes we are unaware of some issues though we are awake. Is it because we are ignorant? Or is it because we are naive with no knowledge. It is not everybody's case to know everything. All of us know about our immediate surroundings and the issues that appeal to us or confront us.

In India, i.e. in our country, what I have noticed as a citizen is different sections of people have different interests. They are just bogged down by their daily chores. How to reach and when to reach their places of work is their main problem as far as the working sections are concerned. The others confine themselves home, doing work that they are compelled to by routine rigmarole of life. None of us have time to think of the burning issues the country is being plagued with. Of course, our politicians also speak what the people want to hear; what they are confronted within their day-to-day life rather than bigger issues of the country that need attention. That's the reason they are being called populist leaders!

I would like to take you back to 1990s and how the life was then and how the people were—to an extent it applies to now also - I am in South India; most of us here do not know about Dodo village in the north-east, Bodo land in Assam, Doda district or Ladakh in Jammu & Kashmir and what issues are terrifying or confronting the people there. J&K is not a big problem for us. We know that it is a part of our country and will not go elsewhere and shall remain so. We have confidence in the central government of whatever dispensation that it will in no way handover it to Pakistan. We have guaranteed it to our minds; hence the issue is over and settled in our minds and hearts. We are not perturbed by the disturbances there like any Indian in the north. For we are physically and geographically far away from the topmost state of India. Our local news carries very little about it (now, of course, with the cable/satellite TV in place J&K comes in headlines). Anyway, proximity also matters. We know (at least the educated sections) that there exists a Constitution for India. But most of us are not aware what is inside it. At least the salient features are also not known to most of the people. They never care to bother about the big things like the Constitution, for knowing that will not provide them their daily bread. Apart from doing their daily job, common people here are interested in seeing movies or indulge in drinking, probably it is some kind of merriment or enjoyment for them. You may ask a question: people of south, are they not educated? Have they not studied geography, history, and civics in their curriculum? Yes, of course, most of the educated have studied history, geography, and civics as subjects. We all have studied about UNO in class V when we do not know what our neighbouring state, city, or village is. Can we imagine UNO at that state of mind? So much so for our education system! The teachers ritualistically teach without knowing what goes into the student's head. If they have any problem regarding what they are teaching, the teachers cannot complain to anyone because the higher authorities are invincible and callous in attitude towards them. In India, the problem lies with individual egos. Hierarchy always comes into picture. Status always counts. People in the higher echelons matter, not the grass-root ones. The higher officers think the lower cadre as cannon fodder and bereft of worth, and to pay heed to them is worthless. This is all okay if the higher officers are really higher in knowledge. It's not so with many. Because they come to those positions by virtue of their seniority in service rather than by merit. Anyway, I thank the government for incorporating NATIONAL PLEDGE in all textbooks.

If it is properly understood and followed, there wouldn't be any differentiation of people, and cases like Nirbhaya wouldn't happen! But it is confined to the opening pages of the textbook only.

As I am a woman, I would like to begin with what a woman does as a daily routine. An ordinary middle-class woman's day starts with getting up early in the morning, washing vessels, collecting drinking water, cooking, going to place of work, working (that includes some amount of gossip also), lunch, coming home in the evening, watching TV, dinner, sleep. Same routine with slight changes follows for days and years together. When are people bothered about the problems of the country? Come elections, people of different sections see to the solution of their immediate problems, not the holistic problems of the country. None wants to go beyond 'me'. My world starts and stops with I, me, and myself. This is the reason why politicians make different promises to different sections. That's fine. Because everywhere in the world, people see to their welfare. The attitude is 'if I have food, if I have shelter, if I have robust health then I can think of higher things'. These are actually the rights of the people. Those who have these rights can talk of other issues. After all, life is not mere survival. It is more than survival. A better survival!

I started bothering about the country much only after I joined the job. A tremendous exposure to the outside world. Sitting at home like a housewife never enticed me after my children could do all their personal work by themselves and go to school. After all, women need to explore their potential other than doing their regular routine in the house. Of course, the working women know the world better. It also gives different perspective of the world to them. They will bring a different world view to home.

I started searching for a job intently. I wanted, out of my own volition, to do a teacher's job. I thought that it would not impair my household duties as much as the other office jobs, with holidays at every quarter apart from the summer vacation. I could be available at home after school hours to my children. It was always my responsibility to make them do their home assignment correctly, given by their teachers at school. I almost re-taught everything that was taught in school. I used to set mini question papers on their subjects to be answered. I also awarded marks to them as a sign of encouragement and discipline.

In those days of late '80s, job scenario in India was terrible. Getting a job was an uphill task. I used to worry that my children would not get job if they did not study properly. So, I was a strict mom to them. In fact, I wanted to join as a teacher in their school so that I would have a first-hand information on their studies and other activities. One day after their school re-opening (after the summer vacation), I went in and gave an application for a teacher post. The principal there read it and cut a sorry figure. She said that some posts, which were vacant earlier, got filled in the summer vacation after scrutiny and interviews were being done. I was late in seeking the job, she said. I was a little disappointed. For I was very keen on joining the same school where my children were studying for the simple reason that I could go along with them and could bring them back with me in a secured way. That apart I could also know their performance in studies from time to time. In general, women are always multi-tasking.

I tried in one or two other schools. I was almost rejected for not having any experience in teaching. That kind of refusals made me pursue the job more vigorously. One of my friends who was working in a school in Hyderabad asked me to apply in their school so that she could talk to the principal there. It was a regional medium school where my friend was teaching Telugu subject. They wanted an English teacher in their school. I have an M.A degree in English and also had the methodology of English teaching in my bachelor's degree of education. Since I was qualified for teaching English I gave an application, they needed an English teacher urgently, so, called me without delay. It was far off from my home. Initially, I was worried of reaching the place. My friend said working needed some compromises. She advised me to get up early and quicken the process of doing household work. And she gave an impression that they pay salary promptly on first of every month unlike other surrounding institutions that delay inordinately. She also convinced me to do for at least a year to get experience of teaching to students. So, I thought of what she said, weighed the options, balanced one with the other, the conditions prevailing, and came to a decision that I should give it a try. As far as my husband is concerned, he left the decision to me. He said, 'Whatever suits you, whatever makes you happy,' a standard answer for all my dilemmas and queries.

There were many women teachers in the school. Among them the Telugu teacher, my friend made the place familiar. She showed me the classrooms, which were pretty big and decent. The blackboards were long, carved out on the wall, and were often painted with black colour for the visibility of letters written on it. The school supply of chalk pieces was abundant, she said.

I took up the job as a futuristic decision to finance my children's education at college, if need be, and to supplement our finances. Of course, my first salary was a pleasure. It was a joy to see my hard-earned money in cash. I paid our house rent from my salary. Then I thought, doing job was not a bad idea. For any employee, the first of the month is the happiest day of the month, provided they get salary on that day. In some private schools, this privilege is not granted by the management as a deliberate policy or due to paucity of funds. Anyway, this particular school paid promptly.

Financial benefit was one part, and exposure to the world is another part. I always felt that there was an activist hidden in me. I started seeing the world before me in a new version. Those were the days of Ayodhya-Ram Janmabhoomi movement. L. K. Advani's Rath Yatra days. Old City of Hyderabad, being a communally volatile place, occasionally, riots erupted. Suddenly, curfews were imposed. Travelling from one place to another, commute from work to home were not easy. At times, life-threatening, if the person was in a communally, highly sensitive place. Situation during rioting period was tense. No one knew what would happen and when. At that point of time, I neither knew who L. K. Advani was nor why he was making the Yatra as I was not an avid reader of newspaper. Leaders of the north were not known much barring a few Congress leaders as the Congress Party had been ruling the state of Andhra Pradesh for a long time.

Slowly, the political picture at the central level started unfolding to me. When I started telling about the BJP, to which I newly started affiliating myself, to my friends and relatives, they used to say wonderingly, 'Oh! That party that says about temple . . . Ram temple'. That was their awareness and reaction. Now the Prime Minister Sri Narendra Modi of the BJP is a household name. (Earlier in Sri Atal Bihari Vajpayee era, social media was not in picture.) Thanks to technology, thanks to media, kudos to the BJP!

The description and narratives given in the book would give an insight into my mind and how it worked at situations. Whether my thinking is subjective or objective, I leave it open. To me, I believe that every individual at some point of his speaking or writing is subjective. None can escape. However, every individual should make a deliberate and fearless effort to think whether what they are saying is right or wrong. I leave to the reader to judge rather than saying myself what my thinking was and how my thinking was in situations given in the book.

CHAPTER 1

Ayodhya—Ram Janmabhoomi Movement

That was the movement that moved the nation and me. The particular mention of 'me' has no special significance, other than a person unmindful of surroundings, or outside world, had begun to observe them. In a nutshell, got 'awareness'.

One can quite confidently call Ayodhya movement to be a grass-roots one. The BJP as a party became known in the south of India because of the movement. Even vegetable vendors (women who carried fruits and vegetables to homes with baskets on their heads), when asked, they also said they wanted a Ram Mandir. 'This time we would vote for the mandir,' they used to say.

Undoubtedly, Ram and Ramayana are popular throughout the length and breadth of our country. The Congress failed to fathom the sentiment. It's easier for parties to snub Hindu feelings than any other minority communities in India. The Ayodhya movement exposed the faux secularism practiced in India. The BJP, in its earlier form, the Jana Sangh, and the RSS have been crying hoarse on appeasement. None cared.

The one and only issue that brought it (pseudo-secularism) to the fore is the Ram temple issue. It showed the place of Hindus next to minorities in preference, as far as secular politics is concerned. Of course, parties could hide under the garb of judiciary and courts in the case of Ayodhya temple issue. But Parliament is in their hands. When Shah-Bano amendment could be done, why could not Ram temple issue be resolved similarly? The age of Constitution is only seventy, the age of Lord Ram and the belief of people in him is thousands of years old. Of course, mine seems to be an emotive argument. However, it touches the chord of the common man.

In the days of Ayodhya temple movement, we, the common public, were told that 'Ayodhya temple issue' was only a sloganeering. For the BJP, it was impossible to build it in a secular country like India. My doubt is this prescriptive, disciplinary, and obscurantist secularism is meant for Hindus in India only? The other minority religions have their own way. Before the might of the minorities, all parties bend; like in a family, parents yield to whims of the youngest child and discipline the elder one. Obviously, the elder one feels discriminated! So, treating on equal footing is important.

The cadres of the BJP did the impossible. The crowd that gathered at Ayodhya for kar seva did not bother about legality or the Constitution. They seemed to be not much aware of them. The leaders who went along with them were stalwarts and luminaries in those legal fields. But they yielded to that force unstoppable! To that tide, the structure was swept. The intelligentsia that made derogatory remarks on the kar sevaks for demolition could not do anything better before. They could not find any solution through their debates. Never had sympathies with the temple-builders. They always viewed them cynically and with full of derision. Never viewed them as their own countrymen. They took pleasure in letting them down. Never felt sorry of their deaths. For a common man of any religious denomination, this country is his ancestral legacy. He is carrying forward their heritage. For generations, he has been living on this soil. Whoever rules this country never bothered him. Whether he would get two square meals a day is his concern. For which he works. He works to fend his family. He has neither the time, energy, or education enough to understand various articles in the Constitution nor anyone for him to educate the salient features. This kind of public the politicians have to deal with on day-to-day basis, not the executive or judiciary. With this kind of scenario in India, let us see how Pakistan viewed the demolition of the Babri structure.

Pakistan's view on Ayodhya Ram temple—Babri Masjid dispute:

Pakistan's people were also very keenly observing the developments during Ayodhya Ram Temple—Babri dispute. When the structure of

Babri was demolished, in fact, they were happy that Indian secularism died with it.

In those Ayodhya temple agitation days, it was written in the newspapers that Pakistanis were evincing more interest on the Ayodhya temple issue rather than on the Jammu and Kashmir, their heart-throb. For this temple movement was directly linked to the practice of secularism in India. Though the Hindus in India thought it to be a pseudo-secular game.

From small tea-shop owners to cantonment of personnel and people of all other hues, Ayodhya-Babri was a hot topic of discussion in Pakistan then. They just wanted to establish that Indian secularism was a fiction and fabrication. When the country was partitioned, India chose to be secular and Pakistan theocratic. So, therefore, they always tried to expose Indian secularism as Sham secularism. They have no clue how our secular political leaders of India tamper with our secularism to please the minorities. With Babri demolition, they thought Indian secularism was buried under the debris of the demolished. The intellectuals in Pakistan thought Jinnah's two-nation theory was vindicated. They inferred the meaning of 'Ram and Rahim can't live together', stated by their tall leader.

However, things proved otherwise in India. The whispers of our neighbours proved wrong time and again. India stood resilient. Both communities convinced the world that they could live together.

The model of the Indian Constitution:

The Constitution has an important role to be the undercurrent of this society. The Constitution is the arti-craft of the policy elite to get semblance in the society. Most of it is a British legacy. A Western egalitarian thought! The Western world view after the World War II learnt how to respect human lives and values. Human rights have been a big issue for them after the disasters of World Wars I and II. Though India was not directly affected by the wars, these values have been coming, as the substrata of Indian society for centuries. I agree that some erosion had taken place in the middle by way of caste, which brought schism in the Indian society. The gaps in the society should be filled with human compassion. Aping the West has become a fad for all English educated. If race is the problem in the West, here they say 'caste' is the grey area. Agreed. No one disputes. But it is magnified out of proportion to please the Western world.

Whenever Ayodhya temple issue comes up, the so-called liberal-minded Indians say, why rake up religion now? Why bring in history of Babur now? Now India is an independent country, a democracy; the baggage of old should not be brought to the fore. We should forget the past and what the emperors had done or not done. Points well taken. We are in a progressive democracy. We do not need any regression. We have given adequate or substantial rights to the downtrodden to assert themselves in the Constitution of India. Then why blame the Hindu society for their past history, what their ancestors had done on any basis? So, some issues of importance to the peoples' lives should be addressed.

Until 1990, I did not know much about the 'Babri' movement and Ayodhya temple—related issues. In 1986, I vaguely remember, when our family was in Vishakhapatnam (known as Vizag), I happened to meet my friend who was a doctor, a gynaecologist. She was working on lean in Gulf countries then. She, in her talk, touched upon the issues of Ayodhya temple and the treatment of women in those Arab countries. She was the first person to introduce Ayodhya issue to my mind. She said people in Arab countries were talking about Ayodhya-Babri Mosque dispute. Until then, I did not know that such a dispute existed. She said it was a hot topic there. I was a little puzzled why the other countries' people were talking about our country's matter. Since it being an inter-faith issue involving Muslim community, it might have mattered to them, I thought later. She explained the controversy though I could not comprehend fully. Afterwards, I completely forgot about it. To worry about anything, you need a context. Even if someone provided the context, you cannot understand unless you are in the context. The context unfolded to me after a few years.

Being a gynaecologist, she also explained about the condition of the women in those gulf countries and how they bear the torture of retrogressive measures of their ruling. One such harsh measure was deprivation of women on birth control. The women could not bear the horror of deliveries. Sometimes, they would plead her to do sterilisation operation without the knowledge of their husbands. As a doctor, she used to wonder at their plight.

During the course of time, I came to know and experience the Ayodhya movement myself after joining as a teacher in a school in old city, Hyderabad. The frequent strikes and curfews drove me mad. The impediments I faced, to reach to school to work, were nightmarish. Every minute was life-threatening. Never, ever thought I would live this longer to tell the tale.

Each time when Advani or some other leader of BJP made a statement my heart, went pom, pom. The situation from 1990 Oct Rath Yatra to demolition was intensely volatile in Hyderabad. Nobody knew when it would erupt. In those circumstances, I really thought, 'Do we need a temple there at Ayodhya with all this violence, that too when so many Ram temples are around?'

In every village in Andhra, at beginning of the village itself, you find a Ram temple. Now they are all in neglected condition, dilapidated with surroundings muddied and idol uncared and temples themselves look ancient. Once upon a time there were activities around temples. Cultural activities like singing (classical songs) and dancing (dance arts of Indian origin) were promoted. Now except a few temples, all the other temples lost their beauty and charm. The blame should go to endowments department first and next to the governments that ruled all these years. Because of communist influence in Andhra, the lands given to temples by donors, especially to the upkeep and running of the temples, were taken by successive governments for distribution to peasants, it is said. So, the temples are left with no money! Would this kind of distribution be possible with any other faith?

The seeds of my conviction, to support, to build a Ram temple was sown by my neighbour Raju, who ran a tutorial in a building next to our house. As a matter of fact, a neighbour. He convinced me totally why it was necessary to build the temple in Ayodhya. He opened the Pandora's box of appeasement politics. L. K. Advani's Rath yatra was an eye-opener to us in south. It motivated us to delve deep into the details of Ayodhya movement. His Yatra made us aware of *shilanyas*— opening of temple doors by Rajiv Gandhi government and Shah Bano case and what the pseudo-secular politics had led to.

In 1990, when Advani's Rath Yatra was taking place, the difficulty I faced was to walk on the narrow lanes of my school. During the curfew relaxations, the whole of the road was filled with people to buy things they needed. Many stabbing incidents occurred when I was in school.

We did not know how to come out and walk on the road after school. Walking on the road was so scary. The school was not on the main road. There were serpentine bends of narrow lanes to reach the main road. Anything could happen at any time while walking. Nobody knew when a miscreant would attack you. 'If something happened to me, what would happen to my young children and family?' This question always lingered.

Basically, what a person needs is peace and freedom from fear. After boarding the bus, I used to feel safe going home. Of course, public transports have public support! One among the many gives strength. Moreover, in buses, i.e., public transport, we see a mini society in our co-travellers. There is confidence that they would come to our rescue in crisis. We are all humans first.

While coming to school, after getting down from the bus, I was frightened to walk in the narrow lanes that led to our school in the old city. Soon after reaching school, I was relaxed. These sporadic agitations, rath-yatras, took a longer span of two to three months in that year. To take leave that long was impossible for a new entrant in a job. Moreover, while we were working in the school, suddenly, news used to erupt that riots were happening in so-and-so place. Immediately, curfew was imposed in other parts also. People used to rush to their houses. There was so much of commotion on the roads. We had no clue of what the situation would be next minute. So much of uncertainty.

One of those curfew days, when I was rushing for the bus on the road, there was so much noise on the road. My heartbeat increased and palpitated as I did not know what was happening around. I was wondering whether there was any firing going on nearby. But it was not the case; those shouts were of some fruit and vegetable vendors. They were hooting at the top of their voice to sell their produce at throwaway cast. 'Do ke das, do ke dus' (For two rupees ten, for two rupees ten), pitched the fruit-sellers. They raised the rant so high so that people would take them fast and they could leave the place. They were in a hurry. They had to sell their goods before they left. The curfew was already imposed. Police were shouting in their toy-like mini mikes for everyone to leave the place. The street vendors' goods were all perishable. So, they had to sell and go. I wanted to pause for a second and buy, but I was scared where suddenly some firing might take place. These daily wage earners face unexpected hardships on such days.

Sometimes, during curfew period, schools were given holidays. We used to rejoice coming to school after a long curfew. They would give us a long gap to see each other. However, we were asked to compensate the loss of work by coming on Sundays and holidays to complete the syllabus. One of my male colleagues from minority community asked me after a long-curfew period, 'Sab teekh hai na, madam. Aap theek hai na, ghar pe teekh sab hai na' (Is everyone okay, madam? Are you okay, is everyone in the house okay?) kind of questions. When I said, 'Yes,' he said these riots were all because of goondas. They were all let loose; they were the ones who were causing the havoc. They kill people, irrespective of which community you belonged to. I thought it might be true. My friend who was a doctor said during the riots time, 'Those who came to the hospital with stabs were all fatally wounded. Only an expert in stabbing could cause such wounds. They stabbed on liver, spleen, and other such vital parts. Hence chances of survival were bleak for the victims'. Most of the riots seemed orchestrated. Those killers appeared to be hired.

One day, when I came home, in a bad mood with all roadblocks by the agitators and lot of chaos on the roads, my neighbour Raju, a young man who was running a tutorial to coach students, asked me why I was so upset. I told him my difficulties while coming and asked him whether there was any necessity to take up yatras by politicians causing immense problems to us. Then he said, 'If everybody thinks this way, how can we achieve anything? Is not Ram temple needed by us, right in Lord Ram's birth place? How long can Hindus' interests have to be supressed? Why this pampering of Muslim minorities by all the political parties, if not for their votes? If everyone sees to the safety of one's self, who will stand up for the causes?' This way he asked me a volley of questions. I seemed to be selfish in my own thinking. Somehow, I thought Lord Ram, whom we revere for all his great characters, needed to be placed where he deserves. That is his birthplace of Ayodhya. For Babri mosque ceased to be a mosque since praying in the mosque was not done. It became a bone of contention between two faiths because Muslim leaders stuck to their stand on not giving the disputed structure in come-what-may behaviour.

We did not know who Mulayam Singh Yadav was till he ordered firing on kar sevaks in Ayodhya. He introduced himself as a notorious person to us, all through by taking pride in killing kar sevaks. He had put a permanent wedge between Hindus and Muslims by his action. He could have taken recourse to tear gas or water cannons. Instead, he ordered for firing, to please his vote bank. Juxtapose the situation: if Muslims were fighting instead in that place, would he have ordered for firing? There are two sets of laws in India. One for minorities and one for majorities.

The RSS had effectively used and shown to the people of the country the massacre and butchering of kar sevaks by bringing out picture posters and pasting them on each house. There was one poster pasted on our wall, which showed kar sevaks lying dead on the pool of blood spread all over. A picture speaks more than thousand words, it is said. These posters did have an impact on the psyche of an average Hindu.

Ram Janmabhoomi movement in India was like a revolution. The BJP had very little presence till that time in Andhra Pradesh. But it established itself as one of the mainstream political parties in Andhra with the Ram Janmabhoomi movement. When elections were conducted in 1991, the BJP had won the Parliamentary seat for the first time from Secunderabad. Inspired by Ram Janmabhoomi movement, I did my bit, i.e., ensured that all my family members voted for the BJP. I informed my friends and relatives by word of mouth how bad it was for the country to vote for parties that practice distorted secularism.

I still remember how I wanted to please my mother-in-law, who was against voting like many people in India, saying, 'Why do I need to go to a polling booth? How does one vote of mine matter?' It became so difficult for me to convince her that every single vote mattered. I told her that if everybody in India felt so, who would vote? I also made clear to her how minorities would vote en bloc. And how small margins made a big difference. I also started doing all the work at home just to please her to vote.

All the work at home included cooking for all the fourteen members in the house. When she noticed me doing all work, she said, 'I know why you are doing all this, you want me to vote. Isn't it?'

'Yes,' I said. And asked her to vote for the BJP. By then, they were all convinced BJP voters, according to me. I saw to it that my mother-in-law got readied to vote. I saw to it that she was dropped at the nearest point of the polling booth. After coming home, she said, 'We don't know who that man Member of Parliament candidate for Secunderabad is, but all fourteen people of the house voted to him'. That was a wave. Many voted for the BJP. Bandaru Dattatreya won the election with thumping majority from Secunderabad Parliamentary Constituency as an MP for the first time.

However, in those elections in 1991, the Congress formed the government at the centre. For in the next phase of election, due to the assassination of Rajiv Gandhi, sympathy wave swept over, and it brought the Congress to power. My electoral mobilisation was one off. I could tell how it fell flat on my face in 1996 with my own mother voting to the Congress to my utter disappointment.

Often, I used to tell my mother, who was paralytic by then and was with less mobility, about the issues that were plaguing the country. When I said the issues of the country, it could be anybody's guess. It was about minorities. My brother, who was in Aurangabad, working as a lecturer in an engineering college, used to come to Hyderabad once a month. He used to tell my mother about the economic reforms that were taking place at that time, how they were helpful for the country and people. And then he used to praise the wisdom of the then PM (P. V. Narasimha Rao) and F. M. (Manmohan Singh). My mother listened to both of us. One after the other, we used to bombard her with our knowledge of current affairs.

In 1996, after the full-term completion of Congress government, in P. V. Narasimha Rao's turbulent governance, there were elections. In the north of India, the BJP party got massive mandate, but in the south, especially in Andhra Pradesh, the Congress won most of the Parliamentary seats. I reminded all family members from my mother's side in Hyderabad to cast their vote. I did not remind them whom to vote because I thought all my tutoring would work well for the BJP.

That day, I did my job of voting early in the morning and started my daily chore of cooking food at home. Suddenly, in the middle of my work, I just wanted to know whether my mother had cast her vote. I rang her up. She lifted the phone. I asked her whether she voted. She said, 'Yes'. I should have remained content with the answer. Instead, I enquired her for whom she voted, though it was not my habit to ask people about their personal preferences of voting. Even my mother never told us when were small children, when asked about whom she had voted, she used to tell us that it was a secret and should not be told. This time around, she said, 'Congress'. I got so wild. I always thought my mother was mine and she would oblige me and what I said. All my imagination and firm belief in her had gone with the wind. I was devastated. I shouted at her, 'Why did you do that when I told you clearly the party was not in the interest of us?' She simply said Manmohan Singh was doing economic reforms, which were good for the country. So, what my brother said worked well with her. Then I retorted that economic reforms even the BJP would do if it came to power. Afterwards, I hung the phone down, saying, 'I will not talk to you here after for voting to the Congress'.

I thought, what was the use of talking to her? When all my lectures got wasted, what's the point in giving again shamelessly? I was really crestfallen. I decided not to see my mother and brothers. I thought they betrayed me. I sobbed bitterly over my mother's decision of preferring the Congress over the BJP in voting. I also cried for my mother not being able to understand what the country was going through with that kind of appeasement to the minorities. My husband and children were shocked to see me crying for a long time, leaving my other duties. My husband, being a practical person, advised me not to take everything to heart. After two, three hours, I got up all by myself. No consolation from any quarter. My mother did not relent. She did not call me back, though I expected her to pacify me. It seemed that she wondered what was wrong on her part to vote for what she thought was right. That, I gathered from her later. For her, though old, as a rightful thinking person, development of the country took an edge over religion. So also, for many in India. Because people do not want to live with inadequate means and facilities. If you want to work properly, you need to have the wherewithal, i.e., to have required infrastructure.

Late in the evening, when I came to terms with myself and reality, I rang up Ram Madhav, an RSS Pracharak then, who gave me a patient hearing of my conversation with my mother. Then he said, 'Why did you behave in that way, it's bad, very bad. Why did you say, you would not talk to her? If you don't talk to your mother, I will not talk to you.' Later, I spoke to my mother normally. She said she never expected me to take things so seriously. Though Ram Madhav gave a right advice to talk to my mother after the event, he did not stop teasing me, for some time, for not being able impress, at least my mother, to vote for the BJP to begin with.

However, in 1996, the government of Sri Vajpayee lasted for thirteen days, followed by a coalition of multiple parties. I. K. Gujral, Devi Gowda became prime ministers. That coalition lasted for two years only. In 1998 elections, my mother faithfully voted for Vajpayee-led BJP government.

Before the 1998 elections, she was glued to television. She listened to news bulletins including the Urdu ones. After Vajpayee became prime minister, she started reading her own books of philosophy rather than seeing the news. We were amazed! One day, we asked her why she was not following news bulletins. Then she said she did not need to bother about the country when it is in the safe hands of Vajpayeeji. That was her confidence! I got an opportunity to see Vajpayeeji personally, courtesy of Ram Madhav. I wanted to tell my mother's feeling to the PM, but in those two minutes of meeting, I could not open my mouth and articulate what I wanted to. After coming outside, when I told the same to Ram Madhav, he said, 'You should have told him, you missed an opportunity'. Really, I missed that opportunity.

During that time, all were moved by Ayodhya movement. The epic Ramayana is a household story in the country. Lord Ram was of royal lineage. He was majestic, handsome, truthful, loving, caring, respecting others, and was an incarnate of dharma. All in all, an ideal person. Many people name their children after Ram so as to get at least some of his characters. The 1991 election of Parliament was almost a referendum for Ram temple. Had Rajiv Gandhi not been assassinated, the BJP would have easily come to power. It was a wave.

One day, knowing my interest in day-to-day politics, my colleague took me to late Sri. V. Rama Rao's (state BJP president) house. That was in Banjara Hills of Hyderabad. Sri Rama Rao was an advocate of AP High Court for a long time and was an MLC of AP Legislative Council for some time. He was an intellectual and had the grasp of the BJP organisation. He was a friendly person and known to be noncontroversial. When the BJP came to power in 1999, he was appointed as governor of Sikkim.

My conversation with Sri Rama Rao was in 1993. Though I was no expert in political field, I talked to him at length. First, I told him, how impressed I was with the BJP after reading Arun Shourie's articles. He was slightly disappointed at what I had said. He said, journalists write in many ways; one should not go by their writings. Later, he answered my questions on ideological front.

Sri Rama Rao said, Ram of Ramayana is national hero, a cultural identity of the country, he had qualities that people of the nation could learn and emulate'. I was a little confused. For I believe Lord Ram to be God, suddenly, how could I make him a cultural symbol in my mind? What he said appeared to me that Ram was born like any great king of the country. Like, Ashoka or Chandragupta Maurya. And Ram led a great life with great characteristics. He was an ancient Indian hero along with Krishna, another great hero. There was no divinity part in it.

'Most of the Indians pray to Lord Ram as God. We built temples for him. We would like to build another one in Ayodhya. Why was all this 'divinity' part missing in his talk?' I thought. After a careful thought, both views, his and mine, appeared to be true. Because Lord Ram, in his human form on earth, had set standards for principled life. His ruling, Ram Rajya, had also become a model to take cue from, for any government even now. For a devout Hindu, certainly, he is an avatar of Lord Vishnu.

Sri Rama Rao also described rivers like Ganga and Yamuna to be cultural symbols and identities of Indians. Like how, in Indonesia, their currency notes have the symbol of Ganesha, their official airline is called Garuda (Lord Vishnu's mount), and the official bank is named after Kubera (the Hindu god of wealth), the BJP likes such kind of cultural identities. They appreciate Indonesia for having such symbols. To me, what matters is the survival of Hinduism also along with its culture. Sri Rama Rao tried to convince me that Ram was a cultural symbol, and I tried to convince him that he was a God to all of us.

The state BJP chief then asked me if I could join the party or at least Sevika Samiti (the women wing of the RSS). I said I was not in a position to make up my mind. However, he advised me to see Smt Vijaya Bharathi of Savika Samithi, a social activist of renown. I did not get much input from him, but it left me with a feeling that I had made some initiative to quench my curiosity on issues of the RSS and the BJP.

Smt Vijaya Bharathiji was another interesting person. She was an excellent orator, spreads the message of the organisation clearly and candidly. She was a loyal and dedicated RSS (Rastriya Sevika Samithi) worker. She used to write columns in Jagrithi weekly (Telugu) run by the RSS (she is still working with all these organisations with same vigour; I used the past tense to her just to refer my connect with her in earlier days). After the state BJP president's visit, I got associated with the organisation Pragna Bharati. I often mentioned to Sri V Rama Rao, the state BJP president, in the course of my talk, how much I was influenced by Arun Shourie's writings, which almost had drawn me to talk to him. It was evident from his face that he was not impressed by what I said. At the end of our conversation, he philosophically said, 'Journalists write this way and that way'.

This is how I started writing to vent my feelings:

In the '90s, there was no social media to have any exchange or sharing of feelings. People talked among themselves and kept quiet. Those who had vehemently strong views had no platform other than mainstream media. Of course, public meetings were conducted by organisations of like-minded people. For a person, like me, who strongly thinks that there is something going wrong around, what does she do? It is a pressure and torture to keep it to myself. She needs an avenue to vent her feelings. Often, I used to share my thoughts with my aunt over the phone for a long time. One day, she advised me, 'Why don't you also write to the newspapers what your feelings are, when you think the other columnists are not correct in their assessment?' That gave me a clue. Then I started writing 'letters to the editor' of local English newspapers.

At that time, either handwritten or typed letters were used. My first letter was published in the local English newspaper of Hyderabad on March 1993. I was quite happy. Because it was my maiden act of writing to the press. A simple one. I just took a rough notebook and jotted a few points of disagreement with the Khushwant Singh's column, Queries Raised by Blasts published on 23 March 1993 in the newspaper. And also another letter agreeing with the letter writer who wrote that Hinduism alone preaches secularism.

First, I drafted and redrafted the letters two three times. I copied by my hand the letters into full sheet white papers addressing the editor. I kept both the letters in an envelope, wrote the address of the newspaper on it. I posted it myself. I did all this very secretively. For I had a fear I would be ridiculed if they were not published. The editor of the newspaper obliged me. My maiden experiment became successful. The editor published both one after the other on two consecutive days. Those letters were before joining the organisation Pragna Bharati.

From then on, I started writing to other newspapers also. I do not still know why I did what I did. In our family circles or friends or relatives, I had not seen anyone writing letters to the editor. Politics is not our cup of tea. Most persons in my circle know a bit of local politics but not much of national. The academic discussion on secularism and other things never mattered to them. But they are capable of judging whom to vote. That's it.

I used to constantly nag my husband to listen to my opinions. I used to read the controversial columns (in my opinion, controversial) to my husband at the dining table while he was having lunch or dinner. I would think that was the ideal time because a person would sit stable at that time. After reading, there was a mini comprehension test for him on what I read. I would ask his opinion on the content. Sometimes, he would say, 'Let him [the columnist] write anything, why are you getting agitated? It is his view and you have your views. Each one is entitled to have his/her view'. Life was never so easy for me.

One day, when I started reading to him a column during his lunch, he said, 'Don't read anything to me, I know English, I can read for myself'. From that time onwards, I stopped feeding him with news. I also told him my crazy idea of appointing somebody to listen to my views and reactions to somebody else's writing by paying salary to the person. This idea I got because I was working and every month, I got salary of my own. All that very long ago. Ever since I got the editors of newspapers to communicate, I stopped troubling others much.

Every day, I would read the newspaper first then go to my job. There in school, during my leisure, I would not waste my time and instead write two to three letters on controversial (as I deemed) topics, get them home, and ask my husband to post them the next day. When he comes home from office that day (or the next day), I would ask him whether he posted. If he says, 'Yes', I would ask, whether he posted properly. Then he would say, 'Yes', and added sometimes, 'I shook the post box also to ensure'. One day, when I gave my bunch (of letters), he said, 'Why don't you take room beside the newspaper office [usually we used to read that newspaper at home and added extra newspapers later]. As soon as he gives the newspaper, you can prepare your letters and give him back.' I got angry at his sarcasm.

In due course, I came in touch with the organisation Pragna Bharati and its organising secretary, Ram Madhav who was an RSS Pracharak in Hyderabad. Unknowingly, what the eminence of Arun Shourie was, I started reading his columns in the local English newspaper on Ayodhya movement and others. In that prevailing situation, I concurred with his views, and they gave me immense strength to what I have had in my mind about pseudo-secularism and other issues.

Very soon in 1996, we got a desktop computer and Internet connection at home. The process of dissemination of information became very easy to me. I started e-mailing the letters to the editor and reports to the organisation. That was the time I was fully into the organisational mode. If somebody wrote something against the RSS or the BJP in the newspapers, I used to get annoyed. Both the organisations appeared to be like my babies whom I (obviously like a mother) should be protecting when someone hurts them. I used to write letter (like nobody's business) on every columnist who opposed them slightly. It was so emotional!

All about human rights, free speech, freedom of religion, UN Charter, rights of minorities, liberty, equality, and fraternity as pronounced and used *ad nauseum* and *ad infinitum* in the Western societies were unknown to me then in detail. We adopted them in toto into our Constitution. We always like wearing borrowed coats, though they do not fit us well. Indians, without explicitly citing, by and large have been living with those concepts (that are now enshrined in the Constitution) for centuries. The West articulated them to a degree.

My letters started appearing in newspapers once a week or twice a week. The frequency increased with my increased facility of Internet. To my surprise, I once got prize money for the best letter of the week also! That particular letter was best for the editor of the newspaper because it did not deal with any politics. It was about some civic amenities. When my first column, a middle in editorial page, was published, I was really elated. So, the flow continued. Many of my articles were published in Telugu newspapers also.

Most of my writings, either articles or letters to the editor, were of rejoinder type. For my reality of life was different from what English newspaper editorials and columnists would say. That was the age of handwritten letters. They have a feel and touch unlike e-mails. But we entered into different era later in 1996 onwards. As I said, my reports to Pragna Bharati were sent through e-mails from home. I learnt driving to go to all meetings on my own. Learning technical things left me less dependent on others.

One day, early in the morning, I was discussing with Ram Madhav over the phone about some news item I read in that day's newspaper. Suddenly he said, being activists—swayam sevaks, they were not able to read so early the newspaper, how was I able to manage? This I wrote to say how much I was engrossed in the activity of viewing the country.

Nowadays, we don't need to read news; updates keep coming on our smart phones. Whether we like it or not, alerts are on display the moment something occurred in the world. The search engines give us details on any issue under the sun. The information feed is so much, it bulges our head. Opinion columns are so many that each one differs with the other, and inferences on the events are galore.

Getting your view published in the newspaper was no easy task. Especially English newspapers in those days. They followed a certain pattern like our English TV channels now. They have their own guidelines to publish, which the common people of India don't understand. I laboured so much to convey my views, which I believed to be correct. I understood one thing. If a person was from majority community, his or her view or criticism on the minorities was unwelcome. Minorities criticizing majorities, however obnoxious, was welcome. That was the freedom of speech or expression then and is also now. I did not know about all these freedoms at that time. Sometimes, I wondered why some of my views were not considered and published.

Most of the Indians are not aware of the Constitutional nuances. I heard about 'human rights' but did not know what it consisted of. I only knew that one should not hurt a human. Other than that, most Indians do not know what we have lifted from the Western egalitarian principles! Even among the educated citizens, the knowledge of basic Constitutional principles are at a low. I seriously doubt some of the elected representatives' basic knowledge on the Constitution of India.

Freedom of expression is not totally the preserve of people in India. There was some censoring on the media indirectly by the left intellectuals and the consecutive Congress governments, at the Centre and State. They tried their best to supress the voice that differs from theirs. In the '90s it was a struggle for us to air our views. Freedom of speech was supressed then mainly because of the left's strong-arm tactics in academics and media. That was an indirect state sponsored repression! For the Congress followed the footsteps of the left in principles.

When all the technological gadgets were not in use, our world was different. Going to Jagriti office and attending in-house meetings personally was, in itself, an experience worth remembering. Usually, the meetings were all in the evening. Ram Madhav used to head the meeting which was called baithak. The complex of Jagriti was so serene with all-flowering plants, well-levelled ground, cool breeze coming from all sides, up above the sky, clouds moving—it was always very pleasant for any discussion. It had traditional ambience of a house. The outdoor meetings were all so memorable, I always feel gone are all golden days. In every meeting, invariably, Ram Madhav was present. Even if he would go outside, he would come back by that time. His opinion prevailed in the end whatever the discussion might be.

The main discussions in Jagriti were monthly reviews. All the members discussed how the public meetings of that month were conducted. They also discussed the extra measures to be taken for the next, i.e., coming meeting, about venues, difficulties in getting them, to choosing the speakers for the next meeting depending on the topic, how to get advertisements and funds for the magazines run by the organisation, delegating work to people to collect ads, searching for a hall for the next meeting, mobilising people, distributing pamphlets, etc. Ram Madhav used to oversee everything. He knew the pulse of the organisation. He cared for each and everyone in the organisation. Each person used to think that he was close to him/her. Each family used to think that he was their member. He was the live wire in the organisation. Pragna Bharati organisation still continues in Hyderabad. Although with a different setup.

My job most often was to welcome guests to the podium in the meetings and to write reports after the meetings. I was a little nervous initially. I told the organising secretary my trouble. But he did not listen. He said, 'We know whom to give what by knowing their capacities. It will always be decided in our discussions, so everybody must abide by it'. If that was the answer by an organising head, who could say anything? So, in my own way, I used to speak with a prior rehearsal. Here and there, with the presence of mind, some incorporations. After the meeting, preparing the report was mostly my part. This gave me an opportunity to sit and listen to the speakers unlike others, in the organisation, busy receiving people, escorting them to places, distributing papers for address slips and for writing questions.

Our organising secretary used to love those who do grass-roots work. He used to say, 'There are many people who can write, but the people who go and work on the ground are more important'. I still agree with his statement.

I always had a feeling that the organising head should know the pulse of the members that work with him. And should allot work accordingly. Organisations need individuals; individuals also need organisation. A kind of symbiosis. The only thing is there should not be any self-interest in people who work in organisations. Reason? If you have no expectation, no disappointment.

Though I do not know much about the RSS, as far as my knowledge goes, the following are the appreciable qualities in the members (karyakartas) of the RSS:

- There is a regularity in waking up early in the morning to go to Sakha for drill and *boudhik*. These *boudhiks* give information about the country, society we live in, and the world at large.
- They instruct all their swayamsevaks to have good behaviour, using culturally polite language with no abusive terms whatsoever. I heard many a time the late Sri Sudershanji (Sarsanghchalak, RSS) saying '*vani samyam*', i.e. one has to be careful of what they speak. To mind the language is an important aspect. It shows one's pristine culture.
- They always partake vegetarian food in their gatherings but would not object to non-vegetarian, if it comes as a family tradition. This puritanical approach has its own benefits. We can very well understand when the world is turning into vegetarian.
- The RSS advises its members to keep away from vices like drinking (liquor) habit. Members in the cadres are, by and large, teetotallers. It is a good sign because any talk or

decision taken at a drunken state of mind is different from a normal one. After all, liquor is not water without which people cannot live.

- Personal hygiene is important. Physical exercise is done in Sakhas. Striving to help the society in personal tragedies and miseries is part of their work. When there are calamities, they do much better job than the local administration.
- They do free service when needed. Their service is disciplined and organised. It's question of humanity when tragedies befall on the nation to help people. They strive for societal participation in all their endeavours.

The ideological hold, with which we did work since 1992, really yielded result in 1996, 1998, and 2014. The BJP came to power. We could see with our own eyes what we dreamt of. The meetings, the seminars, the round-tables organised to discuss issues did go down well. Anyway, it was not the intellectual level that gave the vote. The grass-root level workers, whose motivated work did wonders. It was the Ram temple issue that stimulated the people to think about secularism of India in practice. That issue made many closed minds of Hindus to open up and think whether their sentiments had any respect in this country.

The minorities of India have been very strong and steadfast all through. They are the adherents of the strongest religions in the world. In the case Muslims, the Mughal emperors ruled the country for 400 odd years. Our ancestors were all ruled by them. The British ruled the country for 200 years. In all these rules, Hindus were the subjects only. Until Gandhiji and other national leaders awakened the consciousness of the people, none resisted the rule or their might. Of course, 1857 battle (sepoy mutiny) was also a significant revolt. But it was only a beginning. Always in the history, Hindu majorities were humiliated. The reason? Hindus being a loose group of people divided by caste. The British used this division to the hilt. Thus then policy was divide and rule. Only the founder of the RSS, Dr KB Hedgewar wanted to unite the Hindu community by somehow eliminating the caste discrimination.

By and large, India is a peace-loving country. Even the Muslims in India want peace. In the Constitution, it was written that the minorities can peacefully profess and propagate their religion. But not through allurements and hate. They are pitting one caste against the other in Hinduism. Branding of Hinduism as a bunch of superstitions and Islam and Christianity as egalitarian religions has led the left or Nehruvian Congress nowhere. It, in turn, brought the BJP into power.

Lord Ram, taken as a national hero or icon or God, he has a place in the large section of people in the country. Ramayana and Mahabharata are ever-green epics of this country and elsewhere in other South-East Asian nations like the Indonesia, Malaysia, Thailand, etc. Still, the Ramayana culture is thriving there. The present government's desires to forge these countries on cultural lines. Even the Muslims of this country have reverence to Lord Ram. They call him Imam of Hindus.

The debates in the name of free speech and free expression on the existence of Lord Ram hold no water. Because the characters of Lord Ram in Valmiki Ramayana were certainly great. Before writing Ramayana, Valmiki questions the celestial rishi, Narad, who is always on penance, i.e., meditating—who knows what had happened in the past and what is going to happen in the present, and future (knowledge of three times) --- about a human to be born with qualities of good character, chivalrousness, follower of dharma, i.e righteousness, gratuitous, and who stands on truth. Valmiki wanted that person also to have pleasant demeanour, knowledge, and equality in treating all living beings. He also wished that man to have triumph over anger and jealousy. Even gods should appreciate him for what all he stands for. 'Can I find such a person?' asked Valmiki. Then rishi Narada assured that as a human, Lord Ram would have all those characters. So, people still remember him for 'Ram Rajya'.

In Adhyatma Ramayana, Lord Ram himself explains how to lead a philosophical life on earth. These are all in public domain. I do not think sages like Valmiki and Veda Vyasa misled the people by saying falsehood. Most of the Hindus believe in those sages and their wisdom. Whatever those sages had written is for the welfare and well-being of the people in this holy land. When our faith is being steadfast, flippant interpretation would not matter.

Tailpiece: Ayodhya Ram Temple issue supplied much-needed oxygen to the BJP to expose pseudo-secularism practiced in India. The movement motivated many Hindus to see why they are not relevant to many secular parties. Why the secular parties bend over backwards to appease the Muslim community. Why they ask only the Hindus to surrender their strong sentiments vis-à-vis any Muslim interest for the reasons: (1) to buy peace within the country and (2) to protect the integrity of the country.

****

CHAPTER 2

Influence of Renowned Columnist Arun Shourie's Writings

I started reading Arun Shourie's articles from 1991, without knowing who Arun Shourie was! I used to carefully read his articles with a dictionary (of English) by my side. To me, his sentences were not simple and straightforward. They were lengthy and twisted with logic. Sometimes, he gave such big quotations; while reading, I would forget whether he was saying his own views or quoting somebody else's. I developed a habit of regression to go back to connect the thread. Slowly, I was able to understand what he was writing. Partly, I could not understand in my initial readings because I did not know the background of what he was writing. From the beginning, I was not an avid reader of newspapers. Most of the middle-class women are busy doing household work, routine, and bringing up their children. They may be knowing the overall picture of the affairs but not the subtle details. Heavily loaded Arun Shourie's articles aren't anybody's piece of cake. This was in the context of 1990s, not in the present era of information fogging.

I continued reading Arun Shourie's articles mainly for information and thought; the other purpose was for language and articulation. During Ram Janmabhoomi movement, his thoughts inspired me so much. I read so faithfully his articles; I felt that he was personally writing to me alone or people like me! I read them unmindful of the surroundings I was sitting in. Even if my family members enquired me of something, it did not go into my mind while reading. Fully immersed! It was as if Sri Krishna was imparting knowledge to Arjuna! I may not compare myself to Arjun in knowledge (or gender!), but on devotion part, I agree. I was so much impressed and imbued with his writing sometimes I felt it was my writing! I felt he was writing on my behalf.

I read some of his Ram Janmabhoomi articles to my mother when she came home. She felt so happy for him. She blessed him. She felt he was doing a great service to Hinduism. We couldn't find writers like him anywhere around to support Hindu causes. When I asked my husband, 'Who is this person who is writing so well?' he said that it was Arun Shourie. He also said he wrote articles during Indira Gandhi's (in)famous Emergency days that shook the nation. I know about her emergency. The impact of it was not so much in Andhra Pradesh. I was a student then. As a science student, I was busy in my practical lab work and studies. That was paramount to me. That time, I seriously thought of becoming like Lavoisier or Dalton, a scientist, always doing work in the lab in quest of knowledge. Those were only dreams!

Once I met my friend who worked in CPML (Communist Marxist Leninist Party), her husband was also from the same party. In my conversation with her husband, I told him how much I was impressed by Arun Shourie's articles. He said, 'Oh! You are reading his articles! Why are you reading his articles? He is an intellectual'. It seemed, he meant to tell me that intellectuals were far removed from commoners. They write from certain another plane. However, after reading Arun Shourie's articles, I could not read any others. Some of the articles written by other authors were like a mere desk works and lacked intellectual acumen. They projected their perceptions more than facts.

Article 370, uniform civil code, fatwas were some of the articles that appeared to be heavily loaded with arguments and laws, etc. Probably they were for academic discussions. They were not daily bread and butter problems of common man. One way, Ram Janmabhoomi mobilised people. Even lay people, people on the road connected with the movement. The Congress repeatedly wanted to supress the movement by saying that it was impossible to reconcile with the powerful Muslim community. Often, the party reminded that the matter was pending in the Supreme Court. They did not try for negotiations.

The Congress tried to tell the Hindus to be quiet on this issue and wait for the judgement, albeit for centuries to come. The party did not take a proactive role with the fear that they might lose the powerful minority vote. They did not realise their minority vote was snatched away by Samajwadi Party (and other parties elsewhere) with the same kind of tactics with which they wooed them. They failed to gain any dividends by the benevolent act of Rajiv Gandhi opening the doors of shilanyas site. Of course, they did it to counter and normalise Shah Bano issue by doing this act of kindness to the Hindus. They could not sell or market both the issues because both were conceptually wrong. How they had made a Constitutional amendment in Shah Bano case, they could have done for building Ram temple issue also. At times, it is better to please majorities also. Because they are also the people of this country! Happiness also counts in building up the nation.

By the time I lifted Arun Shourie to a demi-god status in my mind, I felt like conveying the same. Like how a devotee, while praying, conveys all his or her feelings to god with no hitch. In the same way, I wrote a letter to Arun Shourie. This I did before meeting Ram Madhav or Pragna Bharati. First, my husband, at my insistence, went to Jagriti office and subscribed newsletter—*Vande* (Bharath) *Mataram*—and then asked Ram Madhav the address of Arun Shourie and got it for me. That letter contained all my feelings about the things that were going on in the country. Occasionally, I mentioned my 'bhakti' part. For the devotees not only tell their troubles to god, they also express their devotion to him, don't they? After posting it, I was slightly worried if I had made any grammatical mistakes in my English. Anyway, my English was better than some of my contemporaries after reading heavily loaded articles in the English newspapers. But yet such a big man!

In my affection, I addressed him 'Dear Brother Arun Shourie'. For he was like big brother writing all my thoughts to the people of the country! I thought they (the writings) were mine but better articulated by him. They synchronized so much that I adopted them. I was so worried that he might find my addressing him 'Dear brother' to be unworthy of his stature. 'Who am I, after all, to address him so?' I thought. I consoled myself, 'Anyway, what is there in writing to an unknown and unseen person whatever I felt?'. You talk to God the way you want to without ever expecting to see his reaction. Similarly, this!

But to my wonder of wonders, I got a response immediately in three/four days. In it there were three sentences of thanking me. They were, thanks for my words of encouragement and approval, for the trouble I had taken in writing such a detailed letter to him, and for writing the newspaper about how I felt on his interview that was published in it. It was triple-thanks message. Now it has become easy for the celebrated journalists and anchors to thank their faithful followers on Twitter and Facebook.

Earlier, I read an interview of Arun Shourie in the local English newspaper. It was published under 'Social Rendezvous' in '93. The interviewer asked many questions in general and on his personal life also. When the interviewer asked him, 'What makes you most depressed?' He said, and I quote, 'I used to feel not depressed but maybe upset not being able to do much about the condition of our country. I must say I am now reconciled to that condition more and more. And that is a very sad stimulus, but it is eventually true of all of us. It is given in the Chandukopanishad that we are like a bird which is tethered on a string which is made to the ground. For a long time, it tries to flap about to breakaway. And eventually, exhausted, it settles down on the string of fate. So, most of us eventually are forced to that condition. So today I would not be depressed at the fact that I am not able to do much about the country. That is, we are too small and the country is too large. And the people are preoccupied with other things. And even if these are, as I am certain they are, fatal habits for them, there is not much that we can do about it. We are sort of, I think, paralytics watching a rising flood. But for that reason, I am not depressed. And I do whatever I can do. I just do whatever comes to head"[1].

After reading the interview, I wrote letter to the editor of the newspaper thanking him for publishing the interview in a few lines. In it, I wrote, 'As a regular reader of his column, I wanted to know about him. He seems to be a down-to-earth man. His love for the country and his intense desire to do something for the country are quite moving. His detachment to material things and his power of meditation are amazing. A rare personality in the fast society of Delhi. I am sorry to know about his child. I never thought him to be so cool and compassionate as he is very forceful in his writings. His citation from 'Chandukopanishad' is very nice and suitable for one and all.

'His voracious reading habit and his disdain for critics are admirable. He is really a man like Socrates, the Greek philosopher. His simple living, having only a few pairs of dresses, reluctance to handle money, zest for meditation and 'satsang' are really yogic characters. His love and compassion for his family members and his agony to do something to the country make him a karma yogi.'

Later, I came in contact with Pragna Bharati. I became a part of the organisation. Ram Madhav, knowing my cult of Bhakti to a knowledgeable writer, he introduced me to him when Shourie chaired one of our programmes. Thus he became acquainted to me. I did not speak to him much, as I thought I was not competent enough to talk to him. And also, I did not intend to take the risk of exposing my scant knowledge on the subjects he writes. I only said to him that I was the person who wrote that (crazy) letter to him. Then he smiled, and my children asked for an autograph, which he promptly had given.

Once or twice, Ram Madhav brought along with him Shourieji to home, and I prepared some sweets to offer, and he spent some time with our family. This is the way Sangh connects people. I was intimidated by his knowledge. So, I could not speak much with him even at home. He might have felt how dumb I was. That did not matter to me. My position was that of Stephen Leacock's character, in 'My Financial Career' (essay) who gets rattled when he goes in to a bank because he doesn't know much about a bank and bank transactions. Leacock says, in his first-person narration, 'When I go into a bank I get rattled. The clerks rattle me; the counters rattle me, the sight of money rattles me; everything rattles me'. Similarly, I was rattled by the presence of Shourieji in our house. So, I thought of confining to myself. Though he looked at me and wanted to talk too, probably to know the depth of my knowledge, I could not open my mouth. Because I was too shy and not used to elite social circles. To ease the tension, I started talking to my son instead. That was all incoherent. I acted to be busy. So, it was all over. Finally, before Shourie left, our family took a snap with him, Ram Madhav photographed (at that point of time, mobile phones were not in place). Shourie bought some fruits on the way to give us as a mark of courtesy. In my own innocent way, I thought, 'Do intellectuals also follow these customary practices of the world?'

Occasionally, I sent 'rakhi' by post on the festival of Rakhi to Arun Shourie. In South India, especially in Andhra, we are not much used to this kind of celebration. To me, he was the ray of hope in the gloomy, dark, secular scepticism. Slowly and steadily, I wanted to shed the dependency on people and tried to understand things on my own by reading books (of all genres) and viewing and watching programmes on television.

My knowledge on economy of the country was zero at that time. But unknowingly, we all supported globalisation. To put it rightly, it was like moving from a congested narrow space to a much wider space. When I got into association with Pragna Bharati, I did not understand why the Swadeshi Jagaran Manch was opposing it. Like the people in the developed countries, Indians too needed quality products to use. Different things to enjoy. To judge what is necessary and useful, one needs to have a choice. Excessive materialism is not desirable. To say how much is too much is difficult. But how could the supressed Indians for so long know what is excessive? After opening up the economy, i.e. after globalising, I thought India should have done that much before. Why the leaders left us in lurch so long? I thought.

General Agreement on Trade and Tariff (GATT), Dunkel proposals, World Trade Organisation (WTO) were much-debated things in the organisation and outside. At that time, Arun Shourie, in his column writes, 'Recall how the Green Revolution was brought about: the high yielding varieties were developed in public research laboratories, and these were released in the market without claiming any patents. Wouldn't that be the way to break the power of the multinational to blackmail our farmers?

'Recall the shouting at the time the Green Revolution work was begun: the marginal farmers will be disposed and thus immeserised— that was the fashionable word those days, the country's agriculture will become vulnerable—a single pest will be enough to wipe out crop over millions of acres at a time, it was said. The Green Revolution will turn Red, it was proclaimed.

'What happened in fact? Far from becoming dependent, we became self-reliant: not only did the new seeds enable us to feed our growing population, our agricultural scientists acquired the skills and expertise to continue the work on their own . . .'[2] By reading this column of Shourie, I started looking at all kinds of protests with a pinch of salt.

He also lauded our scientists' efforts and farmers' hard work in his column. He writes, 'Five years ago we were in the grip of a severe oil-seeds crisis. By the excellent work of our scientists, by the great organisational and entrepreneurial talents . . . by the alacrity and hard work of our farmers, in just five years we are in a position today to export oilseeds and their products'.[3] All this was for stating that signing GATT was not a bad idea.

On J&K, I only knew that it was like crown on India's map up above. Two lobes of it were cut by Pakistan and China that makes all of us sad. Indian government always shows full on the map because they are still occupied territories for us. I did not know or heard the name Hurriyat or terror organisations like Al-Qaida till I read in Arun Shourie's columns in 1990s. Not only me, my friends, and colleague drew a blank face when I said those names. Teaching small kids lessons in the school, keeping abreast with big, big things that were happening in the country, I felt I was doing something incompatible . Those days in the early '90s, this kind of multichannel TVs and smart phones were not even imagined. Newspapers, Doordarshan, and All India Radio were the sources. But one should have time to read or see. Now, the information is pumped in. Even if we do not want to hear, it is heard by word of mouth or by an alert on a mobile.

Arun Shourie's immeasurable contribution as a journalist for the rise of the BJP

Ayodhya movement and Arun Shourie bond together. He was the only stand-alone journalist who supported the temple cause, in my opinion. At that time, his views and the BJP's were so much synchronised! I used to get a doubt whether he was following them or they were following him. Later, I came to know that he was on their 'think-tank'. For a person who did not know that 'think-tanks' exit, it was all amazing!

To counter the urban, sophisticated English journalists, the BJP needed his service. He was also a convinced journalist of their ideology. There is a saying that only a diamond can cut a diamond. Arun Shourie knew their language, so he could counter them.

The culmination of Ayodhya movement was with the demolition of Babri mosque. The demolition caused shock waves in the country. People got shocked for different reasons. So-called secular politicians were shocked because it disturbed their apple cart, i.e. the Muslim minority vote bank. The BJP seemed to be happy initially but, as a responsible political party, denounced the act. Commoners like us thought, 'Can Hindus do such a daring act? Has the Babri dispute been solved this way?' Most of the general public did not care much. But media carried headlines. Called December 6, 1992, a Black Day, and it is still continued to be called. The Constitution of India and everything was doomed according to them. So-called seculars started giving their own definitions. They compared it with Mahatma Gandhi's Assassination. Throughout Babri demolition the PM was snoozing, as per media reports, following that he became wide awake and started campaigning that if something happened to Indian secularism, there would be another partition. Whenever an act of slight or perceived injustice was done to Muslim minorities, the Congress leaders would say that we were heading for another partition. The Congress should explain why it agreed for the first partition, in the first place, in 1947. Why did their policy of appeasement not work then? Why do they pursue the same failed policy even now?

We, Indian Hindus, want the Congress and other secular parties to treat us all the same with no disparity. Sri Narasimha Rao's, the former PM, campaign after the demolition was because of the BJP's policies, Muslims were getting alienated. He did not know that a major section of Hindus was going against the Congress because the Congress was bending backwards to please the Muslims. He propagated about the second partition of the country so that people of India would be threatened. He wanted to create a fear psychosis so that nobody would touch BJP with a barge pole. It did not go down well with people. Somehow, he could manage to be in power. The only thing that brought a big change in his rule was his economics. Here, good economics is not bad politics. It supersedes bad politics that was shown. Manmohan Singh is renowned more as an economist and finance minister of India.

The Congress government at Centre imposed the president's rule in all the four BJP-ruled states of Uttar Pradesh, Madhya Pradesh, Rajasthan, and Himachal Pradesh by invoking Article 356 after the demolition. I was so upset and thought it was meant to pacify the Muslim community. The first state to get the president's rule was Uttar Pradesh. That was understandable. Then they banned the RSS. Thus the Congress wanted to atone its sin! Then Arun Shourie wrote a column after the ban of the RSS, which gave much needed encouragement to the sympathisers of the Organisation. He called the ban a joke. His column titled 'All right, a Ram Sevak Sangh' appeared in our local newspaper within days after the ban.

At the fag end of his column, he writes,

The decision opens the government to being made a joke of. It has banned the RSS. All right, on the reasoning that now Ram has merged into Rashtra, set up a new organisation, another RSS: the Ram Sevak Sangh. Let its sole object be for its members to meet every day for reading reciting the Ramayana . . . By merely discussing Ram is there anything the members will not be discussing? And will the government be able to ban the new RSS whose members meet to do nothing but discuss Ram? Quite the contrary, were the formation of such an organisation to be announced today, and were registers to be just put at street-corners . . . a mass movement could be created. where would that leave, the government's ban?[4]

Arun Shourie was the only columnist who questioned the dismissal of the BJP governments after Babri demolition. Especially the Rajasthan, Himachal Pradesh, and the Madhya Pradesh's imposition of the Article 356 (i.e. the president's rule). He explained the government's reasoning. He writes, 'On December 15, the Centre dismissed the governments of Himachal, Rajasthan and Madhya Pradesh. The principal ground it gave, the one common to each of these cases, was apprehension that these governments, being headed by members of an organisation which had been banned five days earlier, were not liable to implement the ban diligently . . . the dismissal of the three governments under Article 356 on the apprehension that they would not implement a ban decreed by the Centre—was illegal, that it was an act which the Constitution did not permit'.[5]

Arun Shourie was the one who breathed life into the BJP and RSS at that critical juncture by his writings. Had he not written gutsily in that manner, I would not have been working so zealously in those organisations. Despite all odds, despite the calumny and rancour poured in by other journalists, he stood to the ground and wrote what he believed in. So steadfast was he! When I came to know that there was a meeting going to be conducted on 'Secularism in India' with Arun Shourie as the main speaker, I was curious to know about the organisation that was planning to conduct it. I had to go to Jagriti office to know the details.

Since the demolition of Babri Masjid, all the columnists started blaming the Hindutva forces. There was only one exception among the renowned columnists. That was Arun Shourie. Today, BJP is in power because of his courage of conviction. He supported and projected the BJP as a unique party of distinction. I think Vajpayee government recognised his services. They inducted him into the cabinet of ministers and was made disinvestment minister. I cannot judge his decisions as disinvestment minister because I am not competent enough to judge economics and finance. The terminology and jargon the economists use is quite unfamiliar to me. I was happy when he became the Union minister because I could read through his articles that he was a man of integrity and a financial wizard.

I am a strong believer in people's personal character reflecting in the work or job they do. If a person was honest, truthful, principled in his personal life, that would automatically be reflected in the work sphere. I sent a greeting card congratulating Shourieji for becoming the minister. But I still have the letter he sent on the government official letterhead, a very brief reply to my congratulatory message. He thanked me for my card and good wishes. Further, he wrote that he always looked upon himself as a member of Pragna Bharati and hoped that we would all remain in touch.

Arun Shourie, in his writings, brought another angle to Babri demolition. To him, religious angle did not matter much. He writes Babri demolition brings pseudo-secularism in India to focus. Indeed, it really brought into limelight the pseudo-secular polity of India. P. V. Narasimha Rao did his best to please secularists after Babri demolition. That did not change his already-sullied image among seculars. Among the Congress PMs, only Narasimha Rao knew who Lord Ram and Krishna were to the Hindus and what their cultural significance was. He ignored demolition part. The rest taking action against the BJP, removal of the BJP governments, etc., he did to hold his chair.

For an average citizen like me who knew very little of Indian Constitution and Indian law, the dismissal of four BJP-ruled government was perceived as thoughtless and atrocious act. The imposition of president's rule for six months as per norm and extension for another six months (together, one year) to calm down the people and their emotions did not work. The BJP wave continued, and the BJP got elected with resounding mandate. However, the party lost in Uttar Pradesh as Mulayam Singh Yadav was proved to be a better appeaser than the Congress, hence the Samajwadi Party got elected.

Arun Shourie and his debates on conversions:

The RSS opposes the religious conversions on mass scale. When an individual gets spiritually enlightened and thinks a path or a religion is better than the one he is practising, then he has every right to convert as per the Constitution of India. But to select a crowd and say, 'You are all discriminated in Hinduism because of caste system. Convert to a particular religion. We do not have castes. We are egalitarian, you get social status, you need not change your names outwardly. Keep them for all government benefits. Get your relatives also because they are all in a wrong path. We convert you, otherwise you do not get salvation'—all this kind of teaching is humbug. Salvation is not the sole propriety of one religion. Every religion promises it. In a secular country, when all religions show path to salvation, why jump from one to the other? In a country where equality of religions is practiced, how could these massive conversions to other minority religions allowed on dubious manner?

Caste is a reality in India. The country may gradually move to casteless society with improved education. But right now, in India, people are taking pride in their caste. They openly ask one another, what caste he or she belongs to without any hesitation. Even if people get converted to another religion, they would not leave their caste identity. They carry it forward to their newly embraced religion with pride. Then where is the question of discrimination by caste? If any discrimination is done on the caste basis, there are acts in Indian Constitution against those atrocities. The government should punish stringently those who bring the name of caste or community and discriminate people in the workplace or outside. Of course, existing laws are seldom invoked by sufferers.

Pragna Bharati had conducted a public programme on fraudulent conversions in India. The topic was 'A Discussion on Missionaries in India contributions and controversies' at Sri Sundaraiah Kala Nilayam, Bagh Lingampally, Hyderabad on 04 September 1994.

Though it was mentioned a 'discussion' (in the Invitation card), it turned out to be a debate at the end. The speakers were so powerful! It was between Arun Shourie, the renowned columnist, Magsaysay Award winner and Father Augustine Kanjamala (Bombay). Fr Kanjamala was a Catholic priest and former secretary to the Catholic Bishops Conference of India Commission. He was given the chance to speak first. Fr Kanjamala's argument was mainly on Arun Shourie's book, *Missionaries in India*. He said Arun Shourie, in the beginning of the book as well as in the concluding part of the book, tried to communicate towards the idea that his final concern was to protect the integrity of the nation. But he had a hidden agenda because in the 250-page book, he could hardly find any positive work and contribution of the missionaries in our nation. He raised many points of contention to which Arun Shourie gave a rebuttal point by point. Our organisers felt happy the way Arun Shourie demolished the Father's arguments. The hall was fully overloaded and lively with audience. The speeches of the two lasted for three to three and half hours. A volley of questions was raised by the audience. Both the speakers answered. Christian community was praised for being open to such discussion.

At the beginning, I was asked to welcome the guests and speakers on to the dais by the organisation. The introduction of the speakers, i.e. their biodata, was provided. But welcoming and vote of thanks are such cut-and-dried things even an extra word would make a big blunder on the stage. As I was a novice to the organisation and the job, as our organising head would not spare for minor mistakes like regression and repetition, I was extra tense and extra conscious while doing my job. That particular meeting was lively. The entire hall was packed. Some of the audience could not get chairs to sit. Most of them were standing. Those who could not stand sat in the corridor on plastic rented chairs. Arun Shourie used to praise Pragna Bharati and its organisers, specially Ram Madhav for his organising capabilities.

The discussion in detail was on the book entitled *Missionaries in India: Contributions and Controversies*, authored by Arun Shourie. And the series of articles by Mr. Shourie and Fr. Kanjamala in the local English newspaper had been the source of inspiration for the discussion.

Fr Kanjamala regretted the author's views, findings. and references in the book; Mr Shourie sternly defended the stand taken by him. The writer was vociferous in demolishing the mistaken version of Fr Kanjamala while the Father blamed the author for misconceiving things. Initiating the discussion, Fr Kanjamala eulogised Mr Shourie for his 'noble concern' about the integrity of the nation.

But all the while, he squarely blamed the author for writing the book to appease religious bigots. He took strong exception to the author's comment that the country's integrity was under threat from certain groups of people, including Christian missionaries. He said the book dealt with the activities of missionaries in two different eras—colonial period and post-Independence period. Pointing out that Arun Shourie's literature on Christian missionaries belonged to the bygone age, the Father said that the style of presentation was very aggressive.

Fr Kanjamala maintained that the interpretation and the data in the book was exaggerated. He alleged that Mr Shourie failed to mention the yeoman service rendered by the Christian missionaries over the centuries in India and wondered that there was hardly any mention about the contributions of the missionaries in even one paragraph of the book.

However, the Father confessed that the orthodox missionaries did commit some mistakes and said that he would not mind apologising for them. Mr Shourie was neither appreciative of the services of the missionaries nor sympathetic about the mistakes. Referring to Mr Shourie's comment in the book that there was a blatant attack on Hinduism through inculcating the Christian ideology into the gullible minds of students in the Christian missionary schools, Fr Kanjamala sought to know to what extent Mr Shourie or any of his family members had been influenced or forced by the missionaries to embrace Christianity.

He launched a scathing attack on Mr Shourie for publishing the survey report conducted by the Catholic Bishops' Conference of India Commission in his book. He said that the new technology had brought a 'Copernican revolution' in the very thoughts of Christian missionaries.

He pointed out that the main aim of the missionaries was not to convert more and more people into Christians. Their main aim was only to bring God's love to the less fortunate sections of society.

In his reply, Mr Arun Shourie stoutly denied the charges and defended his writings. He gave a blow-by-blow account to 'demolish' the charges.

Mr Shourie said he was sorry that the Father had not gone through the book carefully and called the presentation of views by the Father 'quite scandalous'. His first attack was on the charge that there was hardly any word of praise in his book for the services rendered by the missionaries in the country. He said that there was no doubt and disagreement on the missionaries' commitment in their service. Referring to the quotation from Mahatma Gandhi used in his book, Mr Shourie said, 'The Christian missionaries have quickened the reforms in Hinduism to set our house in order'.

It was well-nigh impossible for the missionaries to convert more Hindus into Christians because of the content of the 'Hindu brethren' and not because of the 'so-called policy of the missionaries'.

The Father's presentation was quite apologetic, and it was a completely whitewashed version. Mr Shourie said that he had nothing to hide in the agenda. 'But as my own experience goes, none had ever tried to convert me into a Christian as I was stubborn. So is the case with others,' he pointed out.

If one sentence was added in chapter 3 of the Indian Constitution that the fundamental rights were applicable only to Hindus, what would be the fate of the other religions in the country? he asked.

The missionaries failed in achieving their goal of converting more people as Christians as they lost the political power after independence, he observed. To gain access to non-Christian houses, the missionaries used to choose the houses where there was ill health. They used to pester the kin of the suffering to allow the latter to be baptised. If the kin did not relent, the missionaries sprinkled water on the head of the patient on the pretext of administering medicine and utter the word *baptism*, he said. 'This is not a story of bygone age, my friend', he told the Father.

Referring to the comment of Fr Kanjamala that he did not spare even Mother Teresa, Mr Shourie said that her humility and nobility were of saintly order. The compassion and care that she bestowed upon the ill-fated did not allow her to wait to think of the religion and caste of the suffering, he pointed out. Shourie admitted that Mother Teresa's service was noble. However, he said, her nobility was robbed by her converting the people to Christianity.

The document released by the Catholic Bishops clearly passed foul comments on Hindu gods like Rama and Krishna and called them sinners. Mr Shourie sought to know if the document was prepared in the colonial era. He, however, said that the missionaries were unable to raise such slogans as the political scenario had witnessed a sea change.

He derided the Father's remarks that Christianity had undergone a Copernican revolution and asked, 'What did Christians give to Copernicus when he proposed his theory?'

He said that the entire Hindu community should be indebted to Dr Ambedkar, for he displayed enormous courage in embracing Buddhism and vehemently opposing the designs of the missionaries when he was a member of the Viceroy's Council.

However, he, Shourie, complimented Christians in the end by saying these kinds of discussions were possible only with Christians as they were broad-minded in nature.

I invited two university professors of Hyderabad. While leaving the hall after the meeting, they thanked me for inviting and said as a passing compliment that I did my job (welcoming) well! They felt Shourie to be a bit harsh in his argument. On the whole, they liked the programme. Their minor remark on Shourie did not go down well with me. For I always esteemed Arun Shourie very high. I used to take any criticism on him as a personal offence. I thought him to be a standard person and his thought had to be taken as a benchmark.

In our organisation, organisers would meet people of eminence face-to-face to extend invitation to the meeting. If they turn up, the ones who invited would feel happy. In my case, I took the initiative of distributing cards to some important people. I went to the university to invite them. This face-to-face interactions build up rapport much better than by any other means. During those days, telephone invitation came as the next, and then only postal services throughout.

Ram Madhav assigned me the job of taking verbatim notes of both speakers to make a booklet. We had recorded the whole programme. In those days, printed material was read and valued by the readers. Before entrusting the job, he asked my consent by writing a letter. He said in the letter to write at the beginning a few words of introduction in which a brief history of what prompted us to take up the issue and a few concluding words in the end.

Ram Madhav sent me three, four audio tapes of their discussion and question-and-answer session. He asked me to take verbatim of them first, in English, and then to translate it into Telugu so that that it (the matter) could be published in a small booklet form. The whole proceedings of the meeting was embedded in those audio tapes. That particular programme was very lengthy. The speakers—Fr Augustine Kanjamala and Arun Shourie—spoke for more than one hour each and the heated question-answer session lasted for another one and half hours. All in all, more than three hours.

For me, to pause so many times the tape recorder and write the verbatim (word for word) out took more than twenty hours, spanning three to four days. And translating it without losing spirit of what they had spoken took another ten days. Poor Ram Madhav had to make so many proof corrections after the typing and brought the whole thing out into a sixty-page printed book. He also said that I did a good job and it was not easy to get sixty pages in print! In those days, my work revolved round home, school, organisation, newspapers. All newspapers of that time contained material contrary to my views. I was so confident of my views to be correct. Never thought I was wrong, though I heard and read people saying differently. The organisation was my oxygen then. I used to often get a doubt—'Can I live without this?'

I was not like the women of my age then. Never used to find time for any kind of entertainment or socialising. Never found time to go to a movie, though my friends suggested some good ones. I was always serious and thinking about the country. I used to get a doubt why the others were not like me. Even if I went to a marriage, I was not much conscious of what was going on around me. I wrote rejoinders to many articles and write-ups that were published in the newspapers. I wrote letters to the editor like nobody's business! Many were published. I do not think any woman would have written so many letters to newspapers! Here I am particularly saying about 'any woman' because women (of my age and generation) generally bother about their family, children, job, and other kinds of entertainment. But for me, schoolwork, homework, organisation work, newspaper work, and my own educational pursuits and their related work consumed all the time. Of course, all of them interested me! They were all invigorating and energizing me. I was also asked to go through the work already done.

Whatever was sent to me I did sincerely to the best of my ability, though it was like punching above my weight as a schoolteacher. I always felt, like others in the organisation, I could not do the outside work by meeting and impressing the people of intellectual class. So, I have had a very less connect with people within and outside the organisation. My socialisation was limited to school.

Fatwas, of Muslim clergies, were another issue that was debated those days. There were like diktats issued for all and sundry by the clergies. This "fatwa" word was also a late introduction in to my lexicon. I did not hear any such word by such a name for a long time in my life. Pragna Bharati organised a public meeting on the book *The World of Fatwas or the Shariah in Action*, by Arun Shourie. Soon after the release of Arun Shourie's book on fatwas, this meeting was conducted. Basically, it was to introduce and promote the book. Arun Shourie and Moulana Wahiduddin Khan were the principal speakers. I read some of the articles on fatwas written by Arun Shourie by the time I attended the meeting. I did not even know Salman Rushdie had a fatwa on him for his *Satanic Verses* by Ayatollah Khomeini till I read his articles in detail. Most of my colleagues were unaware of fatwas and their existence. Do not misunderstand us. We are all educated, in the sense of obtained degrees, from universities in India but were oblivious of many things. Of course, sometimes, ignorance is bliss!

The impact of fatwas and the Muslim clergy were most common in North India. In the South, Kerala is a place where there is Muslim dominance. As far as Tamil Nadu, Andhra Pradesh, Telangana, and Karnataka are concerned, there are a sizable number of Muslims in different pockets. The chief ministers of these states directly appease minorities by always promising to grant more and more minority religious rights and privileges. Since majorities are a divided lot, they have nothing to say or offer whatsoever to please them!

Arun Shourie did a thorough research and produced a voluminous book on fatwas. I bought the book like a sincere bhakta (follower of Arun Shourie) but I could not read it in my packed schedule. Moreover, the book was very big in size and heavy in substance. I did read his articles devotedly every week. In fact, I used to wait for them because his logic and argument appealed to me then. Sometimes, I used to think that he was my advocate. It was so synchronised! But this fatwas book did not suit my taste. I turned a few pages and read them. It was so tedious to read such a lengthy text and interpretations! So many fatwas, for so many purposes! 'In what way that knowledge would help me?' I queried myself. Even if some clergy would say something, he would say on his co-religionist, not on me, I thought. Even if I understood the suffering of a person (a Muslim) victimised by fatwa, what could I do other than condemning it or sympathising with the person if it impinges on his individual right of freedom? I wondered at Shourie's erudition! How he could unearth so many fatwas even a Muslim of India may not know? He did a great research. When he takes up a topic, he leaves no stone unturned. I personally did not want to go deep down into the entire history of fatwas and their background. I thought it was of no use to me, I got better things to do in my life. None of my friends, relatives, and colleagues knew the fatwas' use or misuse. If I had to talk to them, I would be the odd person out in mid-'90s. Some of the newspaper reading sections knew about the fatwas on Rushdie and Taslima Nazreen. Taslima was from Bangladesh. When she wrote the book *Lazza*, she described how Hindu minorities were persecuted in her country, Bangladesh. It was a bold step on her part. All said and done, Pakistan and Bangladesh are Islamic-theocratic countries. They have their own laws of dealing with things. There are many Taslimas in India standing up for the minority cause. Of course, they are all counterfeits of Taslima!

I shrugged off 'fatwas' as something unwanted and wasteful of my mental investment. I kept my mind free and uncluttered. I searched in the introduction of the book the purpose of writing the book. At the beginning, Sri Shourie defined what's a fatwa. He writes, 'A fatwa is a decree, a ruling.' Then he further states, 'The *fatwas* accumulate. From time to time they are compiled. These compilations become both the high literature of the community, as well as the Islamic version of *Supreme Court Reports*'.[6]

In the introductory part, Shourie wrote why he took fatwas up as a subject to write, which no liberal Muslim or secularist had done. 'The reason is that analysing the fatwas would expose that which neither the secularist nor the Muslims wants exposed. The liberal Muslim has internalised the notion that to bring the truth about the Shariah to light, to put in the open facts about those who are the public face of the community is to "help the enemies of Islam". The secularist is even more reluctant to have these facts put to public view. He has established his credentials of secularism by espousing the very position which the *Ulema* and fundamentalist Muslim politicians have advocated.'[7] In the last paragraph of his introduction to the book *The World of Fatwas* he concludes (by reading his writing and the material in original) they (non-Muslims) would be helping to free Muslims from the thrall of the *Ulema*, they would be helping in their liberation.

The analysis of Shourie appealed to me well in one paragraph (page 663). That paragraph is worthy of mentioning wherein the behaviour of the people is still relevant. He writes, 'There is nothing like the fatwa among Hindus—but surely even our intellectuals know that. The point of such admonitions is different. In this view of the matter, a Hindu should stay clear of writing on Islam. Rather, that if he writes about matters Islamic or Muslim, he should only pen Hosannas—'the religion of tolerance, equality . . .' He should only write books 'understanding', that is *explaining away* the 'Muslim mind'. At the least, if he just has to allude to some unfortunate drawback in it, he must attribute it to some special time and place and exculpate Islam from it! Even more important, he must make sure that he 'balances' his remark about that point in Islam with denunciation about something in Hinduism, anything—the caste system, dowry deaths, looking upon foreigners as *malechh*, at least *sutee* if nothing else fits the bill!'[8] This analysis amply clarifies pseudo-secular mind of our intellectuals.

When I read the above interpretation of the mind-set of secularists in India written by Shourie in his book, it reminded me what Swapan Dasgupta had written in his book review on *The World of Fatwas*. He writes, 'Backed by a formidable array of textual evidence, Shourie provides answers that are both predictable and disconcerting. Predictable because they confirm what many have instinctively felt about a fanatically obstinate streak that runs through political Islam. And disconcerting because Shourie indicates the magnitude of the problem. In the process, he makes a complete mockery of banal, goody-goody secularism masquerading as wisdom.'[9]

One day, accidentally, I met an eminent man in our organisation. He advised me that it was better for me to know certain things about Muslims/Islam before I talk. I asked, 'What kind of things?' He said, 'Do you know *Ummah*?' I said, 'I haven't heard the name. I don't even know such a word (*ummah*) exists'. He sneered at me and looked as if I was worthless. He told me clearly that there was no use of talking to me. So, I had to go back to Arun Shourie's articles collected and preserved by me. My revered guru, Arun Shourie, also wrote articles on 'Ummah'. In it he wrote how Jinnah used *Ummah* to justify their opposition to national freedom movement. He writes, 'Jinnah and the rest began harping on the claim that Islam did not recognise national boundaries, that it was a supra-national ideology, that the loyalty of Muslims was to the international Islamic Ummah, and not to a mere country.'[10] That article had given me some perspective. However, it is my belief that religion alone will not bring unity among people as the founding father of Pakistan Jinnah said. Had it been the case, there would not have been any fights in Pakistan. There were so many words like *sharia, nikah, fatwa, talaq, jihad, kafir* that were all new to me. Slowly, they got added into my repertoire of vocabulary.

First, my enlightenment came with the word *Kafir. Kafir* is the word used for idolaters. The only word I knew before my coming to the organisation was *burqa*. We know that it is a practice with Muslim women. I always wondered how they resist from showing off their beautiful dresses by wearing it. India, being a free country, burqa here is optional cloak for Muslim women to wear. None finds fault with those who wear or do not wear.

In those days, 'Shah Bano' and 'Bofors' were recited like *mantras* (holy chanting) by media. Shah Bano case was not fatwa-driven, I think. The case is understandable. When her husband gave her divorce after being married for forty years, the apex court gave a direction to give alimony to her. That was not in accordance with Shariah, said the clergies. So, Rajiv Gandhi went ahead and made Constitutional amendment to grant wakf boards money from government to give alimony to such cases. This is a community problem related to a particular religion though.

The cases of Bofors and Shah Bano had little impact on South Indian people at large. I did not know, for quite a long time, that Bofors was a gun deal and Shah Bano was a case to be known. I do not think, even now, many people know them in this part of the country. Even Indira Gandhi's emergency had had a little impact on us. I still wonder when politicians keep saying on TV channels how ghastly those days were! I always think, was it so? When I heard about the Bofors gun deal, I thought, why was the deal given outside, could we not make our own in India? I did not know at that point of time that

India had no technical know-how like developed countries do to make defence equipment. So patriotically, we were taught in our schools and educational institutions that India is all great and powerful! In reality, that was all bravado when we could not even make our defence equipment. 'If we cannot make our own weaponry, what are we standing for?' I felt. I feel good now that our PM initiated to make defence equipment indigenously.

Coming to fatwas, whether to follow them or not is that community's affair. People from other communities could question if it affects them or the fabric of the country. Even if information is disseminated through public meetings and printed matter on fatwas, the response from people is miniscule, as far as our region is concerned. Like the earlier public meeting on 'Missionaries in India', this meeting on fatwas also was well conducted and well received. Most of the participants were Sangh activists. Being in Sangh makes them aware of the world. They know what's going on in Turkey, Iraq, Iran, Syria, Russia, Europe, USA, and of course in Pakistan and Bangladesh, in those days, when information flow was not this quick. People from outside Sangh, I mean common people on the road, do not know where these countries are on the world map. They know nothing of what's going on in those countries. As usual, I got the tapes from Ram Madhav for verbatim transcription and translation into Telugu. While writing to get a booklet published, I got enough knowledge on fatwas. As to when, where, and how the fatwas are used by clerics, they were all quite mind-boggling. Now, I completely forgot about them.

Regarding uniform civil code, which Article 44 of the Constitution envisages, Pragna Bharati held a symposium and a public meeting on how to go about it. Arun Shourie was the principal speaker. He pointed out that Shariat was supported and legislated by the British for their own political gains. He strongly supported the UCC for India.

Pragna Bharati's main aim is to disseminate useful information regarding the country to thinking people. There would not be any awakening for the majorities in India had the RSS not been born or established. Indian majorities cannot be compared with majorities of the Western countries. In the West, the majority means proper majorities in the true sense. In India, majorities are in a way caste-ridden and weak. They need to be guided and groomed in a proper direction. The RSS is meant for the purpose. The founders of the RSS established it as a socio-cultural organisation, which is good. Had the RSS been a political body, it would have been corrupted by now like any other party, for the very nature of politics tends to do that.

At individual level, people know that their powers are limited. Here the RSS plays a role. They arrange gatherings where they make people aware of changes that are taking place in geo-political world and within India. They elaborate the conditions and the impending dangers to the country. Earlier, mainstream media would never telecast what the RSS stands for. Whenever they got a chance, they gave a negative picture. Now that social media has given space to people's voice, there is kind of momentum to the right ideology also.

Pragna Bharati encouraged free speech:

Pragna Bharati had conducted many inter-faith dialogues on religious matters, calling eminent people from each side. Often Moulana Wahiduddin Khan was invited to talk on uniform civil code and fatwas and other Muslim minority—related issues. Arun Shourie liked Wahiddudin Khan for the latter's appeal and simplicity. Maulana Wahiddudin Khan was known to be a liberal for the conservatives in the community. He was not combative in his argument. I took some of the invitations for Wahiduddin Khan's programme on fatwas to school to invite some of my Muslim colleagues. I gave to a male teacher the invitation personally after greeting him in the corridor. When I asked him whether he would turn up to the meeting, he deftly refused to attend. He said Moulana Wahiddudin Khan was a docile and compromising man. There was no point in listening to him. The others also could not make it. As usual, I was entrusted with recorded tapes to take verbatim notes from them and translate into Telugu for a booklet publication. I did it dutifully though struggling with other works. Within the stipulated time, I submitted to Ram Madhav.

My whole lot of verbatim (word for word) transcription and translations of Arun Shourie's speeches were on the fatwas, uniform civil code, and Christian missionaries in India and their work—is it useful or harmful to the country? —into Telugu. Those translations were published by Pragna Bharati in two-booklet forms of fifty to sixty pages in 1995. The organisation, Pragna Bharati, got them published and gave me some complimentary copies; that was really hard work converted to print.

Ram Madhav did one more act to motivate me to do work. When Arun Shourie had come to Hyderabad, Ram Madhav apprised him of my work (i.e. translating his speeches into Telugu for publication). At that time, Arun Shourie was pleased to know me doing contribution to the organisation. He was about to leave Hyderabad. He was in Hyderabad airport. He immediately sat down on a chair, opened his briefcase, and took out a plain paper and scribbled on it some lines of appreciation (of my work). That was all told by Ram Madhav to me when he met me later and handed over the paper. I read it and read it and read it repeatedly those two, three lines. That handwritten lines, the kind of concern shown, was worth millions! He wrote that Ram Madhav told him about how much effort I was devoting to prepare reports and translations. He thanked me for all the trouble. I preserved the memorable lines on the paper with me to remain. But for Ram Madhav's efforts of taking my contribution to the organisation to Sri Shourie, my work would not have got noticed. Of course, that was also Ram Madhav's oganisational skill!

Pragna Bharati was closely knit under Ram Madhav's period. He assembled family get-togethers often. On one such get-together, it was a happy coincidence to have Sri Arun Shourie also in the city on that day, 15 November 1995. Sri Shourie had been kind enough to accept the invitation to grace the occasion. He had spent two hours with the families and joined the dinner in the end. In his brief address to the assembled family members, he reminisced his association with Pragna Bharati and stated that he would always tell about the wonderful work that the organisation was doing wherever he went. He exhorted the organising members to keep the light of Pragna Bharati aflame and alive.

Tailpiece: The two books, *Missionaries in India* and *The World of Fatwas* are the major contributions of Sri Arun Shourie for posterity. They could well be used as the best reference books by the generations to come. The thorough research and factual figures documented in writing (nobody questioned the authenticity of the data he produced, hence factual) would remain ever after for the use of inquisitive and spirited young people of this country.

Endnotes

1. 'Social Rendezvous', *Deccan Chronicle*, 31-07-1993
2. Arun Shourie's column on Swadeshi, 'Will heckling halt time?' *Deccan Chronicle*, 10-04-1994
3. Ibid., 'Oblivious of principle' 08-05-1994
4. Arun Shourie's column 'All right, a Ram Sevak Sangh', *Deccan Chronicle*, 20-12-1992
5. Arun Shourie's column 'Fait accompli as law', *Deccan Chronicle*, 17-01-1993
6. Arun Shourie, *The World of Fatwas* or *The Shariah in Action*, p. 1
7. Ibid., p. 4
8. Ibid., p. 663
9. Swapan Das Gupta's column, 'Veiled Truths', Courtesy Financial Express published in Vandemataram Dec'95, Jan'96
10. Arun Shourie's Column on 'Ummah' Deccan Chronicle dated 31-08-1997

CHAPTER 3

An Inspirational Pracharak: Ram Madhav

The office of *Jagriti* weekly magazine, run by the RSS, was in Narayanguda, in the midst of Hyderabad. It was a big and old building, but there was a lot of space inside, as far as the urban standards are considered.

For the first time, I, along with my husband, went there. When I went inside, it seemed to me that it was a residence turned office. All the rooms were occupied with reporters' desks. There were many employees.

There was a separate room for the associate editor of the RSS weekly, *Jagriti* with an office secretary to assist. The associate editor was none other than Ram Madhav, the Pracharak. Usually, organisation magazines are read by dedicated cadres, followers, and sympathisers. Their circulation is limited to that extent most often. But somehow, during Ram Madhav's tenure, apart from organisation's ideological articles, he carried various other items that made the news weekly interesting. They included interviews with eminent people (he himself conducted), book reviews of latest books, opinion-building articles on contemporary issues, movie reviews, beauty pageant contests, of course, with a slight slant of ideology. The beauty contests at that time and the awards won over by the Indian contestants was a design by the West to increase the sale of cosmetics produced in their countries to India. I totally agreed with the journal's view of encouraging consumerism of non-essentials in a big way to the two hundred million middle classes of India, at that point in time when money was scarce. There was a valid reason then to construe in this angle.

Besides his main work, Ram Madhav ran a newsletter 'Vande Bharat Mataram' in English language for the nationalist thinkers. This newsletter, in those days, was very informative. Being himself the editor of Vandemataram (in short), he instantly gathered very good news items to be published. Though a monthly newsletter, it was a loaded one. Ram Madhav had done all these journalist activities passionately, though that was the age of rather slow-pace activities. Above all, he brought out many books. Some of them were written by him and some by others who had expertise to write in the organisation. He was a bundle of energy, who invigorated people with his magnetic personality.

Pragna Bharati was a voluntary organisation to which Ram Madhav was the organising secretary. The content of the newsletter Vandemataram covered the reports of the meetings conducted by Pragna Bharati also. This newsletter was thrown into our house compound by someone sometime prior to my coming to Jagriti. Never thought that magazine would turn my fate. And one day, I would become its publications in charge. On the front page of the newsletter hurled into the compound was Arun Shourie's picture and his coming to address a meeting to be conducted by the organisation. This prompted me to go to Jagriti office to introduce myself and ask for the meeting details like when it was going to take place.

Ram Madhav emerged from somewhere and sat on the lone chair. I and my husband were sitting in front. He was quite reserved. Didn't speak much. He looked at us as if to know the purpose of our coming. We said, to know the meeting of Arun Shourie and to subscribe the magazine for our friends. We subscribed to Vandemataram by paying money for annual subscription for three of my colleagues and my aunt who were interested to read. That was the first time I saw Ram Madhav in person in '94. After giving our names and addresses for sending subscription, there was an informal chat. In between, he said I was already in their Mahila Morcha list. I was perplexed. From where could they get my name? I thought. Later, I came to know there were many Sangh activists working in our locality. I was slightly perturbed at my inclusion in the Mahila Morcha. Mahila Morcha? Why couldn't it be in a general kind of a grouping? I felt. Ultimately, knowing the kind of thoughts I had in mind, Ram Madhav inducted me in Pragna Bharati. A few months passed.

How I became a member of Pragna Bharati:

I did not know that I should be formally initiated into an organisation to be with them to do any work. I thought if my mind was with them, that was enough. It was not so. Ram Madhav, knowing my enthusiasm, told me sternly one day that I needed to take some responsibility in the organisation. I was hesitant. I was already burdened with job and household responsibilities. And I was doing all the work the organisation entrusted, by way of writing reports. Sometimes the whole spoken record in the round tables and seminars was brought into verbatim. It consumed so much of my personal time. But he was clever in finding out my weak point. He said, unless I took up some office bearer's post, I would not be called to meetings. I was very keen on listening to the meeting conducted by the organisation. Never missed one public meeting. I ensured myself to be at the venue of the meet before time so that I would not miss a word. Soon after my association with the organisation, I was made in charge of *Vandemataram* newsletter. All this is to say our organising secretary knew how to use the available resources and in what manner.

Our organising secretary also used to send my reports to the *organiser* the RSS-run weekly magazine *Delhi* for publishing. As an organisation man, he used to make necessary changes to project the organisation's point of view in those reports. When the reports were published in my name, he would send the magazine to me to see. Initially, I was elated. In them the major chunk was mine, but occasionally, the arrangement was different. This way Ram Madhav was duty-bound to encourage several people by incentivising them. To some, he entrusted writing work, to some others doing computer work for the organisation for publishing pamphlets and books, to some others for public contacts, to some for roping in eminent people. It was also his job to talk to all highly positioned persons in the society. He used to meet people of higher cadre on daily basis to impress upon the ideals the organisation stands for and to bring them in.

Later, I was made the associate editor of *Bharathiya Pragna* magazine, run by Pragna Bharati. After two years, in another term, I became one of the secretaries of Pragna Bharati. I had never asked them for all these designations. In my world of things, they have no place. Even without all these so-called positions, I would have definitely done the work entrusted because I believed what I was doing was correct; moreover, it was giving a lot of input to my mind to think on the ongoing situation in the country.

Ram Madhav's regular job was to speak for the organisation in the meetings, write for the organisation, meet people for the organisation on a day-to-day basis. He was the full-timer of the RSS. He did all these jobs quite capably. He was full of vigor and spirited. His presence used to bring life to the organisation. Such an electrifying and majestic personality. Before conducting a big public meeting on issue of national importance, there were preparatory meetings called *baithaks* held by Ram Madhav. How to go about the meeting was discussed. These were held mainly in Jagriti office. The office was, as I said, a residential complex. It had a front yard with colourful flowering plants. Fifteen to twenty chairs were laid. In the *baithak,* the core group discussed how to go about with the proposed meeting. Each member was assigned with specific tasks to be discharged.

Pragna Bharati also had a women's wing. The head of the wing was Smt Vijaya Bharathiji. She did all her work in consultation with Ram Madhav. Even for the public meetings of women's wing, i.e. Mahila Morcha of Pragna Bharati, Ram Madhav used to head the meetings. So much of dependency on him! Selection of speakers, invitations, and arrangements were all done in consultation with him. Ram Madhav's opinion was the ultimate deciding factor. Be it for any meeting.

To me, it was so amusing to see the organising secretary taking up women's issues, though being a Pracharak and a bachelor. One day, while we were speaking on a certain women's issue, he said, 'Shourieji will be in the city at that time, we will involve him, he will also talk on that issue.' I said, 'How can he speak on a women's issue?' (for, In South India, we had a clear demarcation between men and women. There was a kind of segregation of men and women in gatherings also. Generally, men neither know nor speak of women's issues.) Ram Madhav looked at me as if I asked a stupid question and said, 'People like him know about all issues.' I was of the firm view that one should be a woman to know women's problems. It's a kind of experiential knowledge. It is not easy for anyone to talk about anything deeper without a first-hand knowledge. That was the time, i.e. in 1994, women's issues were coming into focus. The leftists were very advanced in dealing with them though their solutions were drastic. That was the time Pragna Bharati conducted a meeting on 'Feminism, the Bharathiya Perspective'.

The work of an RSS Pracharak I have seen:

To make Hindu society strong and closely knit, the RSS Pracharaks and swayamsevaks work with people very closely. Here the Hindu society does not mean any religious connotation. It's generic. It encompasses all religions. As a matter of fact, in the office bearers' posts, there were many Muslims and Christians and other religious people. The RSS Pracharaks have association with families. They gel with family members so well, they become one with them. They try to solve if they (families) have any problems, say comforting words if they are in trouble. They partake food in their houses. They will be with them in trouble and despair. Mainly, they draw children by playing with them and telling them stories. They mingle with the families.

Ram Madhav liked arbitration. I think Sangh taught him this knack to unite people. If there was rift between two people, he would personally go there and sort it out. Thus he fixed many a couple who were on the verge of breaking their marriage. He also arbitrated and settled inter-caste marriages and love marriages. This talent, I think, he used in the formation of Jammu and Kashmir government in 2015. But for his efforts, the odd coalition would not have been formed!

Before being formally part of the organisation Pragna Bharati, I attended a meeting of Ram Madhav, conducted in a school in Malkajgiri (a locality in Hyderabad). As the meeting happened to be nearby for me, I attended it. That was in the evening time at five o'clock. After the meeting, I had to leave for an important work. So, I was tense throughout the meeting. On one side, I wanted to hear what he was saying intently; on the other side, I had to leave on some work. My friend and Ram Madhav's right hand in the organisation, Smt Vijaya Bharathiji, invited me cordially to attend the meeting to gain the knowledge of 'Swadeshi'. At that time 'Swadeshi Jagaran Manch' of Sri Gurumurthyji was at its height, making agitations against multinationals entry into the country! They made the agitation against Enron Power Plant so widely. By then, Ram Madhav and other important functionaries in the organisation conducted independently many meetings in important locations and apprised people what was Swadeshi and what was Videshi, be it in food items or cosmetics. Printouts were distributed. By the time I attended the meeting of Ram Madhav, my mind was saturated with Arun Shourie's ideas of economic reforms. They also appealed to me. Like how a sponge absorbs water, I absorbed what he had written.

That meeting of Ram Madhav was of a small scale one. In those days, these small or mini meetings also had had an impact. That was how movements pick up momentum. It was conducted in a private school premises. There were many trees in the campus. The meeting was under one of those trees. Only twenty-five to thirty women attended. Most of them were schoolteachers and some of them housewives. There were also around ten elderly men who were probably from Sangh background. For often they cheered for whatever Ram Madhav said. That type concurrence we get from the same-ideology people. Only Ram Madhav sat on a chair, and others including me were sitting on the floor in a semi-circular way around him. It appeared to me that Ram Madhav was our guru and we being shishyas sitting around in a gurukul.

At the beginning of the meeting, Vijaya Bharathiji introduced Ram Madhav to the audience. She said he was associate editor of *Jagriti* and was a writer of many books. After introduction, Ram Madhav began his speech. He was spirited in supporting Swadeshi and opposed multinationals entry. He said how bad it was for our country's traders! How they would get affected with the stiff competition. Though I was a Swadeshi at heart and deemed myself a patriotic citizen, this speech of his did not move an inch. 'Why should I have sympathy for our traders?' I thought. In India, there was an impression at that time that our traders see to short-term gains and produce cheap-quality products whereas foreign companies go for long-term gains by making quality products.

The women around me were quite attentive and heard everything that was said to them. They heard multinationals were going to invade our country very soon like how once East India Company of the British did to us. So were cautioned! Next our businessmen would lose their business! They could go into losses. There would be unemployment. 'Why should the multinationals come into potato chips business? Why should they come into Maggi noodles? Indian traditional snacks are much nutritious. Those chips and other snacks are being prepared from the time of our grandmothers. Why the entry of multinationals now?' was the logic given. People should encourage our products, i.e. Indian ones. The listed handouts were also distributed. 'Be Indian and buy Indian' was the message.

There was a question-answer session at the end. None of the women asked any question. The men were happy and contended with the presentation. They showered encomiums on Ram Madhav for defending Swadeshi so well, so thoroughly, and so convincingly. I was the only one wondering . . . why should I support this 'Swadeshi'? My doubt was when I could pay money to buy a best product, why should I care who produced it? Whoever gives quality product for the money we pay, we buy it. The same question I posed to Ram Madhav, unmindful of the audience presence. 'If the multinationals give the product of my choice or requirement, why shan't I buy? My cousin gets things from America that are of fine quality. If the same are sold by multinationals, we would like to buy.'

For the above question, Ram Madhav's answer was, 'We should strengthen our traders to the level of multinationals and then we have to open up our economy. Just because, as you have said, they (our traders) are bad, you cannot ask the outsiders to come and hit them.' Then as a subsequent question, I asked him, 'When will our traders get strengthened (time frame) to face the multinationals? Will it be possible? Why should we wait that long?' For that he said, 'We should have internal competition among our businessmen. That will enhance the quality of their product. And they themselves learn the craft.' I was not convinced like many Indians. I too thought that most of our business people (barring a few) do not maintain quality. The meeting took place in 1994.

The next day, Ram Madhav spoke to me over telephone. He was very sparing in his words. Never called anyone unless the situation warranted. Even if he called, he would confine limitedly to the subject matter he would like to communicate. No extra words. If somebody in the organisation spoke more than necessary, he would cut the line off himself. When he rang up after the meeting the next day, I was stunned. He said he expected me to stay after the meeting to clarify my doubts regarding 'Swadeshi'. I told him that I had an urgent work to attend to. I said to myself later, when 'Swadeshi' itself was a big doubt, where was the question of other doubts?

In RSS culture, as far as I know, Pracharaks come close to families. They like face-to-face interactions. For them, it is not the individual that counts. It is the whole family together that matters. So, they maintain contact with the families. They bring in as many families as possible to Sangh's fold. For which they go to houses, talk to people, involve them in the activities of their interest.

In the month of 'Karteek' they arrange 'Vana Bhojan' (community partaking of food). They also wish the families on the festivals. They attend any event in their house whether good or bad. Part of their humanitarian endeavour is helping the flood victims, earthquake victims, any kind of accident victims and blood donation camps for the needy. The first time when Ram Madhav said he would come home to visit and meet us all, I was so excited.

I cleaned and kept everything neat and ready in the house. Prepared some dishes to offer. All of us were waiting eagerly. My children thought by his name, Ram Madhav, he must be an old man. He did not turn up that day to our utter disappointment. At the last minute, he sent a written message through someone in the organisation saying that because of some organisational commitments he was not able to come home that day. He also stated in it, for a crazy person like him, organisation was paramount and said sorry for not being able to live up to his commitment.

After reading the letter, I felt sorry. With the time, I have detached myself from persons and started seeing things objectively. However, it took a lot of effort on my part.

Organisations cater to the individual needs also. Ram Madhav gifted me many books. Even the new books after his first reading, he would give me. Most of them were from Voice of India publication. He presented me *Bunch of Thoughts* by Sri Golwalkar, quite early when I entered the organisation. By then, I was already a convinced ideologist. Whatever doubts I raised on the contemporary politics then, my uncle used to say, 'You are saying the same, what the RSS says, what the BJP says.' I was unaware at that time that those two entities had been voicing the same as mine. My main point was, at that time—and now also—is, that in a secular country, all the citizens should be treated equally; the state should not appease anyone.

Ram Madhav's way of working with people was unique. Pracharaks of Sangh are actually organisers, as an organising head, he knew how to bring the people to the organisation. And also how to engage them in a useful manner. It used to take time for him to exercise his mind to fix them in some work that suits the organisation. But the amount of pain he took was enormous. All those who came were not that receptive. Even if some were enthusiastic, that would not sustain for long. Ideology was the only glue; otherwise, people have some amount of individual differences. To treat everyone equally and to appear non-partisan is an uphill task for any organising secretary.

Ram Madhav invited me into the fraternity with no qualms. At times, he was slightly sceptical of me whether I could adjust to the organisation setup. He tested me on several parameters. I used to wonder whether that was needed. Once or twice, I asked what was all that endless testing. In any case, but for the organising secretary Ram Madhav, I would not have worked so enthusiastically. To me, he was no different from my own brothers.

However, he in his wisdom encouraged members who had ideological understanding, commitment to the cause, and dedication to work for the organisation. Those were the yardsticks for him to measure his karyakartas.

After I was drawn to Pragna Bharati, I attended many meetings. The very first one was that of Maneka Gandhi's. The organisation conducted a public meeting on Al-Kabir abattoir opposing its cow slaughter. Menaka Gandhi was the principal speaker. It was on 16 July 1994.

During the agitation on Al-Kabir abattoir, there were banners displayed at various places on the roads of Hyderabad saying, 'Stop meat export'.

Al-Kabir is located about fifty kilometres from Hyderabad. Abattoirs cannot slaughter animals in an unregulated way. They need to promote livestock management strategy for the surrounding areas. For animals' management is a part of rural economic development in India.

The agitation stuck the chord with many Hindus because it had a slogan of 'Ban cow slaughter.' A custom most of the Hindus religiously practice.

Usually, working women (like me) would find very little time to attend such meets. At the venue, I found some serious-looking RSS members present, gesturing people to go in, by showing their hand, indicating the direction of the hall. In the RSS hierarchy, it was my observation, members were always serious with no-nonsense attitude. It was somewhat baffling to me. They greet people with formal 'namaste'. Hi-bye type of outside gestures, airs, and graces were unknown and unseen. I found them to be more patriotic and matter-of-fact. This I could say confidently because they think the welfare of the country is paramount to them. Before being in the organisation, I had never seen people who were so steadfast in their commitment to the nation.

Ram Madhav, the organising secretary, was standing along with other senior members, carefully monitoring people who were entering into the venue, as if noting the invitees' attendance. Before coming to the venue, I asked Ram Madhav whether I should attend the meet. He said it would be better if I could. It was not that I could not make my own decision. It was because I have had inhibitions to go to such public meets as a stranger. And I was not used to with no known person there. So, I needed a known person. I took a daring step of going alone in a public transport bus. The meet was in Gandhi Bhavan, Nampally, Hyderabad, a very busy centre of the city. Though Ram Madhav knew me and invited me, he looked at me at the venue as if I was a strange specimen or an alien who had come from another planet. Maybe it was his nature, I thought. His seriousness seemed to be a bit uncordial to me. However, very soon, I realized my purpose of coming there. I just wanted to get an answer to my emotions. Emotion of killing cows in Al-Kabir abattoir.

I went in and sat in a row. It was behind the first two rows that were allotted to the press. I was comfortable sitting in that row. For I thought I would not be visible to people. I did not know why I had that thought that someone would look at me or observe me. I knew I was a small speck in the universe. Nobody needed to bother about me. But somehow, I was always self-conscious. In any meeting, I used to choose some cosy, unseen corners to sit. Those corners used to give me a feeling of comfort. That way, I could concentrate more on what I had to, shedding the inhibition of the sub-conscious feeling of someone overseeing me. So, in that very big hall of Gandhi Bhavan,

I was like a dot in one place, neatly dressed, not caring for anyone around. However, the organising secretary's sharp, searching eyes noticed me. I saw him leaning slightly on a karyakartha and telling something in her ear.

Later, that person came to me and asked me to present a bouquet to Maneka Gandhi on the dais to welcome her. Though I was shy and reluctant to go on to the stage, I could not say 'no' to her, leading to some fuss. I went on to the stage dutifully and handed over the bouquet to her smilingly, saying, 'You are welcome, madam'. As I was coming to Maneka Gandhi, she was looking at me smilingly. I still remember that her smile was so natural compared to mine, which I forced upon me as I was not much used to socialising. Public figures are used to courtesies and niceties! I wondered why Ram Madhav gave preference to me over others to go on to dais for this bouquet presentation. The others were my seniors in the organisation and had been working from its inception. The answer is simple: new ones are encouraged and are made a part by these gestures. To meet her from close quarters and to have a photo with her is a memorable thing to me. Still, whenever I see that photo, I wonder how Maneka Gandhi and I were so young in it! That was the time photo-ops were rare.

The meeting started with *Vandemataram* song sung fully. It is a practice in all Pragna Bharati meetings to sing the song completely at the beginning. I thought Al-Kabir abattoir was meant for killing cows. I did not know there were also other animals that were slaughtered. Killing of cows really enraged me. 'Poor cows, they are so gentle, pious, harmless, worshipped everywhere, why should they be killed? Why are they targeted and butchered?' I thought. We compare a mild and docile child in the house to a cow. 'That girl or woman is as gentle as a cow' a metaphorical usage, those days. To articulate cow protection in India, I never knew one should come through the root of cattle protection. This cattle protection is guaranteed under an article in the directive principles of the Constitution was unknown to me then. I did not know to protect cows. I should cite how the tigers are killed. The tigers are killed for want of sheep (by humans). The sheep are sent to the abattoir to be killed and exported. I did not know how goat grazing is damaging lakhs of hectares of forests and depleting ground table. I did not know every goat eats up grass grown over sixteen hectares before it is slaughtered. I was unaware till Maneka Gandhi

spoke, the Al-kabir had been stealing cattle to run the abattoir. When Maneka Gandhi advocated the people to desist from meat eating, I was immensely pleased.

People are free to eat anything they like—it is guaranteed under Indian Constitution. How many in India know what is in the Constitution? How many have studied it or know the salient features of it? Though elementary principles are written in textbooks, could all the students from all backgrounds relate it to their daily lives? Some people who are not literate—vegetable vendors, fruit sellers, mechanics—do they know about what constitutes human rights? When did this rights issue come into existence?

The way Ms Maneka related the Al-Kabir issue to the killing of cattle to the protection of tigers, i.e. wild life protection and environment effects, the pollution of Ganga due to leather industry in Kanpur City, and of course, the way borrowing millions of dollars to clean it up from World Bank and not being able to clean a drop, and how cattle and sheep are bred for meat and beef, causing enormous harm to the country's economy. That was all enlightening. That was the time the issues like pollution, environment, and World Bank were in vogue as the topics of discussion.

When Ms Maneka made a political point like, 'If the prime minister, who hails from the state, does not do anything to stop the unit, you know what to do', everybody cheered. I went up to the meeting with a cow in my mind, but a whole lot of cattle filled it at the end. I noted all the points. It was a matter of habit. Our organising secretary noticed me carefully noting. His keen eye observed. As an organising head, he sent me a note, to make a report of the meeting. I felt happy to make that report; it was a pleasant activity to make a review of the whole lecture and decide which were important and needed to be highlighted. After all, a report is the summary that brings the essence of the meeting.

The other day, when I presented my report, Ram Madhav had read it and had a satisfied look. He smiled and kept it in the draw. In the organisation, they never applaud people for their work or thank them. I have had the habit of saying 'thanks', 'excuse me', 'sorry', kind of things quite often wherever necessary. Ram Madhav used to ridicule my etiquette. I asked him what was wrong with my behaviour and why this kind of mannerisms were not followed. He retorted by saying, 'Do you thank your family members, if they render any service or help to you? If you think all of us are a family, no one needs to thank anyone. If you still think, you are an outsider, I would say thanks to you for each and everything.' I gave a careful thought to what he said. It was so with most of the Indian families; we do not often thank each other in a family, unless the help is very big or substantial. Whereas with outsiders, we thank even for a smallest help.

Family members help each other, which is natural. But it is not mandatory for them thank each other; it could be the reason. In Indian culture 'help' is a natural act. In the organisational meetings I had seen, if someone makes a speech on important occasions on the podium, after the speech, none would clap or applaud. That person, the speaker, silently goes and sits. To an outsider, it may seem strange, but within the organisation, it is natural.

The report I had given was published in *Vandemataram,* without any edits, in the next issue. It was indeed a great pleasure to see my report in Ram Madhav's paper with my name. In those days, it was a rare sight. Now people of all hues express their opinions, in some form or the other, i.e. either print or electronic media, with so many publication sites available. When I collected the paper, and was looking at my reporting and reading it, I could notice Ram Madhav observing me. His focus was on my reaction. After sometime, he asked me, 'Do you need to read what you have written?' meaning to say, 'You know the content, what's the point in wasting time to read?' In his case, he wouldn't waste his time in reading what he had written. He would jump from one thing to the other, never bothers about the past. He always would say, 'I am an activist, today is important to me.'

This writing of reports made me so perfect that once when I attended our school-conducted workshop on how to bring creativity in students, I prepared and sent a report on it to our higher authorities. They praised it and sent it to all schools of their management. So, I could say that writing reports to the organisation smoothened my hand. So, hard work pays dividends.

Ram Madhav was always happy, forward-looking, enthusiastic, and confident. Whenever I asked him, on any issue, whether he was upset, he used to say, 'I am always happy.' He knew, if one worked hard, things would fall in place. He had no permanent binding with any person, place, or thing. It is said, Pracharaks go to any place, where the top brass of the RSS writes the address. His mind was solely dedicated to the RSS. He had once said if RSS says to forget or cut off relationship with a person who is very close to him, he would do it immediately. This seemed to be scary to me where I would be fired one day. I think he made the remark only to emphasize his abiding loyalty to the organisation.

As a person, I consider myself very independent and individualistic. Because I was born and brought up as such. My mother never imposed her opinion on me. On any matter related to me, first she would ask my opinion, then she would add hers, if she differed. Pros and cons were discussed. The final decision depended on my thinking and my mental framework.

Ram Madhav was committed to the organisation. He believed the higher-ups (whom he called elders) in the organisation and their wisdom. Wherever he was sent to a new place with some new kind of work, he would go there with renewed vigour, would make new friendships and relationships in that place, and would work along with them. He appears to snap ties with the old ones. Perhaps as a general principle, old friendships might cause impediments to a new assignment.

I was not only offered the paper in which my report on Al-Kabir abattoir was published but also my photo presenting a bouquet to Maneka Gandhi. In those days, having a picture with a celebrity was deemed an honour. For like how we have now, there were no digital cameras or cellular phones available then. Film rolls (Kodak times) were prevalent. The year 1994 did not see the potential of globalisation or global technology in India. It was just budding. Now, taking a snap with a person of eminence is no big deal. It needs no one's assistance. Selfies have become the order of the day.

Our organising secretary, Ram Madhav, provided such photo ops with many big Indian leaders. Not that I was crazy of taking photos with those eminent people; it was just for freezing the moment. Just for remembrance. We feel nostalgic when we see these snaps. But for that, there is no other point in taking these snaps. All that taking of snaps had happened when the leaders had come to Pragna Bharati meetings. Introducing and arranging audience with these eminent persons and photo ops with them were also only to enthuse the team members, the backbone of the organisation.

Public meetings of the Al-Kabir kind were the order of the day. For at that time 24/7 TV channels were not in place. However, I could not attend all the in-house meetings as I was a working woman. When I said the same to the organising secretary, he reprimanded me by saying, 'All those who come to Pragna Bharati are busy in their field. We do not entertain idle people here. Those who come here are contributing something or the other to the society.' But somehow, I was not convinced with his answer.

Most of the organisations are male-dominated. Men can pursue their interests more easily than women. They have no hindrances. The greatest disadvantages for a working woman were looking after children at home, doing household work, assisting children in their home assignment given by the school. If there are aged parents or in-laws, that should also be taken care of. For a man in the house, there is no binding to do all this stuff. His contribution at home is optional and voluntary. If a man takes up any one of those jobs at home, either he would do messily or end up in not doing for the fear of criticism. A man needs training to do household work; whereas for a woman, that's natural and automatic.

It became very difficult for me to convince Ram Madhav on all these matters. He did not like people who were argumentative on matters of work sharing. Once he said, 'All these works like report writing, translation, article writing, meeting people, arranging programmes, accommodating, and attending to guests, I alone could do. I do not need help from you people. I am just trying to give you work so that you become part of the organisation. Organisation always needs horizontal growth.'

The two women who worked very hard for the organisation Pragna Bharati were Smt Vijayabharathi of Rastriya Savika Samithi and Smt Parijatha. Their service was selfless and dedicated. They both are still rendering with the same zeal. Then comes Karen Dipankar of Trinidad and Tobago Islands. She loves India. She came to study in India and was deeply involved in the organisation work. She used to work day and night for publication of books.

Our organising secretary was a strict disciplinarian. He was a little lenient in my case. When I asked him why he was being kind, he said that they all came from the families that had the background of Sangh, whereas, I was an outsider. Then I realised that the Sangh wanted people of different perspectives and capabilities with different paces of doing work. They would take from a person what he or she was capable of doing.

I used to abide by the deadlines set by Ram Madhav. I always gave back the work done before the expected time. Once when Arun Shourie's translation work was done and given to Ram Madhav, I still remember him appreciating my sense of commitment as well as timely submission, adhering to schedule. It was a strenuous job. But his compliments gave me much needed relief and helped to forget the strain taken. He was the one and only person who seemed to be a personal friend of everybody in the organisation, knowing all the people's problems and helping them out. Here I would like to humbly say that the work I did was miniscule and insignificant compared to the toil some of the karyakartas, who do day and night, in the scorching sun and heavy downpour of rain, risking their lives, convincing people, helping the distressed, always thinking about the country and her well-being.

Often, Ram Madhav used to send a topic to me to write on. So, I used to read a lot to write on that particular issue. It consumed a lot of time and effort. Yet the activity, I felt, was worth pursuing. I have seen normal people who are always on the lighter side, having fun and frolic, dancing and eating in restaurants, some youngsters boozing and abusing and while away time. Whereas Sangh's youth are heavily burdened in thought and deed. Very appreciable! I can't blame the former because it is their chosen life. I can't call the latter to be superior, for the simple reason I shouldn't be judgemental! I would like to narrate with my limited knowledge what I heard on how an ideology drives a person.

I was worried often of the things that were happenings around in the country, but Ram Madhav always used to look cheerful. Never seem to be worried. He used to work in Jagriti from morning till evening, when he had no tours. Towards the evening, he would go out to spend time with well-wishers. He loved to spend time with children.

When Shankara Singh Vaghela revolted in Gujarat, I was so worried of what would happen to the BJP. When I asked Ram Madhav how could he be so relaxed even when things were going wrong (according to me) in the country, he said that the higher-ups in Delhi would think about all these things; we need not worry. All we had to do was to assist them. Again, I started worrying on how much of torture those higher-ups in Delhi must be undergoing. This is what, now I think, is called sympathy towards a party!

But I had never told in my school that I liked so-and-so party overtly. I would rather say why I liked their ideology. Sometimes, the way I questioned about things that were going on in the country, they could easily make out where I meant to drive them. Though I did not make explicit statements, they recognised what was inside me. I felt school was not a proper place to make debates over some kind of opinions.

Politics is never a polite topic, in an environment where different kinds of people are working. People with different ideologies tend to be at logger heads with one another if that is done. But then for whatever I said, almost all my colleagues, those with different ideological persuasions, also agreed. Generally, the things I talked were all thoroughly researched. When in 1999, the BJP got elected at the centre, my colleagues congratulated me. Of course, it was an ideological triumph for me.

Ram Madhav was liked by many people for his modern outlook without sacrificing the ideology. From dressing to thinking, he differed with many other activists of his age whom I have known. The way he wielded electronic gadgets of latest technology was unusual in the organisational structure in '90s. We knew him from the age of using pager to mobile phone, smart phone, and laptop. After technological advancement, Ram Madhav used to send me through e-mail messages of my work. That shows along with time how Pragna Bharati progressed in communication. He updated himself so well with all latest things when most of his peers in the organisation were still strutting in archaic modes. He is truly a big asset to the organisation.

Among the organisation members, he is much TV savvy, articulate and English-speaking. Some of his counterparts, i.e Pracharaks here in Andhra, do not seem so. Even to take an ideology to people's heart, one needs to be contemporary in dressing, thinking, and mannerism. One needs to be shrewd. In the case Vivekananda, Aurobindo, and Gandhiji, their attire was not important. They impressed with their intellect. All I am saying here is, modernity is not wrong. Ram Madhav used to move with people of high positions and learnt the worldly way of dealing things. He never felt out of place in their circles. Even this comes under one of the competencies to become a leader in my opinion.

Ram Madhav had strong views and opinions as he was thorough with the history of India. He opposed Sri L K Advani's opinion of Jinnah to be 'secular' after his Pakistan trip. Still, I am unable to understand why Advaniji made such a remark. It's an open secret that Jinnah was the person who wanted Pakistan by partition. When Gandhiji tried to stop the vivisection of the country, he was so rigid and reticent to listen to Mahatma. In fact, Gandhiji said he would make him the prime minister after independence for the united India. Yet Jinnah did not pay heed to it. We studied in our history books as he was the villain in the whole episode of partition. Now if a new theory was brought forth by Advaniji, eulogizing Jinnah for his secular spirit, who would listen to? Already a wrong, irremediable image of Jinnah was formed in the minds of most Indians. After all, all these years, nobody cared for Jinnah in India, let alone his good or bad qualities. How do I, or for that matter, many Indians, care whether he was secular or not? I heard that Advaniji hoped that his statement would yield some beneficial results for the BJP.

Sri L. K. Advani made humongous contribution to the growth of the BJP. Undeniably, he was tallest leader of the party. Advaniji could galvanise the party through his rath yatra for Ayodhya Ram temple in 1990s. He could bring into the fold of the party and nurture many leaders of the present. No doubt, he is a dyed-in-the-wool ideologist. In the fag end of his career, he took a moral high ground and tried to prove holier than thou attitude by making remarks on his own party. In any case, Advaniji is still a revered leader of the party.

In my opinion, the Late Prime Minister P. V. Narasimha Rao maintained party discipline by not uttering a single word against his party though there was so much of dissent and discontent on his rule by his own party members. He ruled the country in a turbulent time. The other stalwarts in the party were up against him. He was humiliated within his party and outside after the demotion of Babri structure. But never uttered a word outside about his party men! Being in a party, one cannot take a moral high ground. The people would laugh at you and the party if criticism about the party is made.

Some opine that the RSS has no regard for Gandhiji. I being a follower of Gandhiji from childhood asked Ram Madhav whether the opinion held by many on Gandhiji vis-à-vis the RSS was true. He said, 'Do you think we are against Gandhi? It is not so. Daily, in our early morning Sakhas, we pray. We remember all the great leaders of our country. Gandhiji tops the list'. But for him, Pujya Guruji, the RSS founders Sri M.S. Golwalkar, Dr Keshav Baliram Hedgewar, were the icons. He was born and brought up in that mould.

Ram Madhav knew the interests of the people working with him; knowing that I am an ardent reader of Arun Shourie's articles, he provided an opportunity to me and my husband to meet Arun Shourieji in his guest house. In those days, Ram Madhav used to call me a Shourieite. I just greeted Shourieji with traditional *namasthe* there. I could not use the opportunity provided much by talking to Shourieji for knowing things better on issues pertaining to the country.

Tailpiece: Ram Madhav, when he was offered the BJP general secretary post at the Centre, he rang up and asked me what my advice was, whether to remain in the RSS or to join the BJP. I strongly supported him to join the party and serve the country. Perhaps he sought opinions of many of his close associates to take the final call on the issue.

CHAPTER 4

Life in '90s: Concept of Swadeshi

It is interesting for the new generation in their twenties and thirties to know about India before 1990. Telecommunication was sparse, computers were rare in our households. The kind of houses with multiple facilities adorned with new gadgets were never thought of nor dreamt. Economic status of the people was so low. When we were young, there was a huge gap between haves and have-nots. There were always cases of rich looking down upon the poor in the society.

In those days, we used to wait for our cousins or uncles' trips from USA. For it was a delight for us to see the things they would get to present us. I got a digital watch as a gift from my cousin in 1980. All our relatives looked at it so fascinatingly as it displayed only hours and minutes on the screen. Now they are readily available in India even on a foot path.

Very few people of our generation knew what the outside world was and how the countries other than India were. The wonders of the world were only read in books. It was all amazing! English language was only for the elite. Most of us studied in vernacular medium. Fluency in English was a precious gift. English-speaking people were thought to be intellectuals because they were in the opinion making bodies with hydra-headed ideas.

My life in 1980s was fully dedicated to my family. It was me, my two children, and my husband. The times were different then. My son, the elder one, learnt in his pre-primary (kindergarten) school lessons some of the things that would go well with the society then. Based on lessons, questions were asked like 'Who earns money for the family?' The standard answer was, 'Father earns money for the family'. The other questions followed such as 'What does Mother do?' The standard answer given was, 'Mother cooks the food and looks after the house'. (Now this scenario has changed to a large extent). For my son, there were pictures to pick up in his Social Studies text on what a mother needs and what a father needs. For mother, invariably any child would round off bangles and sarees and other ornaments and accessories while for father, pant-shirt, but apart from that there were books and other electronic things.

My world was confined and defined by my family. Of course, bringing up children needs hundred percent dedication and devotion especially when they were infants. I have experienced both joint and nuclear family systems. Both have their own advantages and disadvantages. In this world, nothing is absolute, nothing is perfect or wonderful. The affection of elders in a joint family is undeniably a plus factor. The elderly people most often hold conventional and established views, which are often difficult for younger ones to digest. But by seeing some of the useful conventions followed by the older people, the young learn unknowingly. Caring and sharing is a part of joint-family culture.

Some people argue that in a market-driven economy, nuclear families are good for consumerism. Industries get benefitted. More, more fridges, TVs, mixers or grinders, and other electronic goods are sold as more and more people require them for their independent families. That would boost the manufacturing sector and people could get jobs. But it's (family system) a complex issue. Later, I thought that kind of consumerism would lead to unbridled capitalism, which India cannot afford. Of course, we cannot prescribe in life what suits for an individual. At the best, he himself could be guided by his innate wisdom. All in all, joint family is much more economical and culturally suited for Indians.

It was the then Prime Minister P. V. Narasimha Rao's government in 1991 that started liberalisation of economy that ushered in a new era in Indian history with Manmohan Singh as his finance minister. With the liberalisation of the market, the products which we had never seen before flooded into the market. Swadeshi Jagaran Manch objected to the products of international market. They said Indian traders would get affected. And this type of 'opening up' of economy was not in the interest of the Swadeshi traders and Swadeshi goods.

The SJM (Swadeshi Jagaran Manch) started a movement that was supported by the left parties but did not join hands to make a combined effort. However, they agreed in principle that inviting Multinational National Companies (MNCs) meant bringing in East India Company again to colonize India. They opposed opening up of the markets. This kind of protectionism was rampant then. The agitators wanted, first, the liberalisation to take place within India internally to strengthen the competition among Indian traders. Then to open up for other players from other countries to compete. Their motto was to strengthen internal competition. Even a lay person like me also felt why stopping liberalisation that was due for a long time just for our internal trade when both (internal and external liberalisations) could be done simultaneously. In any case, India can wait endlessly, but the world cannot wait. It goes at its fast pace. To catch up with the world becomes difficult for India with this kind of procrastination on all issues.

The SJM was spearheaded by Sri S. Gurumurthy, Joint All India Convenor, who did vigorous campaigning for the cause. Many people have had their doubts about what Swadeshi was. The movement did not gain as much momentum and people's participation as it had had in the pre-independence era. Before independence, the fight was with the enemy, the British. Now with the multinationals doing trade in India, the multinationals were demonized. They were portrayed as if they would gobble up India one day. At that stage, globalisation was still nascent. None of the common people could decipher what they were saying.

Swadeshi Jagaran Manch (SJM) was an all-India organisation. It was an off-shoot of the RSS. The RSS and other opposing groups wanted to make the movement widespread. By word of mouth, by writing articles, by distributing pamphlets, by conducting lectures or speeches in public forums. They wanted to bring awareness of using Swadeshi products by rejecting multinational goods.

In one of Arun Shourie's columns, I remember him questioning Swadeshi proponents to specify what *Swadeshi* meant instead of making sweeping statements about this way or that way. He urged Swadeshis to be more specific in pointing out the areas where they could lay safety nets. During that time, Shourie wanted the ruling and opposition parties not to make sweeping statements on issues pertaining to liberalisation of the country.

SJM gave a list of items that were Swadeshi and Videshi in two columns so that people would know what to buy and what not to buy. It was so shocking to see products that we had been using for decades that had been the household names were Videshi. They were all indiscriminately used in the Indian households irrespective of who produced them. They were ubiquitous in all Indian markets. For example, the most common soaps, toothpaste, toothbrush, shaving creams, talcum powders, cool drinks had all been videshi. The list was exhaustive.

The list given by organisers consisted of too many things for one to remember. But the above-mentioned were some of the common things which we use in our daily lives. In fact, the pamphlets contained a table demarcating ours, i.e Indians and outsiders for the common patriotic citizen to know! In regular Indian houses, in those days, Colgate was synonymous with toothpaste. Surf was synonymous with detergent, Bata shoes and slippers were widely used. So also, Brooke brand tea and coffee as early morning beverages which are videshi[1]. I think, if I am not wrong, they have been coming from the British time, colonial rule. Our markets are basically consumer-driven. People buy their choice of things without inhibition. They do not find imminent danger to the country by buying the products they want. There are higher technological things like computers—PCs, laptops, desktops, tablets, and other hardware components are all from outside the country. Most of them are made in China. Can anyone stop them? How can we stop such high-end products right now? Unless we develop them on our own. Yes, India should be made self-reliant. Otherwise, all this Swadeshi cry becomes wailing in wilderness.

Seeing is believing:

Those were the days, Swadeshi movement of SJM was at its height. One day, I read about a meeting of Atal Bihari Vajpayeeji that was reported in the newspaper. It was huge pre-election meeting. The crowd was large. After the meeting, the audience and the leaders left the venue. A reporter took a photo of the place with all empty cans of Coke/Pepsi strewn all over the place. The reporters questioned the youths who had come to attend the meeting wearing Reebok/Nike shoes and drinking Coke/Pepsi, 'Is this what Swadeshi meant?'—a query as the headline. I showed it to Ram Madhav and asked why it was so. He said, 'I did not understand the spirit of Swadeshi.' However, he supplied some organisational books to me to give some perspective. They were the occasional gifts to me. One of which was *Third Way* by Sri Dattopant Thengadi.[2]

Sri Dattopant deliberated on what Swadeshi meant in a chapter of the book. He writes, 'It is wrong to presume that "Swadeshi" concerns itself only with the goods or services. That is more an incidental aspect. Essentially, it concerns the spirit determined to achieve national self-reliance, preservation of national sovereignty and independence, and internal co-operation on equal footing . . . Swadeshi is the outward manifestation of patriotism. Patriotism is not considered as isolationism—particularly in our tradition which stands for integral humanism according to which, on the level of human consciousness, internationalism is the further flowering of the spirit of nationalism.

'Proponents of Swadeshi are not prepared to endorse the view that the western paradigm is the universal model of progress and development worthy of being followed by all the peoples of the world. While they recognise the fact of cultural intercourse, they insist that every people have each of their own distinct culture, and the model of progress and development for each country should be consistent with its own cultural ethos. Westernisation is not modernisation. Modernisation should be in keeping with the spirit of national culture. They oppose the move for stream-rolling all the various cultures and national identities in the world in favour of the West'[2]. This brought to me some kind of ideological understanding of what it was.

If I am not wrong, Swadeshi movement of '90s was not against trade with other countries bilaterally. They were against the new GATT (General Agreement on Trade and Tariff) agreement on the so-called Dunkel Proposals. Sri Gurumurthy of the All India Swadeshi Jagaran Manch was interviewed in a newspaper. I'll reproduce two, three questions in the interview and the answers that were given by him that unfold the objective of the movement:

In those days of GATT, Gurumurthyji said Swadeshi was the alternative though not limited to economics; it was also against Dunkel

Proposals that sought to homogenise the world and as they being just not limited to trade. There had been attempts to homogenise the world on the basis of religion, statecraft, and legislative process earlier, he said.

Homogenisation through free market was the culture that was sought to be spread by the west. 'If it is good for Europe (or USA) then it is good for other countries too.' Their (the West's) aim was to introduce common habits by introducing a common lifestyle[3].

He perceived Swadeshi as something that fosters indigenous skills, opposes some pernicious trends, and introduces certain fresh elements into the working of our economy. He also said experts like Alvin Toffler agreed that MNCs foster a worse kind of bureaucracy. Toffler, in fact, referred to small-scale family businesses as the trend of the future.

To elaborate the above views on Swadeshi in the interview, I would quote some of the important points made by Sri Gurumurthyji in his speech in our organisational meeting at that time. In his words what 'Swadeshi' meant,

> The Swadeshi movement, reinitiated by the Swadeshi Jagaran Manch (SJM), was in response to the mindless globalisation of the national economy. The Western economic and industrial policies would not hold good for Indian conditions, said Sri S Gurumurthy, noted columnist and SJM organising secretary, while delivering his lecture.

He observed that economics could not be separated from life, money, and neighbours. 'The Indian system is different from the American and the Indian consumer is not as intelligent as his American counterpart.'

Mr Gurumurthy said that while America, with 4 per cent of the world's population, had 40 per cent of its resources, India, by contrast, had 40 per cent of the world's population but only 4 per cent of its resources.

'The tendency to convert waste into wealth is Indian economics and the country's economics is linked with the lifestyle of the masses, which has evolved over the centuries. Therefore, one cannot discard the cultural and traditional differences', he affirmed. 'If the Americans' economy cannot generate employment in that country, why then are the economists here recommending it for India,' he wondered.

Speaking on the 'Role of the Banking Industry in the Changed Scenario' (1995) in the country, he felt there should be separate institutions, one following the market course and the other the 'social course'. Rolling both into one would mean continued floundering from one adhocism to another, he remarked.

Mr Gurumurthy suggested that the funding of these institutions could be through two streams of depositors—one getting lower rate of interest but higher tax benefits and the other higher interest but no tax benefits. Money could thus be made available for social cause too with people going in for tax benefits.

He said there was enough household saving in the country due to its 'inherent social system'. Savings in India were among the highest in the world with 82 per cent of these coming from the household sector and amounting to Rs 120,000 crore per annum (at that time).

'Swadeshi' movement was said to fulfil the dreams of Mahatma Gandhi in bringing complete revival of Indian economy based on the 'Bhartiya Model'.

In a series of meetings on Swadeshi, in those days, Sri Gurumurthy stressed that bringing the economic model of the West by free trade, without bringing their culture into India, was not possible. So liberalisation was not purely economic question and development question, he said. It was thought to be altering the foundations of the mind, style, and fashion of living in India.

Sri Gurumurthy said with the organised sector, i.e. public sector and private sector, put together, the employment was less compared to the un-organised sector, which was spread all over the country like the handloom industries, small-scale industries in urban and semi-urban areas, village, and cottage industries (that were providing more employment). Their (the un-organised sector's) strength was equal to total employment in Germany then. He also said that that 80 per cent of the exports were from the unorganised sector, i.e. from handicrafts, weavers and farmers that gave 80 per cent of the foreign exchange for the country. The West was on an unsustainable basis for development. They knew it (that theirs) would not sustain. Yet they preserved it.

When Manmohan Singh took over as finance minister, there was foreign exchange crisis and so new economic policies were required. Without new economic policies, we might be finished. New economic policies meant borrowing from World Bank (WB) and IMF (International Monetary Fund). In 1980, India borrowed 4.5 billion from IMF, in the same year our carpenters, masons, nurses who went to Middle East, those ordinary people remitted 23 billion dollars. So, the strength of India is its skill and man.

Our jewellery, is the largest single item of export for India. Indian carpentry skill is more efficient in the world. Unfortunately, they were not recognised since they had not received any certificates from schools or colleges. Thirty per cent of our population gets cured by homemade local Unani medicine. Informal medical system sustained here for so long. It was wrong to think that English medicine could only provide cure.

In the West, the nature was standardised, colour was standardised, only twenty varieties were available (in the eco-system); but in India, there was so much of diversity available not only in terms of human beings but also in terms of nature. In the West, there were only rice, wheat, and barley, etc. So, their influence forced other countries to eat them only. Ragi in India was protein-rich and useful in many other ways. However, the use of Ragi was dropping out because less people were taking it. So, Swadeshi meant survival of our food and eating habits also.

'We need foreign technology but not their culture. We have our own technology. It could be improved. Swadeshi means, we must understand to recreate alternative values which are required not only for us but for the west also', Sri Gurumurthy stated[4].

Arun Shourie had also agreed with Swadeshi Jagaran Manch ideology of innovation and indigenous technology. And the idea to make India self-reliant. And he also espoused the cause of competing in the world trade and patenting technology and products. Those days, I was an intense reader of Shourieji's columns. So, I quote from his columns how India was treated badly by the USA in the front of technology transmission and how the treatment led to innovation in technology and that in turn led to India getting due recognition by the very same USA.

'What would really be Swadeshi' by Arun Shourie

Shourie writes, 'Today technology is perhaps the most powerful instrument of domination. We must therefore be self-reliant in this vital sphere. When we are not, others will twist our tail: recall how the US prohibited the sale of super computers to India, how it pressed Russia to renege on the contract for supplying the cryogenic engine. Conversely, when we have the capacity to produce the thing in question on our own, others who can also do so will bend backwards to supply it to us at the lowest possible price: the US prohibited the sale of super-computers to us four years ago; now that our scientists and engineers have acquired the ability to put one together, the US has decided just last quarter to review its ban . . . the current advocates of Swadeshi— have been right. There is a point therefore in assessing Dunkel-type provisions in the light of their likely effects on our abilities to acquire and develop advanced technologies[5].

'While approving with apologists of Swadeshi he also gave a caution thus: technological developments abroad—in actual fact they are leaps—are not going to stop by our seceding from the arena and shutting ourselves up like Burma. Second, no country can win, none can even hold its own by merely sitting on what it has—be these plants or patents; continuous invention and innovation and application alone will keep its head above water . . .'[6]

In his series of articles on Swadeshi, Shourie writes at a place, 'The critics (of Dunkel proposals) are right in that these changes are weighed in favour of the developed countries. But they are wrong . . . in the cure they are suggesting—that we not sign the treaty in April, that we leave GATT etc'[7].

'Indian government was seeking to have the Draft altered . . . But even the other developing countries did not back India up on them. India was isolated'[8]. So, India, by not being a powerful and self-reliant nation, it was being marginalised and humiliated.

The former two proponents of Swadeshi (Gurumurthyji and Dattopantji) were ideological. Arun Shourie was practical and showed the hard realities of the world. Now at present, we have made so much of progress in the field of technology. Indian Space Research Organisation (ISRO)'s satellite launching programmes created ripples in the world. India has become capable of helping our neighbouring Asian countries like Sri Lanka, Nepal, Burma, Bangladesh, etc., through our satellite system by sharing information to know forecasts of weather, tsunami, and other kind of natural disasters. This is all a goodwill gesture to our neighbours. Indians have used liberalisation and globalisation to their advantage. With the globalisation, Indians could easily get technology transfer and work-culture transfer from the West, which was a good sign. After globalisation, many of our software engineers went to the West to make a living. Culture is permeable. By seeing the Indians and people from other Oriental countries, the West has also learnt the importance of family and family values.

The pre-Independence Swadeshi of Gandhiji was for the country with the motive of encouraging and empowering India's artisans. The British, because of their industrial revolution, flooded Indian markets with their goods and textiles. Which, in turn, affected our artisan. Gandhiji, the proponent of Swadeshi, led his life by example. He did what he said, he said what he thought. That is, he was 'one' in thought, word, and deed. A very rare personality. It is difficult to find another Gandhi for generations to come! In the present-day world, people are so manipulative for political correctness, they twist and turn words. Gandhiji stood for Khadi (hand-woven cotton cloth), promoted Khadi, and wore Khadi. That was the real Swadeshi! Indian home-spun cotton by Indian weavers against the mill-cloth (though cheaper) produced and imported from England. That Swadeshi was close to heart because people then had a revivalist nationalism. They wanted to give the imperialist British a befitting lesson by rejecting their industrial goods and mill-cloth although they were affordable.

Now after so many years of independence, people have become conservative in their nationalism. They have no reason to think that the nation could be at peril if they bought foreign products. Gandhiji, himself took a charkha and spun cotton spindles with full dedication without wasting his spare time; people followed. He wore cotton; the Congress party followed. The women at home followed Gandhiji in weaving with charkha. With the spindles they made, they earned money. In that way, Gandhiji engaged and created employment for them. They were participatory in nation building, in some useful earnings for their families. To intellectuals at intellectual level, to traders at traders' level, to politicians and social reformers, lawyers, spiritual persons at their plane, Gandhiji discussed and argued. He had answers for all their queries. Gandhiji was the one and only leader in this country who could impress so many!

Though my writing of Swadeshi may appear to be not so favourable, I used to argue with those who opposed and ridiculed the concept of

Swadeshi in those days. Once my friend said, 'What is Swadeshi when we are sending our children to foreign universities to study and using foreign goods so crazily.' I did not like her statement. I asked her whether she liked pre-Independence Swadeshi. She said, 'Yes'. 'Then why not now?' was my question, for which she could not answer.

So, I told her, the Swadeshi of pre-Independence and the post, which had been taking place at the moment, were conceptually 'one'. But the former was to show the solidarity of the Indians against the British. It was a weapon against the British imperialism. The latter was to consolidate the solidarity of our culture against cultural invasion. For both the premise is to benefit the country.

I asked her, showing some minor aberrations, was it right to ridicule the concept that promotes indigenous talent? Was it worthy or right to condemn the very idea that the things made in the country should be given priority over the outside ones?

Swadeshi proponents were not asking for shutting the doors completely to the multinationals. They just wanted a kind of semi-permeability in their entry. It was a kind of quality selection. If Swadeshi was understood in terms of hatred towards foreign goods or education, it is faulty. It was to promote the talent and art that is Indian and to reduce the crave for unnecessary and unimportant things.

I told my friend, by ridiculing the very concept, as to whether she would expect the country to progress. I also asked her was it right to condemn our own people and our own concepts of the country so sweepingly without giving leverage to discussion that leads to a kind of understanding. I said to myself, 'Should there not be a degree of acceptability and unanimity in our thought for the good of our country?' My friend just listened. I still have no clue whether she agreed with me.

In my opinion, Gandhiji did little preaching and more practising in his entire life. While espousing Swadeshi, he boycotted the mill-cloth of the British industries and wore only Khadi of Indian weavers. Similarly, he led the 'Dandi Salt March' by going on foot to the spot to make salt. He did not teach anything which he himself did not personally follow. The tendency of the Indian mind is supposed to be in favour of individual perfection or individual reform before bringing a social change or social reform. The foot marches (*Pada Yatras*) to meet people were Gandhiji's contribution.

In fact, higher education was and is, a personal choice. No democratic government bars it. I do not think the World Trade Centre agrees to the semi-permeability that I talked about way back. Every country has to follow the norms laid down by the WTO. People are not obliged to go by the governments. They could choose the products of their choice. Hence Swadeshi proponents always appeal to people of the country. This momentum is picking up now elsewhere in other developed countries also. This they call protectionism and isolationism. India, being highly populated, has to create employment to many of its citizens. So, therefore, we call Swadeshi as a concept for the promotion of indigenous talent and for the self-reliance of Bharath.

The initiative, to promote handloom by the central government and the PM himself taking up the cause was laudable. PM Modi himself did the job of running the charkha! Nearer home, in Telangana and Andhra Pradesh our own handloom weavers are in distress. Many of them who have been traditionally on that job are committing suicide because of losses and no encouragement to their products in the market. Both the governments started encouraging the weavers by subsidising their products. By providing amenities to work. The Western malls are stuffed with our Indian cotton shirts and other cotton dresses, which are quite expensive there. People in those countries buy them fondly. And that appreciation should come from consumers. The PM sitting along with weavers and spinning the loom to give a boost to the artisans was an effort by itself. Instead of saying what to buy and what not to, blindly in a prescriptive way, living by example is better.

Enron project was a big issue then. SJM head Sri Gurumurthy spearheaded the movement against Enron power plant also. This was to highlight how the multinational companies work. And this in a way strengthens the cause of Swadeshi. He said, 'Political system abetted by bureaucracy helped Enron to loot. Civil servants would often say, if you touched Enron no foreign investment would come. Yes, we want foreign investment in power sector because we do not have adequate power. But we do not have a mechanism to stop global forces if they went wrong'. Some of the columnists also wrote Enron-type deals necessarily bypass our own electrical equipment industry, which was among the best in the world, but which had been starved of orders. A world-class technologically strong company like BHEL could easily be brought to its knees if it was deprived of orders.

SJM's campaign on Enron deal was a noteworthy one. They made an extensive movement against it. Finally, it was closed by its muddy corrupt deals. SJM has powerful constituents like Bharathiya Kisan Sangh and Laghu Udyog Bharati. At that time, some other movement that SJM took up were highlighting fishermen's problems, slaughter of animal wealth (Al-Kabir symbolized that). They recognised handloom weavers and beedi workers to be two of the largest employment intensive categories in the country. They conducted conferences as a means of creating public awareness.

The SJM movement, for Swadeshi, did continue, after the Vajpayee-NDA government came into power also (in 1996). The SJM launched Swadeshi Chaitanya Yatra in Andhra Pradesh to take the movement forward. Symbolically, it was started at Sri Mahatma Gandhi Gyan Mandir, Koti, Hyderabad on 2 October 1997. It was a fortnight long yatra to educate people of the country. The then Union minister of State for Urban Development of the time, at the beginning of the Yatra, ridiculed the parties, which ruled the country since Independence for ignoring the concept of Swadeshi and encouraging foreign goods. He also said, with the entry of the multinationals, the small-scale sector in the country was badly hit. Sri Dattatreya blamed the government for allowing the export of meat to foreign countries, thereby destroying the animal wealth of the country, upon which the poor people and agriculturists were largely dependent.

Now with the technology acceleration, and artificial intelligence (AI) robbing off the jobs of daily labourers, it's is interesting to see the direction of the movement. India is a world player now. The growth of information technology revolutionised the world. India cannot be isolationist. The much-feared cultural invasion and cultural flow has been taking place but not to the extent of being glorified then. By and large India, is resilient to changes. The world is also learning a lot from India. Yoga is one such contribution to the world. Indian culture proved its resilience time and again. To a minor extent, though India changed, it has not been swept by the Western culture.

Tailpiece: During India-China stand-off at Doklam, near trijunction of India, China, and Bhutan, in the year 2017, Swadeshi Jagaran Manch threatened to intensify its boycott campaign of Chinese products. They at least wanted people to ban Chinese crackers to mark a token protest and to encourage Indian traders. At the time of near-war situation, the appeal was well-taken. It had also touched the hearts of people. All over the world, the trend in trading has changed. Their own version of 'Swadeshi' is encouraged. Even in the United Kingdom, there are proponents who ask for buying products from the British markets only. In USA, after Donald Trump assuming office, the fad goes, 'Be American, buy American' or 'America first' campaign.

End notes -corrected form

1. Swadeshi Jagaran Manch, pamphlet in Telugu
2. Dattopant Thengadi, *Third Way*, pp. 194–195
3. Gurumuthy interview, Courtesy Business column, DC
4. Swadeshi is Cultural Question Not Just Economic, Pragna Bharati, AP Publication
5. Arun Shourie's column- 'What would really be Swadeshi', *Deccan Chronicle*, 10 and 17-04-1994
6. Arun Shourie's column- 'What would really be Swadeshi', *Deccan Chronicle*, 10 and 17-04-1994 (same column)
7. Arun Shourie's column- 'Will heckling halt time?', Deccan Chronicle, 10-04-1994
8. Arun Shourie's column- 'Will heckling halt time?', Deccan Chronicle, 10-04-1994 (same column)

CHAPTER 5

Minority Assertion in the South India

South India is a bastion of minorities. There are certain villages where you do not find families of majority community. Persecution of minorities is more of a propagation than a reality in the south of India. Majority Hindus are not a solid monolith to persecute or harm any minority community. There are no right-wing activists as such in India to protect the interests of Hindus. Only the RSS seeks to bind India by cementing with Indian culture and heritage. There is very less space for activism in Hindu society.

To Christian minority, missionaries in India, not allowing them to proselytize itself is a great persecution. The founding fathers of our Constitution were magnanimous in granting rights to minority religions to 'profess and propagate' their religions peacefully. A naïve step. It's keeping food before a hungry predator. Many in media argue that the percentage of Christians is measly two-point odd. The problem with Christians is most of them are crypto.

I am going to narrate two incidents that I was a witness to of Christian teachings and bias. In our school, a panel had come for annual verification. That was an inspection kind. There was an officer and three other members in the panel to inspect. All the staff was busy. Most of the teachers were busy preparing teaching aids and other work for the inspection. All of them wanted to show the best of their performance. The intention was to have nice remarks in their reports.

Some were nervous of whether they could show their performance up to the satisfaction of the panel or not.

I finished my class meant for inspection and was sitting in a vacant room. One lady from the inspecting panel came and sat before me. In an informal chat, she asked my name and which subject I teach etc. It was obvious from her face and manners that she was a Christian. Mine to make out was easy as I wear *bindi*. In her talk, she eulogized Christianity and said Christ was the only saviour. I had no issues with what she said. For the followers, their faith is paramount to them.

She started narrating incidents. She said sometime back, one of her neighbours became sick. That man in bed was pathetic. And his situation was hopeless. They (the patient's kith and kin) prayed to God for his health. She said, they prayed and invoked Lords Vishnu, Shiva, Ganesh, etc. None answered their prayers. None relieved the pain of the man on bed. In the end they called Lord Hanuman, asked him to show mercy. Nothing changed. Ultimately when they prayed to Jesus, as advised by this lady, their prayers were heard. The patient was slowly, little by little, relieved of his pain and regained his health. 'So, who was the ultimate saviour? What did Hindu gods do? They were all a waste. Only Christ could do wonders! He is the only real god', she said. I was dumbstruck. I did not know what to do. I did not know why she was narrating all that to me. I did not ask her the question straight because she was one of the panellists. By being in the panel, she was one step above me.

Anyway, her narrative appeared insipid to me. I know that people pray in their weak moments to God rather than when they are on strong state of mind. Randomly, their wishes are fulfilled. That means we should assume they are sometimes heard, sometimes not. Strange providence!

Being a Hindu, I myself do not give much importance to all those gods, as projected by her and depicted in the pictures. They are taken symbolically, representing certain powers. How could she, being a Christian, believed God Hanuman's existence, his coming and not coming to the patient's rescue? Even I doubt Jesus's saving. If the God's only job is to cure people in the world to prove himself, why does he make them fall sick in the first place? What's this 'my god' versus 'your god' theory? Going by reason, these are all our own creations. This example is a drop in the ocean. The missionaries go to gullible Hindus with fanatic arguments. These are all secular acts in India!

One day, in my college-going days, I asked my mother whether Ramayana and Mahabharata were true. Whether Ram and Krishna existed. As stories, Ramayana and Mahabharata are interesting. They have stories within stories. Each has its own contemporary moral and ethical values. When it comes to the question of faith, I got a doubt. Then my mother replied that Ramayana was written by Valmiki and Mahabharata by Veda Vyas. They were rishis (sages), and they would not tell lies. So, faith comes through family tradition.

People pray to God to have a good and trouble-free life. It is between them and God. They may not say it in open. It is too personal. Comparing gods will not augur well for the society. I was the captive person in that situation. It was not fair on her part, coming from a government education department to propagate a religion she believes in to others. Christian missionaries in the south of India leave no stone unturned to increase their numbers.

Another incidence in the school. All the teachers wanted to take loan of some bulk amount in thousands, which could be paid in instalments, from a bank. A young lady, who came to our school, said about this loan details to them. She also said she was an agent for the work. Most of the teachers wanted to buy something or the other with that big amount. They were all willing to pay instalments. They filled up the forms of loan and paid some amount of money to her. The whole amount came up to a huge sum for her. She took the amount, took the forms, promising she would be coming soon; she went off. She did not turn up for two, three months. Then they realised that it was a fraud.

So, they thought of nabbing her. Somebody among them had her phone number. So, they dialled. She said the delay was due to some transactions in the bank. They called her to school saying some more people were willing to pay and take loan. She came with all hope. They made her sit on a chair. All of them surrounded and asked her questions about the money they had given. They said they did not want that loan and to give back the money she had taken. She said she would give it later. They said, 'We do not allow you to move an inch without money, if you do not have money, give your gold chain and ring. We will give them to you back when you get the money.'

She started crying. She said she had not got the money to give them back. She said she was not the agent; some other man told her to do this work. She took out the Bible from her bag and showed it to them and said she was innocent. Then two of my Christian colleagues backtracked immediately. After showing the Bible, they did not like to coerce her anymore. The others pursued the matter till the end. So much sympathy with a co-religionist! Their malpractices could also be condoned!

Mulk Raj Anand's novel *Untouchable* perfectly depicts the dilemma in the mind of an untouchable youth who was approached by an evangelist to convert him when he was demoralised. The conversation between them is very interesting. After reading it, one knows this conversion business has been taking place in India for centuries! It had its roots dating back to pre-independence era.

The conversation between *Bakha,* the protagonist of the novel, and *Colonel Hutchinson,* father of Salvation Army, an evangelist, had many aspects of the society to take note of at that point of time and now.

Bakha, whose job was manual scavenging, was an outcast. His father and mother did the same job. They were looked down upon and none cared for their feelings. One day, Bakha was downcast and demoralised. He expected Ram Charan might come and console him or someone from the outcasts' colony. He was surprised to see Colonel Hutchinson (of Salvation Army) coming to him. Bakha's narration about the colonel (a British white-man), an evangelist goes this way:

'He felt flattered that he should be the object of pity and sympathy from a sahib. Of course, he at once recognised the Colonel. Who didn't know the missionary? But it was the first occasion on which he had found himself face to face with him. Being of a very retiring disposition and full of a feeling of inferiority, he had never talked to Hutchinson . . . His father, he recalled, also talked of the *sahib,* sometimes if he saw him in the distance, saying that the old sahib had wanted to convert them to the religion of Yessuh Messih and to make them sahibs like himself, but that he had refused to leave the Hindu fold, saying that the religion which was good enough for his forefathers was good enough for him.'[1]

The last sentence that Bakha's father says, though an outcast, is the spirit of a true Hindu heart. Most of the Hindus never question the wisdom of our ancestors for being born and following the religion of their birth. We always think, when it was good enough for them, it is good enough for us. Sowing the seeds of separatism in a religious community and converting people to another to increase their fold is an earthly material activity, not a spiritual one. If there are discrepancies in one religion, they are so in any other.

No religious group could claim it is infallible. When someone is demoralised or crestfallen, converting the person to another religion would not bring a permanent solution. When dealing with worldly materials, solution should also be from the worldly matters. There is no dearth for mental solace in any religion. If, really, that is needed, Hinduism has an oceanic depth in bringing solace to mind.

Let me continue the saga of Bakha with the colonel as written:

'Sahib, who is Yessuh Messih?' Bakha persisted with Punjabi directness.

'He is the Son of God,' answered Colonel Hutchinson, coming down to earth for a moment. 'He died that we might be forgiven', thought Bakha. 'What does that mean? He is the son of God if God, as my mother told me, lives in the sky. How could he have a son? And why did His son die that we should be forgiven? Forgiven for what?'

The colonel saw Bakha lagging behind and, realising that his new follower was losing interest, exerted the peculiar obstinacy of the enthusiastic missionary in him and dragging at the boy's sleeve, said, 'Yessuh Messih is the son of God, my boy. While we were yet sinners, He died for us. He sacrificed Himself for us.'

He sacrificed Himself for us, Bakha reflected. His idea of sacrifice was something very certain and definite. He remembered that when some calamity brooded over the family, such as an epidemic of sickness, or starvation, his mother used to make offerings to the goddess Kali . . . Now, what did this sacrifice of Yessuh Messih mean? Why did He sacrifice Himself?

But he (Colonel Hutchinson) began garrulously, 'He is our King. He is the Son of God. We are all sinners. He will intercede with God, His Father, on our behalf.'

'He is superior to us. We are all sinners. Why, why, is anyone above another? Why are we all sinners? Bakha began to reflect.

'Why we are all sinners Sahib?' he queried.

'We were all born sinners,' replied the Colonel evasively, the puritan in him shying at an exposition of the doctrine of original sin which seemed called for.

'We must confess our sins. Then alone will He forgive us, otherwise we will have to suffer the eternal torment of hell. You confess your sins to me before I convert you to Christianity.'

'But, Huzoor, I don't know who Yessuh Messih is. I know Ram. But I don't know Yessuh Messih.

'Ram is the god of the idolaters,' the Colonel said after a pause, and a bit absent-mindedly. 'Come and confess your sins to me and Yessuh Messih will receive you in Heaven when you die.'[2]

Though it was Mulk Raj Anand's protagonist speaking, it was subtext of all Hindu minds.

I always think sacrifice means, in the living world, to forego some material thing at the altar of some higher goal or objective. The Congress party and its leaders always say that Indira Gandhi and Rajiv Gandhi sacrificed their lives for the country. Nehru-Gandhi family is the epitome of sacrifice! I still can't understand what they meant by sacrifice. Those who come into politics come on their own volition. Agreed, the risk to life is very high in politics. That's the reason for politicians' security cover. Politicians get name and fame. They get limelight all the while than any other professional or an expert in any field. When their job gets so much lustre to them, the other risk is incidental.

Through the character of Bakha, the author could bring to light how the economic and social disparities prevail in the society that give scope for missionaries to work. Bakha and his father thought that the religion that was practised by their forefathers in their wisdom was good for them. Really, this belief system in the wisdom of their ancestors survives the Hindu religion for centuries. Though the British did not interfere much with the Hindu religion as Moghuls did; the British rule had let loose missionaries for the task. It's amazing how Hinduism could survive the onslaught!

There is not much for me to say on the matters of missionary work. Arun Shourie had clearly stated the data of Christianisation in the country in his work *Missionaries in India*. He also gave a vivid picture of missionary work and the dubious ways in which they convert people.

Delivering the third Dr L. M. Singhvi Memorial Lecture on 'Secularism and Rule of Law in India', justice Sathasivam said the state has a right to pass laws restricting conversions if such activities created public disorder. The Supreme Court delineated the boundaries of the right to propagate in the context of state legislation prohibiting forcible conversions, said Justice Sathasivam . . . But the bench chose to modify it after several Christian Organisations termed it uncalled for and demanded its withdrawal.[3]

Tailpiece: The silent voting for the BJP and Modi in 2014 was not only for the development of the country but also for growing excesses minorities in India have been committing. Since the minorities in India are vocal and have the support from within and outside the country, they are much emboldened than the Hindus. Here the onslaught on Hindu religion could also be taken as violence. The patronage the secular parties give to the minority religions is not found in any other secular country.

Endnotes

1. Mulk Raj Anand's novel, *Untouchable*, pp. 137–38
2. Ibid., pp. 142–146
3. Dr L. M. Singhvi Memorial Lecture, *Hindustan Times* 27-02-2011, m.hindustantimes.com>delhi>conversions

CHAPTER 6

Population Issues, Sardar Patel, Cow Importance

Population Issues Perceived Demographic Changes in India:

When Indira Gandhi incorporated in the Constitution of India the words *socialist* and *secular* in 1976, no one posed an objection. Because the Hindu population at that time in India was high. And certainly, they were the majorities. They did not bother labels. The country, they felt, implicitly belonged to them. It is so with every majority in every country. For they are the major contributors and major beneficiaries in that country.

Whenever I talked to my friends about secularism, they would say, 'We wanted India to be secular'. 'We' here meant for them the Hindus who are the majorities. It could also be all Indians to some. When I asked my friends from the minority communities, they showed their loyalty to the first prime minister and their most favourite iconic figure of secularism, Pandit Jawaharlal Nehru. Some of the minorities answered that the Constitution and its founding fathers granted them this bonanza. The last answer seemed to be correct and more appropriate to me. For it does not attribute the credit to a community or a person.

After the demolition of Babri Masjid, the Indian political scenario changed. Before that, secularism was not an issue with the people. Ever since appeasement policy touched its zenith, ever since the numbers of Hindu majority are dwindling, people awakened to the reality.

Demographics are affecting secularism in India:

Most of the Hindus saw the benefit in family planning. To give quality life to their children, they confined to limit their numbers to two. Even the downtrodden followed the same pattern. Occasionally, the hard-core leaders from among the RSS and the BJP voice their concern on depleting Hindu population and the growth of the minorities in India.

Most of the minorities in India either by not observing a planned family or by religious conversion tend to increase their numbers. Hindus in India know what the troubles were with a big family! How difficult it was to bring up children in a big family according to their, i.e. children's, expectations. How difficult it was for parents to see children doing menial jobs in a country where dignity of labour had been absent conspicuously. How pathetic it was for a parent to see children half-fed, ill-clad, and working on small errands. It was so difficult to be in a condition where the basic need of the child was not met and his intellectual growth was stymied. To give useful citizens to the country, planned family has been their practice.

At that time, decades ago, in our circles at home or on any gathering of our relatives, we always used to vociferously support family planning and how the country needed to contain the growing population. My younger brother always used to ridicule the girls who got married and very soon became pregnant and came back within months to their parents' house to get the baby delivered. He used to curse the population growth of the country by saying that 'India's population is growing day by day'! However, in most cases, they would only have two. They had seen the comfort in bringing up two children, educating them properly, doing job themselves, exploiting their potential, and contributing to their families' kitty. There was sense of responsibility in them towards their family and the nation at large.

Family planning is one thing that goes against religion. Even for the majorities. I asked my mother about this issue as I myself did not know what was laid down in Hinduism. She said, 'No religion on earth says to stop procreation. Even Hinduism does not say to stop giving birth to. But we go by conditions and circumstances around, i.e. as per time and place'. She espoused the need to change according to the changing time.

Later I had had a discussion with my maternal uncle, whose knowledge and eminence I highly esteem. My uncle, was a professor in an engineering college. I explained to him plainly that by planning their families, majority Hindus were doing a great service to the nation, weren't they? That was my impression then, way back. He said, 'The government advises—as a family welfare measure—to all the people of the country. It never imposes or makes it mandatory on any one community. Some follow and some don't. It has not imposed on Hindus either'.

'Then what's the use of following? We should get an incentive for abiding by the government counsel', I argued. There were so many doubts raised in my mind, if Hindus were only one section of the country's population, if the secular India was shared by everybody, if the country belonged to all, all have the same responsibility!

'It is you who have to decide what is good for your family. The government of the day never forces', my uncle added. The government took up this advisory position after a careful thought. It was said that during the Emergency Sanjay Gandhi took up the family planning issue so ruthlessly, it became one of the issues for the downfall of Indira Gandhi's government. I was ambivalent on whether the government imposed on us, or we ourselves wanted a planned family for our benefit. Then I came to the conclusion that it was useful in both ways.

Let me tell you another aspect: majorities mostly became affluent and comfortable by following family planning measures and by having only two children. The increment for those working in the government, as an incentive, was a meagre one, and it was not a regular increment either. It was an additional one limited to the government servants alone. What about others? They were willingly undergoing birth control because they saw some merit in it.

It is really appreciable to see how Telugu middle classes, like most of the South Indians, aspire to see their children to study in IIT, IIMs, or at least in BITs Pilani. Of course, it is taking toll on young minds when he or she is forced to prepare for those tough entrances. It is indisputable that there is a direct link between number of children and their well-being. What do people get out of burdening the country and themselves? The country progresses only when everybody feels responsible. Onus does not lie with only a section of the population? What's sauce for the goose is sauce for the gander. If restricting the size of the family as is advised by the government is good to one section, it should be to all. I think the educated among all communities realised this fact and are making their choices now. After all, a society has interests that are over-arching and customs over-lapping.

Sardar Vallabhai Pater: Tall Stature, Tall Statue

As Pandit Jawaharlal Nehru is to the most of the minorities, Sardar Patel is to the majority Hindus an iconic figure. Many Indians wish he was the first prime minister of India. If that had been the case, India's fate would have been different. He was a man of iron-will. When I was a student in school, I studied things about Sardar Patel, which are still memorable. I would present the anecdote from my memory of Vallabhai Patel's lesson.

Sardar Patel's life and anecdotal references from his biography had a place in the textbook lessons earlier. I still remember studying in school as to how Patel sacrificed his hard-earned university seat in London for his brother. Vallabhbhai Patel worked very hard to earn some money to do barrister course in London. In those days, barrister course was done only in England. Sardar Patel obtained seat in the course and was about leave for London. However, he found his elder brother who was also very keen on doing the course. Both their abbreviated names with initials tallied completely. So, Sardar Patel sent his brother to London to do the course first, as he was equally qualified. Later, at the late age of mid-thirties, Sardar Patel also pursued the course and obtained the degree.

Sardar Patel was dedicated to his work. Once when he was arguing an important case, he got a wire. Somebody brought it to him in the middle of the argument. He saw the telegram and kept in the pocket of his coat and continued arguing to win the case. After successful completion of the argument, he broke down to the astonishment of the audience present. The incident showed his iron resolve to pursue the important case at hand, despite the saddest news of his wife's death did not deter him from the resolve. So, therefore he was called an iron-man, as was written in our textbooks. Now, such lessons are not found on national leader like Sardar Patel. These leaders are the right persons for emulation. However, they are neglected by curriculum framers.

Sardar Patel, with his strong and steely determination, galvanised this country into one republic. Unlike Pandit Nehru, he had no vacillation in taking decisions. He played a stellar role during the independence struggle of India and after that. But for his too early demise after independence, India would have been the strongest nation like Patel, the strongest man. He was rightly called the *Loh Purush (man made of steel)*.

Sardar Patel integrated all Indian states into one. When he was the chairman of the minorities sub-committee, he was successful in abolishing communal representation granted to the Muslims by the then British in 1907, which would have caused a permanent wedge between the two communities for ever in Independent India. That was the greatest achievement after the integration of states. The evil effects of communal representation were so patent that the authors of the Montagu-Chelmsford Report could not justify it. They observed, divisions by creeds and classes mean the creation of political camps organised against each other and teaches men to think as partisans and not as citizens . . . But they concluded that the pledge given to the Muslims in 1907 could not be repudiated. Mr Ramsay Macdonald's (the prime minister of Britain) Communal award not only confirmed but extended the system of communal representation. This was repealed by Patel, was challenging and a no mean task.[1]

Patel was so pragmatic. That pragmatism (of anticipating flare-ups between the two major communities of India) was clear when he had given the advice to both communities soon after the Independence of India. He appealed to them to forget the past. The New Nation of India will not tolerate disruptive tendencies in any form. Sardar Patel had foreseen some disruption from the major communities in India with a foresight, as he had seen the partition of the country on religious lines, from a close quarter, being an important functionary in the Congress. However, he did not envisage that the real disruption comes from his own party, the Congress, in the long run by creating a wedge between the communities, with pseudo-secular politics and an eye on elections. As Gandhiji said, the Congress that made the movement of independence should have been dissolved, instead of turning into a political party and willy-nilly making schemes to win electoral battles.

Now the younger generations of Muslims and Hindus have another advice from the same Vallabhbhai Patel on another occasion to remind. Because these younger generations are born in India. Hence, they are constitutionally and legally Indians. Earlier there was ambiguity because of separation into two nations.

Patel's advice to Muslims was, 'It is your duty to sail in the same boat and sink or swim together with the rest . . . Make friends with others and create a change in the atmosphere. You will then have more than your quota . . . if you really feel for the country in the same manner as the other people.'[3]

Sardar Patel balanced his advice to the Muslims with a similar one to the Hindus, whom he told: 'Forget the past, because it is a manly virtue to do so . . . every Muslim should feel that he is an Indian citizen and has equal rights as an Indian citizen. If we cannot make him feel like that, we shall not be worthy of our heritage and our country.'[2] He never hesitated to call a spade a spade.

Pragna Bharati Organisation of Hyderabad celebrated the golden jubilee of the liberation of the Nizam's Hyderabad State in September 1998. Late Sri. Nani A. Palkhivala, senior advocate of Supreme Court was invited to speak on that occasion. However, the eminent advocate could not attend the function. But sent a message, which says,

> 'The younger generation of today—the students in particular—would never know the sacrifices made by the stalwarts of yesteryears whom we had as our leaders prior to, and during the independence struggle. In the twenty-five years between 1922 and 1947, India had a galaxy of talent combined with sterling character. Undoubtedly, Sardar Vallabhai Patel was in the top rank.'

Sardar Patel was one of the founders of our Constitution. Luckily, the Constitution was drafted by the Constituent Assembly, which was not elected on the basis of adult franchise. First-rate minds were hand-picked from all parts of India for their knowledge, vision, and dedication.

The Sardar's life-work has been the consolidation of India. In the five thousand years of its history, India was never united; it had always been a group of different states. Vallabhbhai wanted to bring into existence a united, homogeneous India when it became a republic in 1950. To him, the unity and integrity of India was of paramount importance.

Unfortunately, the nation has not realized the greatness of Vallabhbhai as it should have done. We have all but forgotten him.'[3]

So, therefore, Sardar Patel contribution to unify India was immense and immeasurable. For, the tallest leader, tallest statue in Gujarat is a rich tribute. The RSS and the BJP have been showing reverence to Saradar Patel for a long time. It's not a new phenomenon.

Endnotes:

1. Montagu-Chelmsford Report http://en.m.wikipedia.org
2. The *Hindu* newspaper, Sunday, 28 June1992
3. Late Nani A. Palkivala's message, Golden Jubilee Celebration Nizam's Hyderabad State-liberation, Pragna Bharati dated 14 July 1998, Bombay.

Cow Importance Discussion

One day, while coming from school, I saw a procession going by with drum-beating and slogan shouting. Many muscular young men sporting tilak on their forehead and saffron turbans tied to their heads were walking along with the cart in giant strides. There was a box atop the cart. It was pasted with massive pictures of cow on all four sides. The cart was drawn by bullocks slowly. That was all, a procession which was against some abattoir that was killing cows along with other cattle, of course. By seeing the picture of the poor cow taken in a procession, I felt suddenly a kind of sympathy for it. That sympathy was out of religious sentiment or otherwise I could not fathom.

Immediately I thought of all animals; cows should not be killed. My mind agreed with the agitators. 'Cow is a docile, domestic animal, why it should be killed unnecessarily?' I thought. Moreover, it is venerated. On all auspicious occasions, it is brought in and worshipped. With us Telugu people, especially when we build a new house, it is religiously mandated, at the auspicious time of house-warming ceremony the entry of the cow, first, in to the house is a part of the ritual. The cow should be taken into the new house, and it should tread in all the rooms. Then the house becomes purified for humans to live in.

Before taking into the newly built house, it is worshipped with all grandeur. When the cow walks through all rooms of the house if it drops dung or urinate, the house-holder feels so happy and thinks him to be blessed. It is treated as a good omen, a nice foreboding. So scripturally, it has its place.

Later when I went to a function, I met my cousin Raghav, a young chap. He did his engineering in IIT and was about to leave for USA. I just wanted his opinion on cow slaughter. At that time, even I was young and naïve. I said, 'Don't you feel bad when a cow is taken to be killed? I saw people on the road doing an agitation against it. I felt sorry for the cow. Why it should be killed?'

Then he said, 'What about chicken? Small chicks, they will be roaming on the road playing, look cute! Why should they be killed and eaten? What is wrong with them? Poor things! Don't you feel sorry for them? For that matter, even a buffalo? Why should it be killed? Or any animal?' He rationalised all animals as one, not one above the other. If killing was bad, killing any animal was bad. I had no answer when he equated a cow with a hen or a chick. He wanted to show that my anger was misplaced.

Ethically, all animals have life and all should be treated as the same. Hindus do worship cow on religious ceremonies in their entire life. Beyond life also, a cow has a role according to the scriptures. In obsequies ceremonies, the priest asks to donate a cow so that departed soul would catch the tail of the cow and cross *Vytharani*—river. Believe it or not, we paid money to buy a cow and donated it to the priest who was performing ceremony to my parents when they died! Though rationality and faith are incompatible, faith prevails over rationality in some matters. Emotions cannot take a back seat. 'Parents give birth, loving and caring, and decent education to the children, when they pass away, can't we do this much to them?' is the question many children ask themselves, taken over by emotion on the death of their parent. So, many religiously follow the rituals. This way, cow is different from other animals for Hindus.

When I told my uncle about what Raghav said, placing all animals on the same footing, my uncle replied, 'It's strange! Raghav doesn't know the difference between a cow and a chick? Cow is revered and worshipped by all Hindus throughout the length and breadth of the country. That apart, cow is beneficial for the society. Cow's milk and the by-products of the milk like curds, butter, cheese, ghee have tremendous health benefits. It is scientifically proven that cow's milk is wholesome. The milk of a cow is better, easily digestible, and more nourishing than any other animals by way of proteins and vitamins. Cow's urine as medicine cow dung as manure are very useful. Cow has its own prominence and importance in our country both culturally and scientifically.

'Cow is specific to India. We have been worshipping it for ages. It is a sacred animal. The cow is equated to mother. People call *Gaumata*. Whereas buffalo is a hybrid and brought in late into the country. Though useful as an animal, cannot be kept on par with cow on value. If you go for ahimsa, even a cockroach should not be killed'. Hindus respect the life in all beings. Hindus see god even in animals from the time immemorial. These conversations happened a quarter century ago. Now, time elapsed. Still taking place in a more vociferous form. The Gau-rakshaks are hell-bent in protecting them. India is different in its heritage. To me, cows should be protected in this land

and should not be killed even if they are old and sick. Like how the majorities in India respect the minority sentiment, even the minorities should do so by reciprocating in a befitting manner.

When the RSS calls for cow protection or beef ban, it is religious for the opposing parties. In that case, they could listen to environmental activists who are crying hoarse on eating less meat, especially red-meat, to contribute to combating climate change. There are well documented health benefits of a plant-based diet. A shift in diet is one step for the sustainable future of the planet. Plant-based foods can drastically cut carbon footprint. 'The beans for beef' should have to be the motto. We can even control environmental pollution by not slaughtering cows.

CHAPTER 7

Faux-Secularism in India

The 'idea' of India for so-called secularists:

There were many intellectual debates on secularism in India and how it had been practised. The arguments that were made earlier, if I mention now, they seem to be the battered ones. For instance, for the Congress secularism is skin-deep. Its commitment was displayed in the Mizoram elections when it promised to rule the state by the Bible. Again, it amended the Constitution in the case of Shah Bano! The Communist party created the Muslim-majority district of Malappuram in 1968 in Kerala. So, these mistakes were committed by those parties for others to highlight how pseudo their secularism was! Given a chance, given a majority, they repeat the same in a more forceful way. Because they were not aberrations of secularism as is perceived by others. In actual sense, they are the party policies.

The secular governments in India, as a principle, pursue policies by 'pleasing and pleading' the minority religious leaders perennially with an eye on the votes in the next election. Otherwise, those leaders would heckle and make a big hue and cry that their community is under threat. One cannot expect this appeasement of minorities ended with Uttar Pradesh elections of 2017 by the big win of the BJP. For there is every possibility that the trend may bounce back once there develops a discontentment in the people and their aspirations or the people may be carried away by the gullible secular parties with false promises. So, with this victory of the BJP government, one cannot expect that the so-called secular forces are defeated forever. And the debates on secularism could be stopped. The 'idea' of India for the Congress is this pseudo-secularism that they have been forcing on us.

People of the minority community, like others, lead normal day-to-day lives. Only leaders with their visible community look make shrill calls and appeals to the community to take any issue related to the community to heart and fight the secular-governments head on. In this regard, All India Muslim Personal Law Board that was set up in 1973, ostensibly to protect and interpret Muslim personal law, should take action against those who call for irregular religious practices and communal disharmony. Though headed by educated and eminent lawyers, the board never condemns fundamentalists' arguments and seemed in a way supporting them with erudition. I wish even the majorities have a such a board to protect their secular (not religious) interests. For in a surreptitious environment of the secular parties wooing the minorities, the majorities are at a weaker wicket. Even the courts are not able to judge as the Parliament of India is the supreme body in making legislations.

The so-called secular governments always had come on to their knees, leaving the other governmental vital activities to plead with the minority mullahs and maulvis what more religious rights they needed other than they had already been granted on them lavishly. It may be pointed out by many that they would do in the same way with the Hindu majority community leaders also. Yes, they had done it in a minor way.

In any given situation, the religious leaders from the majority community are unaware of the secular rights they have to ask for, for the welfare of the Hindus. Whereas minority communities' leaders are clear in their minds. First religious rights, then secular rights and demands.

I am convinced that secularism is good for India. The Hindutva, which the BJP says is almost similar. However, the word *Hindutva* is abominable and unacceptable for certain sections of the country for the simple reason, the word *Hindu* has been a part of it. The secularists of India have made it a hate word.

Now, of course, that trend is changing for good with the BJP emerging as a force to be reckoned with. The secular political leaders have now become pragmatic and started wooing majorities by going to their place of worship devoutly. The innocent gullible Hindus fall into trap, the so-called secularists gain power and take India back to square one by applying reverse gear, thinking their 'idea' of India to be good, and people voted for it.

Of late, the Congress realised the fact that a section of Hindus is averse to their appeasement of the minorities. So, the Congress party, whenever it tried to include Hindus of India, the media immediately reprimands by saying that the Congress party is too soft peddling on secularism. And call it, the party is playing soft-Hindu card. This soft and patronising secularism, if done, to the so-called minorities, the media will never show a finger-pointing. In the recent Gujarat assembly elections (Dec-2017) Sri Rahul Gandhi hopped from temple to temple to show that he also practices Hinduism. Can he replicate the same devotion-template in 2019, throughout India? One has to wait and watch whether his spiritual touring is genuine and heart-felt. The Congress is trying this route of soft-Hindu card, only to empower minorities again coming to power, this, the majorities should ponder over.

People in India vote for different reasons. Some for their daily bread, some for jobs, the farmers for the solution to their problems, some for freebies, some others for primordial loyalties. The secular parties appeal to all, to cater section by section, in the end, if their party wins, they say 'secularism' has won! How many common, ordinary Indians on road know what secularism is which the intellectuals of India are not able to define! They say their daily lives will not be transformed whoever comes to power, which is true. Of course, I should admit here that there has been substantial change in the situation and thinking of the people than earlier because of media and technology and information flow.

During the Ayodhya-Babri movement, when it was at its peak, there were statements emanating from many secular leaders on TV channels. My mother-in-law, who listened to all those statements, asked me naively, 'Why do all the leaders advise us, Hindus, to give up the stand on temple issue, why not even one leader advised Muslims?' She was correct in her own way. She did not know the legality and constitutionality of the issue. What she knew was the religious aspect of the issue at hand. It was apparent by her statement that there was a disconnect between the spirit of India and the Constitution of

India. This gap is in all secular democracies. Secularism envisages a principle that state should dissociate itself from religion. However, this gap is more in India. For the other secular countries have a state religion as undercurrent; we have nothing. Minorities in India are not only protected but also granted religious rights by our Constitutional luminaries. Hindus are asked to remain secular. This is the 'idea' of secularism in practice in India!

As far as minorities leaders in India are concerned, almost all are aware what is secularism and how it could be bent to suit to their needs. The majority of the majorities in India do not know the wrongdoings of the secularists in the name of secularism and what that could lead the country to. Here I would like to mention my personal view point. The concept of demarcation of people into two camps, i.e. majority and minority, in India in itself is faulty. Till yesterday, a person in a majority community, suddenly if he converts into another religion the next day, how could he become a minority? Which secular country in the world recognises religious minorities? Other progressive Western countries have ethnic minorities, not religious.

If Hindus are only a section of people in India,
think of the following propositions:

It is implicit, in any country, the majorities have a say or a voice. In India, it is to the contrary. Majorities are merely relegated to a section. They are made into sub-divisions and sub-sections so minutely dissected to suit the whims of the so-called seculars to rule the country by appeasing other bigger religious chunks by shedding false tears for them and introducing the ideas of fear and discrimination into their minds to pit them against their own country people. They, as a mission, grant all rights to the minority, which they ask for. Since the fractured majorities have no PR (public relations), they are kept aloof. Otherwise, which secular country has given the following rights given in India to their minorities.

Permissions to Haj and Jerusalem on tax-payers' money. The Haj subsidy has been coming from a long time. A colonial legacy like Sharia. As it is mandatory for that particular minority community to visit the holy site, this religious right is granted by our so-called secular governments as a goodwill gesture. However, it came into question by the apex court of India in 2006 (when the Congress-led UPA government was in power). The court asked as to whether secularism, a basic feature of the Constitution, allowed it to grant largesse for the annual Haj pilgrimage. The bench cited the constitutional provision mandating the government not to discriminate on the basis of religion.

Now, with the changing time, there have been many private airlines that are willing to board the pilgrims for cheaper prices. It is pragmatic to change with changing time on secular issues, if not with religious ones, for the leaders of the community. This the Hyderabad Member of Parliament grasped. It is in the news that the amount allotted to the pilgrimage by the government be utilised for Muslim girls' education. Of course, I cannot comprehend what prompted him to make that appeal, but apparently a good move.

Former chief minister, the late Sri Rajasekhar Reddy, the hot favourite of the Congress party and its high command, himself from the Christian minority community, promised Haj-like subsidy to Jerusalem and implemented in his own tenure. This is a secular act by a secular party, the Congress! He promised none to Hindu pilgrimages. Naturally, when Hindus are relegated to one section of people in the country by the secularists and the media, sharing the country with other sections who have equal rights or more rights, this kind of questions arise. Day in and day out, all English channels say to Hindus that they are only 'a section' of people in this country, and India is not a Hindu country. So, there is nothing wrong if that section is asking for equal rights with other sections.

My friends in secular parties may ask, 'What happened to the arrangements of Kumbha Mela and other pilgrim spots?' Hindu temples with huge donation are managed by the governments. They use the funds for secular purposes also. There is no transparency in utilisation of those funds for a common Hindu to be aware of. Moreover, the Kumbha Mela at Allahabad and Ujjain takes place once in every six or twelve years. Except for making provisions for maintaining law and order, hygiene, and erecting tents for stay of pilgrims, the government does not give concessions in terms of fares in trains, buses, ships, or aeroplanes.

When we copy Western countries in our secularism, which dissociates religion with the government functioning, it has to be applied in India also. Hindu endowments are milking cows. The money could be used for other than Hindu purposes also! There are noises that started, though in a subtle way, among Hindu groupings if waqfs, mosques, churches, and gurdwaras can be managed only by bodies composed of people of those faiths, then Hindu temples should also be managed by Hindu bodies. Of course, I am not a supporter of this theory for the reason that earlier, i.e. way back, they were mismanaged by the temple trustees. However bad the secular governments are, people still trust them. A degree of transparency and an iota of empathy for the Hindu community that is contributing such huge funds is needed.

There are several articles in the constitution that guarantee the minorities either the right to propagate religion or to run educational institutions or to promote their religion. The right to run educational institutions applies to linguistic minorities also. Even a miniscule of linguistic minorities are not invoking the article. In India, the term *minority* is almost synonymous with Muslims. No caste from majority community can come close to 18 per cent of minority Muslims in India. These terms, *minority* and *majority*, are convenient terms for secular governance for the secular leaders.

For a particular community people, 12.30 timing- permission every week and 4.30 on festival days could be given magnanimously. Even Western countries do not object for prayers by Muslims or any other religions as long as their work is not impaired. They have 'silent rooms' in offices as well as malls. Entry is for any religious person to pray, not particularly to a religious group. Hence in India, Hindus may also have that privilege when they are relegated to a section along with others sections.

There is no country in the world where a privilege and right that is given to one religious group is not available to another. So therefore, Hindus think they are discriminated against in their own land because, while other religious communities can start educational institutions with certain privileges and exemptions that are not available to them. If a Christian minority establishes educational institution for teaching the Bible, it is perfectly understandable. So is the case with Muslims. But for the majorities, there is no such choice. My job is not to find fault with the minorities; they can enjoy the rights given to them legitimately in the Indian Constitution. My question is how far India is secular. Why an organisation like the RSS, when it wants to knit the Hindu society into 'one', the secularists feel the pinch.

The emboldened secular leaders stop Hindu procession for minority prayers, openly saying that it disrupts communal harmony. When Hindus are only a section of people like the other sections with equal or less rights, only this section is asked to oblige. The principle, dubious or otherwise, 'Be strong to the weak and weak to the strong' applies here. The vote banks come under priority for the secularists. Because they are a vociferous minority. This is secular polity in India!

Because majorities have no collective voice, earlier in my childhood days, our secular leaders neglected us on our important festival days. Anyway, we did not take it seriously and made strikes. In those days, milk, electricity, and water were supplied by the government. They were not available outside to buy. We had successive Congress governments. For us in Andhra Pradesh, even if we wanted to buy extra milk on festivals, supply was limited and sometimes less than the normal. Even on important festivals, sometimes, the water supply was not released. To use grinder or blunder for preparing some cooking items on festival days, power supply was interrupted for a longer time than the normal days. None of us had complained. Because the leader turned deaf ear to the complaints of the majorities. However, on minorities festivals, the secular governments ensured that there should be no deficiency of supply on any of the afore-said facilities. We could not understand whether governments had done those arrangements out of fear or favour to them.

Now the situation in India has changed. There are counter questions from the Hindutva parties. In both Telugu-speaking states, leaders are ensuring that everything reaches to everybody on all festivals. Freebies are given to the weaker and poorer sections among the minorities and majorities on certain important festivals such as groceries and clothes to the ration-card holders. Of course, the CMs of both states are schooled in the same 'secularism' practiced in India but are doing a fine balancing act at present. This appears to be a strategic move to contain the growth of the principal national party the BJP.

Earlier, the secular parties effectively divided Hindus into caste camps. They know what is Tower of Babel better than anyone! So, each caste started talking of its own interest. These so-called secular leaders take an oath on the Constitution to protect it. The founding fathers of the Constitution wished to foresee a casteless society. There is no effort on that front but there is a tremendous effort to dissect and shred into pieces the Hindu society. This is all in the name of secularism! Now with the emergence of the BJP along with the RSS, there is some amount of Hindu consciousness in the society.

Now coming to topic of secularism per se, the Constitution of India was drafted in secular spirit, i.e. state and religion shall be separate in polity, it applies to only the majority religion in India. The founding fathers of the Constitution who were all intellectuals wished India to progress in a secular or worldly way rather than by the diktats of the religion as in theocratic societies. The 'scientific temper', which Pandit Jawaharlal Nehru envisaged for India to develop, was good. All of us have had our education with that temper. But even the noblest ideals could also be questioned if they become dogmatic. The Ex-PM, Pandit Nehru, being educated in the West and to an extent adopted the lifestyle of the West and developed the mind-set also of the West, he regarded Hinduism to be a bunch of superstitions. Hence, to transform India, he wanted scientific outlook and temper. Taking this as an advantage, the leftist intellectuals removed whatever the worthy ethics and morals Hinduism had taught, from the curriculum, in the education field. This left the majorities bereft of self-worth and self-esteem in their own country.

Democracies are party-based, not voter-based in the sense the percentage of votes. Whichever party comes to power, it propagates its policies and ideologies, naturally. All Indians, most part of their life, have seen the Congress. The most aggrieved people in the Congress regime after their long rule are the Hindu majorities, some of them were very loyal voters of the Congress earlier. As far as minority Muslims are concerned, whichever party says most of the time secularism as *mantra*, increase their reservations and rights, throwing Constitution of India to winds, and brings conveniently the same Constitution to chide Hindus and try to shut their mouth, is liked and voted. Elite Muslims and elite Hindus from the cosy comforts of their houses see this drama and enjoy, occasionally, given a chance, to come to the TV. Studios and say a few words of what was going on in their own terminology. While speaking, they would not lose sight of their phonemes and morphemes of English to have been properly used.

The Samajwadi, Bhahujan, Trinamool, RJD, and others literally snatched away Muslim minority votes from the Congress. As far as majority of Hindus, they have cosied up with the BJP. In the latest political equations, Shia Muslims are coming nearer to the BJP, a positive gesture. Hyderabad's MIM has national ambitions. There is a confusion in the Muslim minority camp as too many parties are enthusiastic to embrace them. They, in fact, are trying forge an alliance for them sacrificing their personal and ideological differences!

What went wrong with the 'idea' of India that the Congress stands for

The words *secular* and *social* were incorporated in the preamble of the Constitution through 42 Amendment Bill by the Late PM Indira Gandhi during emergency for the reasons best known to the government of the day. Even before the incorporation, the spirit of the Constitution of India was secular. However, since Independence, successive Congress governments at the Centre and the state have been using the word *secularism* in breach.

Bringing religion into public space and getting clash in the public sphere between the communities is no good for any democracy. Not so, definitely, for the good of India and for the sustainability of this nation. But the successive Congress governments (here the mention of the *Congress* is merely to question it for ruling the country so long with that idea), used it for political expediency to gain power to rule the nation. For instance, in educational institutions where I have seen preference is given more to minorities whether the institution be of any kind. To elaborate it or to drive home the point, suppose an institution is run by majorities, minorities are always given preferential treatment and their sentiments and religious rights are valued. Whereas in an institution run by minorities, the majority community people (though their status is that of a minority) are not treated with any such feelings.

In a majority-run institution, our principals would request us to see that they (minorities) were given permissions and privileges. In a minority institution, the principal would ask us always to toe their (minorities) line. In both ways, the majorities are a causality. In both (majority and minority institutions), minorities of India get the benefit. These are secular acts of secularists to patronise religious groups like kings earlier did in feudal system, whimsically whomever they liked. The hidden reason? To take their bloc votes. The state-sponsored policy of appeasement is transferred to officials. A top-down policy!

The Kashmiri pandits being refugees in their own country is secularism! They are humans. They have been living for more than a decade in their hutments. No action to restore their dignity of life. But the so-called secular heart bleeds even if inanimate structures of minorities are damaged!

When it comes to the question of minority rights, the minorities always give credit to the first PM Jawaharlal Nehru. But never, ever admitted to the magnanimity of the majority community. As is said by the secular liberals, India is not a Hindu country; it is shared by all religions. In that case, Hindus are only a section of people. Why could that section of Hindus not be treated equally with others, is always my question.

The 'idea' of secularism has become, in other words, appeasing the minorities. This policy of appeasing was miraculously hijacked by the other so-called secular parties and reduced the Congress to a bonsai status. Anyway, the Congress has no patent on secularism.

The Congress, in its helpless state, all along tried to forge alliances with those parties (that forcibly took away its vote banks) to come to power. It did succeed in 2004 and 2009 to an extent. The hotchpotch coalition led to mighty scams. The former prime minister, Manmohan Singh had become their strength and weakness. Ten years of rule, although scam-tainted awarded them the bonanza—Hubris syndrome! The dilemma for the Congress was to resurrect itself with the same old buddies or alone. To be a mainstream party it needs to rethink and re-orient. As Donald Trump said in his inaugural address after becoming president, 'The forgotten men and women of their country would be forgotten no longer'. Here in India also, from the majorities, there are forgotten men and women who were once with the Congress.

The BJP has emerged with the backing of the RSS as tallest party to take care of the Hindu interests. There is nothing wrong in being recognised with a 'Hindu' label according to secularism practised world over. Even in the secular Western democracies there are parties like Christian Democratic Party, which Angela Merkel represents in Germany, and Christian Socialist Parties in Europe. Abortion and LGBT rights are major religious issues in politics. The secularists should not drag Hindus to this level of stooping to religious connotations in India. The UK and USA, though secular, have an official faith: Christianity. They are inclusive of their right-wing parties. In India, the *so-called secular* parties shudder to promise any demand of majorities. To them, equal rights for majorities is equal abolition of rights to minorities. This is the 'idea' of India to them!

My main grouse in the entire business of secularism is it is oversold to Hindus and less taught minorities. It is an established fact for all secular parties in India to treat minorities as born secularists and majorities as born communal with some exceptions. Sometimes, they mouth shibboleths like Hinduism is a tolerant religion, etc., because they are also voters like their dear minorities. And other times, to say 'Hindu' is an abominable thing. Earlier, way back, it was a taboo word. Like the forbidden fruit, it should not be put in mouth, i.e. mouthed.

The 'idea' of secularism of appeasement variety is so injected into the nerves of majorities, they are getting an aversion syndrome. The so-called secular parties, knowing the pulse of the people, are inventing some diversionary tactics like economic growth, jobs for youth, farmers' problems, etc., for jumping into the saddle through back-door methods. They know pretty well that they have no magic wand for all the problems ailing the country.

'Secularism' per se is not a bad idea to rule India. However, it needs slight modifications here and there to suit this countries' culture and civilization. Elsewhere in the world, we see secular countries invoking their majoritarian cultural values. The parties that came to power recently in 2017, be it France, Germany, Netherland, etc., want to accommodate their right-wing ideologues also. In India, the Congress along with other like-minded wants to carry the smoky mantle of secularism as the party's preserve. Of course, that is the 'idea' of India for the party.

Comparisons and contrasts make a concept clear to mind:

My entire problem is with the secularists. Not with the minorities or the Muslims of India. The secularists, the left liberals are saying time and again, 'India is not a Hindu country. Hindus in India are only a section of people sharing the country with other religious groupings.' Agreed. To give confidence to minorities that they belong to this country, you are alienating the majorities. It is a shared country for Hindus, not theirs ancestrally. Even after partitioning the country on religious lines and giving away magnanimously a piece of the land forever, the

Congress claims, it's the party that has brought independence! Now striving to get the confidence of the same minorities and make them believe it is their country, though nothing wrong in principle, often browbeating Hindus, that they are only a section of people whose sole motive should be to forego their temple endowments and other privileges and be second-rate.

Though Hindus are divided by caste, they have one unified force— that is their gods and symbols. They have been worshipping them for ages with reverence. Even the British did not touch them, though felt the practices being pagan. During Ram Janmabhoomi movement, the Hindus became united as their daily worship symbol was not given importance by the Congress to appease the Muslim leaders. So, it was looked upon as a minority-appeasement party.

The British came for trading and looted the country. They had not tried to disturb the majority Indian from their deep slumber and idolatry. Many Hindus, even now, are least bothered about worldly matters. They are immersed in their religious practices and rituals. This is the case with the most educated and those who held the highest positions in the government. Even the Muslim rulers, barring a few fanatics, dared to touch or criticise the Hindu practices. The Hindu faith does not deal with day-to-day worldly things. As fundamentalism begets fundamentalism, some of the Hindus learnt activism from other religions. This is going to cause repercussions in the long run. Here it's pertinent to mention what Syed Karimuddin, a member of the Constitution Drafting Committee of India warned,

> 'India has been declared a secular state. It is in the interest of the minorities of the country that this secular state should exist. If any community wants to say that there should be communalism or that communal activities should be allowed to be practised, then the majority cannot be prevented from preaching communalism which will go to the great detriment of the minorities in this country.'

Here, the minorities are not communal per se; it is the secular parties that are promoting them to be so. They joined hands with the so-called left liberals in denigrating Hindu feelings. They have no qualms in criticising and slinging mud on Hindutva forces. I wonder why people make this phenomenon as a sole objective in life as if there were no better things on earth to do!

Hindus in the BJP rule:

One may get a doubt why I am raising these issues at this point of time (2017) when the BJP government is in power. No doubt, the government emboldened Hindu pride, i.e. being a Hindu, one need not be apologetic in this country but had not done substantially yet. For instance, in education, to incorporate certain ancient value-based literature. For I, being a language teacher, think that lessons in languages leave an indelible impression on pupils' minds in tender, impressionable age. We talk of human rights, human dignity, and to have empathy with the *divyang* (people with physical deformities). There are excellent stories in Indian cultural heritage. For instance, one story I would narrate. It is the story of Ashtavakra. The essence of this story is physical appearance should not be given importance.

Long, long ago, there was a sage by name Astavakra. *Asta* in Sanskrit means eight (8), *vakra* means curves. That man had eight curves on his body. That means, obviously, he was deformed. But he was a very knowledgeable person. He was a genius in *Brahma Gnana* (knowledge of universe or Brahman). King Janaka (father of Sita in Ramayana) wanted to conduct a *Vedantic discourse* (a philosophical discussion) and invited Astavakra to his court. The discourse was about to start. All were serious of the proceedings. Some of them were discussing, sitting in their luxurious and comfortable chairs, waiting for the discourse to take place.

Astavakra entered the palace and greeted everyone sitting there. They raised their heads, looked at him, and laughed loudly at his awkward shape. Astavakra felt bad. He wanted to leave the place immediately. He turned to Janaka, the king, and exhorted, 'Oh, King! I thought you invited me to a forum where knowledge of *Brahman* would be discussed, and I expected that Pundits (scholars) would be present. I never thought I would land up in a place where there were mere cobblers.' Janaka stood up and requested him not leave the palace with anger and tried to pacify the sage with folded hands. Then King Janaka said that the august panel was full of scholars. To that, Astavakra retorted, 'No, how can that be possible? They all seemed to be cobblers. For they only knew the beauty of skin.' Then Janaka understood what Ashtavakra meant, pleaded him to remain with an apology. Astavakra obliged. From Astavakra story, it's learnt that one should not go by external appearance. One has to look up to beyond the body—external.

These stories are gone. They are nowhere in the lessons. In India, though Ramayana and Mahabharata are cultural texts they are treated as religious ones only. None of the good stories from ancient Indian culture are ever present in school curriculum. Even if some stories of Ramayana and Mahabharata are placed in textbooks, they are dressed in such a way to suit the modern, secular slant with the message and essence dropped.

Languages are really a must for a student. For in a language class, they read poems and prose lessons of renowned authors whose thought is profound. A physical education teacher gives strength to the body by making them exercise. But a language teacher imparts strength to the mind. The thought in poems and prose treatises appeal to the mind. The impressions laid by such thought percolate into their life. The essence of it is to inculcate values in life. When they are in any crisis, this knowledge gained at school level comes to their rescue. The language teacher also enjoys what she is teaching, though she is teaching the same syllabus year after year. Each time, each year of her teaching, she gets a different dimension to the interpretation of the text.

If a tonic is given to a boy as an extra nourishment, it nourishes the body. Similarly, the mind of a child gets extra supplement from the language lessons through the thought concealed in them. The *dohas* (versus) of Tulsidas, Nanak, Kabir and stories of Buddha, Chaitanya, Mahavir give an essence of Indian values and heritage. Those great people shunned materialism. They deliberately embraced poverty. The Indian youth chasing after material things madly, if not achieved, going into depressions and committing suicides is pathetic.

They should know the real values of life and also their individual talents and strengths. Instead of going on a wild goose chase, they must be able to judge themselves in the light of what they learnt in their early childhood. As grown-ups, we always remember the things that we learnt in childhood by way of psalms or poems or anecdotes of value. They come to our rescue when we are at low spirit. Sanskrit is our heritage. It is rich in its text, grammar, and syntax. Mahatma Gandhi himself said in his autobiography that every Hindu child should learn Sanskrit. To me, it appears that it would be easier to understand the scriptures when they grow up. Reading original works is always better than translations, which sometimes distort the actual version of the story and the spirit of the writer.

I assume that the government should appoint a commission to look into these aspects of discrimination and disparities between communities. Otherwise, the majorities may not find any difference between the Congress and the BJP but for the Hindu pride and assertiveness granted. For the time being, the Hindus should be content with their pride restored. The forgotten men and women have got a voice. 'Equality to all and appeasement to none', this slogan has gone down well. Foreign Contribution Regulation Act (FCRA) regulations have become stringent after the BJP has come to power so that the non-governmental organisations that are funded by foreign countries would not misuse their funds for other purposes (like colonial civilizing missions) other than they are granted for. The Uttar Pradesh government and other state governments elsewhere are sending poorer sections among Hindus to Hindu pilgrimage centres in the lines of Haj subsidy.

In the Congress regime, minorities were patronised. The Congress had sent a feeling that being minority in the country is an advantage. I have had a conversation with my uncle on this issue. I present a bit of it. It gives the feeling of desperation of being a Hindu in India. Because this religion has no governmental support like other minority religion. The conversation was a very old one. Yet pertinent.

I said to my uncle, 'To be in a strong community with stronger communal ties is more advantageous. People get united and voice their concerns. What's in Hinduism? None cares. There is no societal binding. There is no one voice to raise issues. The government only pays heed to minority religious demands. I think, one book, one prophet, and one god unites people. What is the point in being a Hindu for anyone?'

For a moment, I felt Pakistan was better, where there is unity of language, religion, and identity. I appreciated Pakistan for being declared a theocratic state with no qualms. I appreciated, for a moment, their one specific religion rather a bunch of divergent principles in Hinduism. In Hinduism, there is nothing fixated, I thought.

The certainty of how to deal with things of life is not as explicit as in other Semitic religions.

Those thoughts and realisations have had a background. After independence, successive secular Nehruvian governments sacrificed the values of Hindu religion at the altar of minority religions. Like kings and feudal lords, they patronised minority religions by providing religious sops. They completely wiped out whatever values Hinduism stood for in school curriculum. Hindus, by their education imparted by these secularists, have nothing to be proud of. They have no self-esteem now. They are emasculated. The majorities, bereft of self-worth, cannot do anything worthwhile. Are secular governments in India run for the minorities and by the minorities?

When I just expressed my thoughts outwardly to my uncle, he detested the very thought of liking Pakistan for it being theocratic. He reprimanded me by saying, 'What an awful thought to have to like Pakistan.' He made me clear how Pakistan and India were so incomparable and incongruent. He said, 'India is such a great country, how could you think Pakistan a better place? India is country that has been there existent for more than 5000 years, people have been tilling this land for thousands of years, yet she is capable of feeding, even now, more than a billion people. She could withstand so many ups and downs. She has sustained her culture and traditions even after facing so many upheavals and onslaughts. She was resilient in ebbs and tides. If I were to have a hundred births, I would still like to be born in this country Bharath!' he exhorted.

I was moved by his patriotism. To my religion-related emotive question, he went ahead and said, 'Do you think religion brings unity? If it is so, Pakistanis would not be fighting among themselves. Look at the plight of Muslims who migrated to Pakistan from India when partition took place. They are treated as second-rate citizens in Pakistan still. They are called Muhajirs. They are fighting for their rights even now.

'Our pluralism is our strength. Hindus have, polytheism which makes them accept other faiths. Most of the Hindus do not mind adding one more god to their pantheon. That is the kind of Catholicism Hindus follow.' When I asked my uncle what happens to this country with this kind of appeasement-oriented secularism, would it survive? To dispel my worries, he said, 'May be these so-called secular leaders would not take it that far, that something happens to the country. But whom are the Muslims voting for?' he questioned. And he himself answered that they were voting to Hindus only, the majority community!

The kind of religion with one god, one prophet, and one book could not get unity among themselves but got unity when they are pitted against other religious groups. The Semitic religions keep the people in a straightjacket! There is less space for horizontal thinking. By being a Hindu, there is a lot of space for a person to grow. He could be religious, an atheist, or an agnostic. He need not necessarily go to a temple, necessarily fast for a festival, necessarily pray or celebrate a festival. Everything is his choice. The freedom of mind prevails. Freedom of mind without fear is supreme according to Hindu Upanishads. The whole race of Indians can be called 'Hindu' with no religious connotation. In fact, that gives recognition to India in the comity of nations, I thought at the end.

The kind of philosophy Hindus practice always keeps them at defence. They never come out to confront worldly problems with adequate passion that is done elsewhere in the world. It became very difficult for the RSS to get Hindus to the forefront to air their views. Activism in Hindus is limited to intellectual and spiritual activities, not of mundane. I do not find fault with their *upasana* or rituals practiced by Hindus instead of fighting worldly battles. This country, I think, is surviving because of their intense prayers and devotion. To an extent, activism in the worldly things is desirable. But by aping the West, many have become activists for meaningless all and sundry causes in India. Anyway, it is their right and their freedom and their wish to do so.

CHAPTER 8

The Congress Rule at the Centre and State of Andhra Pradesh (United)

I am bound to write about the much loved and adored Congress party in Andhra Pradesh (United). I would not be doing justice to my political treatise otherwise. Having lived a long time under the Congress rule at the Centre and the state Andhra Pradesh (United), we, in Telugu states, can claim that our knowledge about the party is greater than that of others. In any case, I would not claim that I am the representative of all the Telugu-speaking, but that does not stop me from writing my view.

Long ago, when much of these media buzz was not pervading, I went out for some marketing and returned home. That was the day of Andhra Pradesh state election results. The electoral fight was obviously between the national Congress party and the regional Telugu Desam Party (TDP). Though I wanted to know the result, I was not very keen on it because it was a paper ballot, and it took longer time to count. The kind of alerts which we get were not present then. As soon as I entered the house, my brother also came in. I just casually asked him what the election results could be as it was the counting day. He immediately said the Congress won the election. I asked him, 'Where did you get the news from? Is it correct?' He said, 'I am also coming from outside, so I did not hear any news from any channel, but I could make out by the mood of the people on the road, they are rushing here and there, none of them is caring traffic signals while driving. Most of them are jubilant.'

The inference of his talk is the Congress led lenient governments. People want lenient governments rather the stringent. In any case, the TDP was strict on law and order and on corruption compared to the Congress. As a teacher, I can say more authoritatively, students want a teacher to be lenient, not strict. Of course, the benefits of being strict and rule-abiding are aplenty. The Congress stands for 'everything to everybody'. In the due process, nepotism, favouritism, caste, and community equations have been promoted. So, there was no complaining. Everyone used to get their own by pulling strings. This eventually led to corruption.

Ex–prime minister, the beloved masses of Andhra, Smt Indira Gandhi called corruption a global phenomenon. She wanted to normalise and neutralise the malaise of corruption by saying so. Her statement became politically incorrect, though not an untruth. However, in other countries it happens at high levels. In India, it is spread throughout the length and breadth like cancer. Which part has to be annihilated? is the question.

It is very difficult to tighten or plug loopholes and control this institutionalised corruption for any leader. So, people thought, what cannot be cured should be endured. Of course, people are also part of the problem. They have found ways and means. Instead of endless waiting to get their work done in the offices, they are resorting to bribe to get their work done. Once they learnt the art to bribe, it would not be a bad idea for them to get bribed. So, it is a vicious cycle.

Every cloud has a silver lining. The silver lining here is going online. For the online payments and transactions have brought in more transparency in the system. But 'the old habits die hard' adage has still place! The system is not fully sanitised.

The most loved party, once upon a time, in Andhra Pradesh was the Congress party. The party's leaders were adored. Even after the late PM Smt Indira Gandhi's infamous emergency, also people of Andhra Pradesh were loyal to her and voted to her. Emergency and its excesses were unknown to most of the Andhras in South India, barring a few newspaper-reading sections. All India Radio used to give some filtered news. Emergency did not impact us much. When someone says fundamental rights were curbed at that time, press freedom was scuttled, it took time to comprehend. For the impact was predominantly more on North India.

I had once seen, when I was very young, Smt Indira Gandhi, the ex-PM, physically and heard her short speech when she came to Hyderabad to inaugurate Durgabai Deshmukh Educational Institutions in early '70s. Durgabai Deshmukh, from her early life, was associated with Indian politics. When the Indian National Congress had its conference in her hometown of Kakinada in 1923, she was a volunteer and placed in charge of the Khadi exhibition, which was running side by side. Her responsibility was to make sure the visitors of the exhibition were not allowed without a ticket, and even forbade Jawaharlal Nehru from entering. When the organisers of the exhibition saw what she did and angrily chided her, she replied that she was only following instructions. After the organisers bought a ticket for Nehru, he praised the girl for the courage with which she did her duty.[1]

Smt Indira Gandhi, former prime minister, also had a personal rapport with her. Hence, she had come to inaugurate her educational and medical institutions. It was so pleasurable to see the frail and dainty-looking, yet a stern and determined, woman prime minister Smt. Indira Gandhi and listen to her sweet voice.

After the emergency when Smt Indira Gandhi was defeated by Raj Narain of Janata Party from Rae Bareli, it was so shocking. The Janata Party that came to power, though ruled well, could not survive for long. Again, the Congress was installed by another election in two years' time. Smt Indira Gandhi ruled another term.

After Smt. Gandhi's assassination followed by the sympathy wave brought the Congress to power with a full majority. Sri Rajiv Gandhi's rule's initial euphoria died with Bofors, *shilanyas*. and Shah Bano. Again, his assassination led the Congress to power in 1991 with Sri P. V. Narasimha Rao, the prime minister. Mr Rao, though an astute politician, had vacillation on every issue. His like Shakespeare's *Hamlet* 'to be or not to be' kind of wavering resulted in Babri demolition. After the act of demolition, he became wise suddenly. To regain his party's vote bank he took up several jerky steps. One was to impose Article 356 in all four BJP-ruled states, the other was to enact a special law under which, inter alia, the demolition of even such super-imposed mosques, built in the period of Muslim rule in India's history, will attract stiff punishment. These acts neither satisfied his party nor the party's most loved minority vote bank. He remained as an unpardonable sinner ever after these measures in the eyes of the chaste (so-called) secularists of India!

Sri Narasimha Rao's biggest contribution to India was 'economic liberalisation' with a vigorous momentum. He went on with reforms in a big way. He and his finance minister Manmohan Singh were a great combination. Later, Vajpayee government took the economic reforms forward, keeping the momentum and pace the earlier government had set in.

The appeasement-oriented secularism of the Congress party haunted the ex-PM even after his death. Late Sri Narasimha Rao was not absolved of his Babri sin, while living or after his death. His dead body was packed and sent off from Hastinapur to beyond Vindhyas to an unknown destination unlike for other former PMs who had had memorials in sprawling grounds of Delhi for the dignitaries and commoners to visit. No sympathy for the ex-PM who kept warm and alive the Congress' PM chair for five long, turmoil-filled years! That was the treatment meted out to their ex-PM for the singular mistake. Of course, for the Congress, it was Himalayan blunder for losing their largest chunk of minority vote. That was all done by the Congress for the noble cause of protecting the (ever-so- fragile) secular fabric of India!

Sonia Gandhi-led Manmohan Singh government of UPA (United Progressive Alliance), being a coalition, with too many stakeholders was not smooth sailing. All desperate parties came together for power in the name of secularism. Andhra Pradesh (United) was instrumental in placing the national Congress in power twice in 2004, 2009. But the Congress betrayed the trust reposed by the coastal Andhra and Rayalaseema by granting Telangana state unilaterally and thrashing the Andhras mercilessly. I have not seen such callousness and ingratitude anywhere in history. Sonia Gandhi was completely ill advised. Even if she wanted to bifurcate the state, she could have done it in a more dignified way. In her bifurcation process, she singled out Andhra people and jettisoned their affection for the party.

Coastal Andhra is known for its fertile, delta land basin. It is an agrarian state and is very rich. The people of Andhra supported the

Congress through thick and thin. The Congress alienated them in one stroke. The Congress's defeat in Andhra Pradesh in 2014 was its nemesis.

Sonia Gandhi and the Congress had expected a win in Telangana by giving separate statehood. Similarly, the BJP thought it would benefit by the bifurcation as it had been making noise for smaller states for a long time. However, the people had voted for TRS (Telangana Rastra Samithi) and for the man who fasted unto death and had a close call on life.

The decline of the Congress dynasty started with the death and demise of Rajiv Gandhi. Sonia Gandhi could sustain the party with the help of the left parties and other so-called secular parties, but not on its own. The Congress party is a true Nehru-Gandhi dynasty party. The other minor dynasties elsewhere are not much powerful. The glue or combining force of the Congress party is its dynasty; otherwise, the individual members have no connect. The Pradesh Congress presidents of AP (United) were always unknown entities to us. The high command of the Congress thrust on us all weird candidates with no grass-roots work culture.

To me, *dynasty* means successive generations. If a present, first-time, politician's son is to contest for election, it may not be dynastic representation. When they have Constitutional right to stand, none can point their finger. Anyway, dynasts have edge over others. They have a ready platform to board. However, others also have a place in the politics of India. I think dynasts are only a few in number.

Law and order in the state Congress regime:

Earlier, whenever there was the Congress rule in Andhra Pradesh, there were communal riots in Hyderabad. NT Rama Rao, after coming power, contained them by strict implementation of law and order. Now in the media, I see debates in which panellists from political parties argue over political killings. If the person dies from the majority community, the secular governments attribute it to the 'law and order' problem; if the same happens to a minority community person, it's 'communal' killing. Here, I am reminded of an incident in the Congress government in 1990s.

Mohammad Sardar, a famous rowdy sheeter's death in police encounter in 1990, caused a lot of commotion in parts of Hyderabad.

Riots started on a very large scale, and then the Congress chief minister declared that politicians opposing him were behind the riots. In those riots, many innocent civilians were killed and many others were injured and curfew was clamped.

A high-ranking police officer worked very hard, throughout day and night, indefatigably, and won the hearts of people in the city on those riots and curfew days, following the rowdy-sheeter's death. For we were all watching him work devotedly to restore normalcy on our TV screens. He nabbed and rounded up many rowdy sheeters from the riot-torn places and kept them in lock-up to ensure law and order in troubled areas. Such efficient officers make an indelible impression on the minds of citizens. They grab the eyeballs, and a kind of hero-worship is developed among the youth.

However, in the on-going religious (communal) tensions, a young police constable from the Muslim minority community shot dead his superior, the said officer of the majority community, while on work. That was late in the night. The police officer at that time was standing on his jeep and overseeing the situation around, unaware of the shot. The police constable was taken into custody, but the Congress government of the day was soft on him by declaring that he was mentally deranged and acted so because of the heavy work day and night on those curfew days. Finally, the riots stopped after the chief minister stepped down. Though the killing had communal angle, the government declared it to be an aberration and came under the investigation of law and order. That argument of the government was in a way apt in that situation. However, the yardstick has to be used on both sides, the same.

Endnotes

1. IdealPerson-DurgabaiDeshmukh//Rajahmundry   rajahmundry.me> rajamahendravaram

CHAPTER 9

My Ideology, My Reality

A set of ideas become ideals. All ideals put together becomes ideology. An idea is so powerful as John F Kennedy said, 'A man may die, nations may rise and fall, but an idea lives on'.

My experiences and my convictions led me to the organisation Pragna Bharati. It was Ram Madhav's initiative; he started the forum first and took it to heights as a body of nationalist thinkers. The forum, as an NGO, had spread throughout the state of Andhra Pradesh (United) with branches all over the districts. Many youth joined and took it forward with zeal and fervour. India does not lack nationalist and patriotic youths. The only thing is one should channelize their potential. I am very careful here in using the words *nationalism* and *patriotism*, now, as they are abominable words to liberals of India, especially the *nationalism*. But I do believe nationalism and patriotism are much needed, if not oversold. To compare nationalism of Germany during Nazis, and saying, ' patriotism is the last resort of a scoundrel' are unnecessary parallels.

Pragna Bharati is a true nationalist forum. True in the sense, wholehearted devotion of the people who work in the organisation. If a national or international scholarly person of repute was invited to Pragna Bharati, Hyderabad, he was invariably taken throughout the state to other Pragna Bharati units of importance in Andhra and Telangana. Those days, electronic media was not so omnipresent to cover and disseminate the information. The only way to spread the information was to conduct lectures, seminars, symposiums, round-tables, etc. Pragna Bharati did all this with due diligence.

The chairman of Pragna Bharati, Dr T. Hanuman Chowdary, is the backbone and driving force of the organisation. As a chairman, his services are un-paralleled. He has versatile knowledge on all subjects, though by career a telecom engineer and IT professional, has been for decades studying India's history, society, politics, and philosophies and writing and speaking profusely about them. Apart from being chairman of Pragna Bharati, he held many high positions viz: director, Centre for Telecom Management and Studies; fellow, Tata Consultancy Services; former information technology advisor, government of Andhra Pradesh; chairman and managing director, Videsh Sanchar Nigam Ltd; adviser, Satyam Computer Services.

Pragna Bharati is only a discussion forum on issues of national importance. The issues discussed and points raised by the panellists are to give vent to their feelings freely. It's like exercising their freedom of speech and free exchange of ideas. Things expressed, in toto, are not binding on the BJP government at the Centre or the states. People of different ideological perspectives also air their views on issues of national importance in the public meetings held by the organisation. There is space for ventilation of thought of different viewpoints and ideological perspectives. There is always scope for audience participation in all the meetings in a disciplined manner.

Need for establishing the organisation:

- Pragna Bharati, Hyderabad, Andhra Pradesh (United) was established with noble objectives such as to uphold India's hoary and continuous civilization and also abundant material and mental resources.
- India has its own integrated philosophy of life which enables Indians to form a concrete opinion and judgement of every aspect of life. To see life, truth, and nature as a continuum is the hallmark of Indian outlook. In contrast, the Western view of life sees mind and matter, faith and reform, man and nature, religion and science as separate.

- Indiscriminate and rapid spread of the Westernised mechanic civilization with its 'Cartesian division' has not only resulted in a crisis of human values in our society but also endangering the very existence of the human race at large.

[I would like to clarify briefly here, what 'Cartesian division' meant before going further, for general understanding. Because initially I used to wonder about the term 'Cartesian division' as I had not heard earlier before being part of the organisation. I made a search myself in some dictionaries and encyclopaedias as online search engines were not available then. To me, it is clear now that René Descartes postulated some revolutionary theories that promoted new mechanistic sciences of the day. In his philosophy of dualism, mind and body are two separate entities. The mind can exist outside the body and the body cannot think. Descartes wrote volumes of books which deal with his revolutionary theories. So, therefore his theories were divisive.]

- It is an irony that independent Bharat, instead of learning lessons from the Western experience and following the basic inspiration of its own freedom struggle, has been forced to blindly follow the Western model.
- There is an urgent need to correct this trend, to take stock of our own moral and intellectual resources and use them in concerted manner to formulate a plan of our own for national regeneration.

Thus, it is time the country needs a powerful moral and intellectual movement to

(a) present, in modern idiom, the sublime philosophy evolved by the ancient Bharathiya genius and the social system aiming at the evolution of the man into a superior being, by pursuing the Indian holistic approach, which is based on the concept of fundamental organic relationship between man, his environment, and the cosmic process.

(b) analyse, assess, and suitably re-orient the existing social structure, which has become distorted and disoriented during the prolonged period of foreign rule and promote a dynamic forward-looking social setup founded in our universal sanatana life values.

(c) strive to bring modern science and technology in harmony with Mother Nature and higher human values by encouraging a comparative study of the scientific and technological knowledge acquired by mankind during the last few centuries and the Bharathiya perception of nature, science, and technology.

(d) raise the people's thinking from narrow loyalties to all-encompassing loyalty to our country, our people, our culture, and, indeed, to all mankind.

(e) strengthen the resolve of the nation to fight against tendencies detrimental to the unity and integrity of the country.

(f) develop studies and thought among our people about economics, politics, history, ethics, scientific, and technological applications bearing upon life and welfare of our people.

Activities and programmes:

To translate above aims into practice, Pragna Bharati would:

(1) prepare an exhaustive list of intellectuals of the area.

(2) conduct periodical group discussions, seminars, symposia, round-tables and invite competent scholars to deliver lecturers followed by a 'question and answer' session on topics relevant to the objectives of Pragna Bharati.

(3) set up a library of reference books and magazines for study and reference.

(4) publish important lectures delivered at our fora and other relevant material.

Pragna Bharati, Andhra Pradesh (United) started its activities in early 1991 (became full-fledged in 1992). So far, it has conducted many seminars, symposia, lectures, etc., on national and international issues like secularism, nuclear option, Indian Constitution, economy, human rights, Swadeshi movement, common civil code, Hindutva, and other relevant issues of the country from time to time. It has over twenty branches all over Andhra Pradesh, including all university centres and important towns.

To facilitate its functioning, Pragna Bharati, AP (United) operated through the following wings:

1) Vignana Bharathi (for scientists and doctors)
2) Maharishi Bhardwaj Institute of Vedic Sciences and Technology
3) Centre for Developmental Studies
4) Centre for Women's studies

These wings have also been taking up various activities and projects relating to indigenous science, technology and medicine, women issues, and development.

Pragna Bharati AP has published a monthly newsletter in English, 'Vande (Bharatha) Mataram' for few years after its inception, later the Vandemataram (newsletter) became Bharathiya Pragna magazine. Besides, it also published yearbooks, souvenirs, and monographs on various specialised topics.[1]

Some of the Pragna Bharati programmes, after my association with the organisation and after being the in charge of some publications work since 1994, I summarized here. My presentation covers mostly my reports of those important meetings published in house journals of the organisation. They belong mainly in three important categories—ancient Indian Culture: Vedic studies, contemporary ones viz. Jammu and Kashmir; uniform civil code, Hindutva; women issues: feminist movement—dos and don'ts for India (a discussion that was held way back).

******

To me, what went wrong in a secular set-up: The association with the organisation immensely helped me. I came to know that the 'ancient Indian culture' has still place in the modern Indian society and discourses. Here I should laud, particularly, the RSS and its frontal organisations like the Pragna Bharati that have been doing yeoman service. The patronise that the successive secular-Congress governments have given to minority religions is conspicuously absent in the case of promoting ancient Indian culture, values, and heritage. More than the earlier Nehru-Gandhi dynasty rulers like Pandit Jawahar Nehru and Smt. Indira Gandhi, the successive aspirants of the dynasty now, seem to have no clue of what ancient Indian wisdom or heritage stood for and can the modern society blend at least some amount of the ancient culture.

As far as Vedas go, my knowledge of it is from my parents. It is said that Vedas are *apaurishyas* (*'a'* in Sanskrit means *'not'* or *negative connotation, 'purusha 'means 'man' that includes human race*), i.e. not defined by man. The four Vedas—the Rigveda, the Samaveda, the Yajurveda, and the Atharvaveda—are considered to be of divine origin and to have existed from all eternity. The *Rishis* or sacred poets to whom the hymns are ascribed being merely inspired seers who saw or received them by sight directly from the Supreme Creator. They are preserved and transmitted, orally, by reciting from generation to generation.

Each of these four Vedas is divided into two distinct parts, one the mantra containing prayer and praise, the other the Brahmana containing detailed directions for the performance of ceremonies at which the Mantras were to be used and explanations of the legends connected with them. The end of Vedas is Vedanta (Veda+anta= Vedanta, `anta` in Sanskrit means end). The Upanishads are the endings of Vedas that contain the philosophy of Hindus which is called Vedanta.

Veda, meaning literally knowledge which is taken as standard and which formed the foundation of the early religious belief of the Hindus. In colloquial use, most of the Hindus say, 'That book is not a Veda, whatever he said is not a Veda' meaning to say, 'That book or what he said is not the standard thing'.

'The Veda has a two-fold interest: it belongs to the history of the world and to the history of India . . . As long as man continues to take an interest in the history of his race, and as long as we collect in libraries and museums the relics of former ages, the first place in that long row of books which contains the records of the Aryan branch of mankind, will belong forever to the Rig Veda,' said F. Max Muller.[2]

Many of the European scholars, especially German-Indology scholars, studied and interpreted Vedas into English. But Indians' works and translations and interpretations of renown are scarce. While interpreting the great texts, the 'freedom of judgement' always remained in their foreign hand. However, most of the translation and commentary was based on Sayana's work. The great scholiast Sayana, was the prime minister at the court of the king of Vijayanagar, now in Andhra Pradesh.

Sayana is regarded as infallible by many pandits and Indian scholars and has a wide acceptance. No arguments by any Western scholar who laboured so much to understand the most ancient and venerated books are likely to shake this belief.[2]

The European scholars went by rationality to suit their domain by dissecting the externals rather than catching the spirit, which the ancient seers held. However, the European students and interpreters agreed that their work on the Vedas must not be supposed to claim anything like infallibility, completeness, or finality for the results to which their researchers have led them . . . as Professor Max Muller says, 'So in the explanation of the Veda complete success, if ever attainable, can be attained only by the labours of generations of scholars'.

In the modern-day world, Dr David Frawley's understanding of the wisdom in Vedas is comprehensive and unparalleled as it includes the ancient culture of yoga, Ayurveda, and astrology. Frawley's works give us ample evidence of his scholarship and the spirit with which he grasped the true essence of Vedas rather than the European scholars.

Endnotes

1.   Objectives of Pragna Bharati, brochure Pragna Bharati, 1995
2.   Preface to the First Edition, *The Hymns of the Rigveda*, Vol. 1, Ralph T. H. Griffith, May 25, 1889, The Chowkhamba Sanskrit Series office, Varanasi, 1 www.sanskritweb.net>rigveda>griffith

CHAPTER 10

Vedic Culture and Promotion

Pragna Bharati arranged a Public speech on 'Message of the Vedas and Modern Times' by Dr David Frawley, director, American Institute of Vedic Studies in 1995

The Vedas were not only for Hindus. They were also for humanity, for any culture or civilization. The Vedic view of truth is universal. It transcends time, space, and person. Religion is just an aid to know ourselves. The purpose of all religions is spirituality, said Dr David Frawley of American Institute of Vedic Studies, New Mexico, in his message on the Vedas in modern times. He added the Vedic civilization is indigenous to India. The Vedic culture was the culture of river Saraswati dating back to 5000 years.

It was wrong to say that the Aryans had come to India from outside. There were many objective factors in the Vedas, which proved that India had had a very sophisticated culture. The Vedic and Aryan people could be found in Harappan times, he said. He also made a passing remark on how Egyptian and the Arabian cultures had slithered away while the Vedic culture still sustained.

Unleashing a scathing attack on those who separated science and the Vedic quest, he said that science was merely a paradigm in which Vedic understanding of the universe was there. Here he mentioned Schrodinger, the quantum physicist, who used Vedantic base to explore physics (or scientific phenomena).

The much-touted Western culture was based on human arrogance and exploitation of nature. Nature should not be separated from man. Even animals would have consciousness and feelings. The consequences of the Western mentality we had been seeing, instead of imitating the West, we had to learn from the West what not to do, advised Dr Frawley.

There was hardly anything for Indians to learn from the West. The spirituality emanating from the West is but a reflection of the Eastern thought, he reminded. He praised India for being homogenous. He said as a proof, if one travelled from the north to the south of India, one would know that the culture of Sanskrit prevailed all over alike.

Referring to equality of different religions, he said, 'All roads take to the same goal' was wrong. 'A path can take as far as it can go and can't go beyond that', he said. Elaborating his view, he said, moksha meant liberation from ego and samsara (i.e. recycle of births) which is possible only from Hindu thought, 'the Vedic knowledge of knowing thyself.' No other religion would teach Bhakti and yoga. Islamic Vedanta and Christian Vedanta were not known. Vedanta, Hinduism, and Santana Dharma had been synonymous and would give universal truth, he said. He condemned the view held by Semitic religions that they had the exclusive hold on the truth, adding that we should not sacrifice individual human self for institutions and churches.

Hinduism is the greatest religion in the world. It has got everything—richness and diversity. Hinduism should come more to light and be more communicative and expressive, he opined.

Dr David Frawley said that Hindus were said to be more tolerant people in the world; it was not enough to simply take pride in being so. They should condemn the lot of things that were carried out in the name of Hindu fundamentalism. Otherwise, the Hindu tolerance would be construed as cowardice. He also said when Hindu temples were destroyed, no one knew about them. But when a disputed structure was demolished everyone in the world came to know. However, it was not needed by the Hindus to aggressively change the trend. It was possible for them to express Hinduism in a convenient way. Hindus should not be too passive or too tolerant was his advice.

CHAPTER 11

Ancient Submerged Cities of India: Dwaraka and Poompuhar

(A programme of 1997)

Eminent archaeologist and Oceanographist Dr. S. R. Rao, former deputy director general, Archaeological Survey of India spoke on the subject. Dr. S. Kalyana Raman, president, Saraswathi Research Centre, Chennai, gave a speech on the subject, 'Recent Findings on River Saraswati'.

Former deputy director general of Archaeological Survey of India Dr. S. R. Rao, in his speech on ancient submerged cities of India, Dwaraka and Poompuhar, demonstrated slides and video recordings to buttress his point.

Dr S. R. Rao said, knowledge of ancient Dwaraka, and about the oldest findings of the time, had been interesting to Indians and more so for the scientists, to know what was stated in the 'Puranas'. Some people opine that 'Puranas' had no scientific evidence or base, but it was not so, he said.

In the pioneering research to conserve and preserve old places and things, the National Archaeological department started exploring sea by way of marine archaeological techniques. Initially though, it was difficult for the archaeologists of the land to unravel the things in the sea by diving into it and taking pictures; they learnt it later to prove and corroborate the evidences of the Mahabharata.

Dwaraka was supposed to be a complete island, but it was not so completely. The city Dwaraka had big buildings built with pillars and beams, which were corroded heavily now. There was modern building in front of Dwaraka temple, when that building was removed (for it had to be removed) with permission, the archaeologists found underneath its platform an earlier temple of ninth century, which carried sculpture of Lord Vishnu. The archaeologists could see two more temples below this, the last was the fifth temple, i.e. Dwaraka temple, one below the other, they could find five temples of fifteenth, thirteenth, and ninth centuries, etc., showing pictures and described how it could occur.

Before making a search for Dwaraka, they (the archaeologists) wanted to find a spot from where they could start, as the sea is such a vast area; and moreover, they did not want the exploration to be a wild goose chase. They proposed to start from Samudra Narayan temple, for people from olden days offered prayers there before going into the sea. Hence the archaeologists thought that it was a place proper because the movement of the people was high at that place.

The civilization, pictures, inscriptions, things like porous jars and other evidences of Ved Dwaraka and Poompuhar tallied and were similar to that of Mohenjo-daro and Harappa, stated Sri Rao emphatically. When went deep into the sea, they found interesting structures in Poompuhar, a very prosperous and big city. The submerged cities showed our cultural heritage, he said.

The inferences drawn by studying the city Dwaraka, amply proved it to be the Dwaraka of Mahabharata, i.e. Dwaraka of Srikrishna. Explorations in the sea were indicative and paid rewarding. Dwaraka was fortified; it was called 'Vari Durga', i.e. the fortress in water in Mahabharata. Harappan civilization was seen while observing the old things, stated Sri Rao.

Recent findings on river Saraswati were expounded by Dr Kalyana Raman, president, Saraswati Research Centre, Chennai. The marine discovery gave us protohistory.

My view: Many of us, were elated to see the presentation with visual slides on the screen. In those days, even television documentaries had also elaborately presented the underwater marine coverage of Dwaraka of Sri Krishna. Indeed, it was a great adventurous excavation by our Oceanographist.

CHAPTER 12

Origins of United Vedic Culture

(National Seminar, 2001)

A minister of state in the Union Cabinet inaugurated the seminar in which Dr. David Frawley, Veda Acharya, USA delivered the keynote address.

The minister in his inaugural speech read out the following text:

'I am pleased to be with you this morning. To be associated with this seminar on the profound subject of the Origin of Vedic Civilization is indeed a privilege. I am delighted that men and women of science, history and archaeology devoted to the exploration of truth and its propagation are assembled here.

1. India and its history and civilization have been very much tampered with and *in fact have even been fabricated by interested parties.* Until the middle of the 18th Century, no one has anywhere ever heard about the existence in the past of an Aryan race somewhere in Europe and its invasion and incursions into India. The Indian people themselves have never had any such memories of having come from somewhere outside India. In the Vedas, in the Puranas, in the Ithihasas and the whole of Indian literature, there has never been any mention of.

2. The European imperialists and colonialists who first came to India lured by its wealth, on the pretext of trade established their dominions over India. Some of their scholarly persons discovered the greatness of the Vedas and Sanskrit. They wanted to establish that such great civilization, literature and magnificent language could not have been developed by the indigenous non-white people. It must have had European origin, they said; because these colonial conquerors were Europeans. Because the European languages have structure and words from Sanskrit, they thought that on this basis, they should write a history to establish that Aryans were a race of Europe who had gone to India to conquer that land and to settle down there. It is significant to note that it was the British India Company which commissioned the Christian missionary, Max Muller to establish that the Aryans had their origin in Europe and it is they who took the Vedic civilization to India in the process, defeating and driving out indigenous peoples, the so-called Dravidians, to the South. The European "oriental" scholars of the imperialist and colonial countries which were conquering the fabulously rich India and other Asian countries picked up the fabrication of Aryan invasion as it served the twin purposes of white man's supremacy and the legitimacy of further conquests of India by the colonialists.

3. Unfortunately, the theory of Aryan invasion and destruction of Dravidian civilization had been lapped up by the Indians who had no means of independent research and scholarship. Later on, when the evidence was mounting against the Aryan invasion theory on the basis of archaeological findings, on the basis of attempts at deciphering the Harappan script and on the basis of satellite imagery of the dried-up course of the river Saraswati, many scholars especially in the United States i.e not of European origin have started countering the Aryan invasion theory. Indian scholars basing their studies in Sanskrit, Vedas, and indigenous literature and tradition, and on archaeology, astronomy and language arrived at the Truth. And by now, it is reasonably established that the word Dravidian refers to geography; that the Harappan civilization is part of the Vedic civilization itself; that the Saraswati river dried up because

its tributaries like the Yamuna changed course to the East and that in consequent the Harappan civilization declined and disappeared. Hundreds of sites have been discovered, all like those in Harappa, Mohenjo-Daro etc. All of them suggest the falsehood of the theory of Aryan invasion of India and their settlement in India after defeating the native people. It is regrettable that today the only supporters of the intentionally fabricated theory of Aryan invasion are leftists and their collaborators who are progeny of those who later on came to India as conquerors and tried to convert the people here. It is significant to note that the white European imperialist settlers in South Africa have also written a history that says it is not only they who have come as immigrants to South Africa, but that the native blacks in South Africa also had themselves come from the North! The white settlers have therefore, stated that they have as much right to the land as the Blacks themselves! It is obvious that all the colonialists and invaders and occupationists would like to fabricate history to show that the conquered people were also not native to the land and that they themselves had been immigrants conquering, subjugating and absorbing the earlier settlers. It is fantastic that some of the fabrications of history has said that even Dravidians were not native to India but that they have come from the Mediterranean lands. According to all these fabricators of history, India was a vacant land and it was immigrated by various people, in wave after wave! Those colonial, imperialist fabrications of history require to be expunged once for all in the light of thorough scholarship and multifaceted evidence.

4. I am glad that the Pragna Bharati of Andhra Pradesh which has been putting in tremendous efforts in order to enlighten citizens on different aspects of History, Economics, Ideologies and Politics has organised this seminar and that so many scholars are speaking here. I am so glad that the Indian Council of Historical Research which hither to has been hijacked by a set of people who had a missionary zeal in negating Indian history and fabricating it in order to sub-serve certain interests and ideologies is at last seeing light and that it is extending support for this Seminar.

I thank all the scholars who have come from different parts of India and also from abroad. I welcome all the participants and I hope that together, they would be able to broadcast the truths so that the fabricated history gets buried. I congratulate the Pragna Bharati for organising the seminar. I wish that they will arrange for the general public also to hear the eminent scholars.

Thank you!

Thus, he concluded his introduction to the seminar.

In his key note address, Dr David Frawley stressed on the measures to be taken to take the country forward. They are still pertinent. I have immense respect for Dr David Frawley, for he could understand India better than most of the Hindus. Frawley did a thorough research on Vedas, Ayurveda, astronomy and Vedanta. Frawley tried to highlight the importance of Hindu traditional medicines, traditional sciences, traditional philosophies from Vedas. For him, it was wondering to see how passive the majorities in India were, being lame to the facts! He wanted Indians to be intellectual Kshatriyas! For which he wished Indians to use intellectual argument to take forward their age-old wisdom and culture more aggressively.

Dr David Frawley wanted the education system to be revamped. That way, the coming generation will know the values of this land and the proud inheritance. For that he suggested the following:

1. Rewriting history is not wrong. It is similar to writing science again with new research and findings.

2. Indianisation of history, though called Saffronisation by opponents, is much needed, as the textbooks in India have not changed for the past fifty years. History of America and Africa are re-written from time to time.

3. In India alone, the history change is trampled. Today, Indian textbooks are filled with dominant Marxist intelligence, for they (Marxists) have been in academia for a long time. Though Russia and China got rid of it, Communism failed in the rest of the world ten years ago, India has not been able to resist it totally.

4. Active missionary work in India is going on today. The missionaries proclaimed the Aryan-invasion theory. Caste system got converted into class system. History has been frozen

for last few years. Distortions that have been going on should have been removed ages ago.

5. It may be questioned as to why is it important to know that had happened 5000 years ago. It (the history) is important in this country than anywhere else. The rich foundation of the tradition goes far. Indian civilization and culture have spiritual values over material values. Those values reduce or prevent the influence of consumerism. The rest of the world can't understand this, hence degenerates.

6. In Africa, America and East Asia, there is no indigenous culture.

7. 'Aryans lived in Central Asia', 'Caste-system prevailed during that time'—these accounts may be found in the textbooks—no such traces are ever found archaeologically when the skeletons of different periods were examined.

8. Saraswati civilization was the largest civilization that included Mohenjo-daro, Harappa, contemporary regions of Mesopotamia and Egypt. The 'Swastikas' symbols of those days are very famous in European side. There are many factors that connect. Mythical winged, several-headed animals create a very curious situation.

9. Vedic literature is the largest in the world. Greek's Homer and the oldest accounts of Bible are only 2000 years old.

10. India has the largest literature and tradition that is continuously maintained. This 'Aryan invasion' and other related ideas have no connection whatsoever.

11. I challenge any scholars who say that Vedas are nomadic. Rigveda is filled with *mantras, dharma, karma, gnana, shakthi, and yoga*. Vedas are very sophisticated. People like Dayananda, Vivekananda, and Aurobindo studied them with reverence.

12. Now (at present), the nature of debate on Aryan invasion changed. The new theory or issue debated is called 'migration of language'. The theory—Aryan language of Central Asia was imposed on nomads—had changed.

13. India has a great unparalleled national, cultural text—the *Mahabharata*. The traditions in it go all the way back to Vedic traditions. There isn't any great China text or great Europe text in those countries.

14. The fact that India has different linguistic groups that different people had come to settle here is a fallacy. Very strong connections and associations of Tamil lay with Sage Agastya and the twenty-five sutras in Rigveda culture comes from South India also. On the linguistic count, there are many issues to counter.

15. The problem in Indian context is Hindus have apologetic approach. They must build genuine, sincere, and positive nationalism based on Vedic, Vedantic, and Buddhist traditions.

16. When we are bringing out indigenous history with massive evidence—for any group to say that we are politicizing history is something fundamentally wrong.

17. India caters to greater spiritual wisdom—a spiritual humanity. Mahatma Gandhi said Westerners lack this Indian experientialism and universality of feeling. For they indulge themselves in personal enjoyments.

18. Tilak and Aurobindo drew spirit from Vedas. That spirit is Bharata Shakthi. Rigveda permeates in all this. Bharath is Karma Bhoomi, i.e. the land of action, civilization, and spiritual culture.

Chairman, governing council of Pragna Bharati, Sri T. H. Chowdary said in his introductory remarks, Macaulay-type of intellectuals who were wedded to colonial theories have brought in the myth of Aryan invasion. 'The unfortunate thing is every invader feels the others are also invaders,' he opined.

In the following sessions (session 1 was on 'Antiquity of Vedas' chaired by RVSS Avadhanulu, the deputy director, NIMS), what each speaker spoke are all my reporting after listening to the seminar carefully and noted the points.

Speaking on 'Antiquity of Vedas,' Prof K. I. Vasu, former director, CECRI, said Vedas evolved from mind and Vedic traditions were preserved in various parts of our country.

According to Sri Vasu, the greatest movement of people took place, essentially by nomadic people with the discovery of 'fire'. People understood 'the diet principle when they cooked grains, meat, etc., on fire.

Natural fire became 'community fire' later. That should be the origin of *Yajnas*. To make it (the yajna) continuous, sitting around the fire with best posture was important. The science of yoga evolved from that to higher consciousness. With Patanjali Yoga sutras, the intellect evolved to the highest degree possible, Sri Vasu said.

The best way to preserve the community fire was the shape of the hearth. The designing of hearth led to the science of geometry. *Yagnasalas* were built with mud and brick that paved the way in making ceramics. In Neolithic age, the science of metallurgy and ceramics came out of these *Yagnasalas*.

Prof. Vasu also pointed out that people saw the movement of the sun and the stars during night. Thus, science of astronomy was reflected in the Vedas. The science of agriculture is a product of *Yagnasalas*.

Community fire, i.e. *Yagna* fire—sitting around it the *Yogis* chanted mantras—these mantras were collected by Veda Vyasa and codified them in a scientific way. In Vedas, one finds the spiritual and material values together. The Upavedas are the sciences, viz. political, social, and engineering part of it, stated Sri Vasu and added Ayurveda, Gandharva Veda, are the scientific components. Vedas contain quite a lot of astronomy and everything on linguistics and grammar. From the geological, cosmological, literature, and traditions of various parts, one needed to study and give the antiquity of Vedas.

The whole of science and the whole of human knowledge is available in Vedas. In the *Bhagavad Gita*, Lord Sri Krishna said that Vedas existed, noted Prof K. I. Vasu.

Sri Avadhanulu, who chaired the session, said Sri Vasu analysed Vedas in the modern scientific way. There was a strong traditional point of view, which as a chairman he briefed. He said Vedas cannot be perceived through direct perception.

Session II. Saraswati Civilization: New Findings

Dr Kalyana Raman, director, Saraswati-Sindhu Institute, Chennai, said, 'When we speak of the Revival of River Saraswati, we must keep in mind three things or components: (1) the discovery, (2) the revival going on, (3) the importance of discovery and revival for understanding the nation, Bharath.

Dr Kalyan Raman said, on the banks of river Saraswati, Rigveda culture flourished. He mapped the river sights on the map and presented in the seminar the course of river Saraswati. Rigveda is the source to tell how river Saraswati traversed. He concluded his long lecture, full of evidences, by saying river Saraswati was not a myth; she was a 'ground truth', that was what the geologists and satellite pictures proved.

Session III. Open Session on Strategy: Countering distortions and Projecting True Copy

Sri N. S. Rajaram, in his brief exposition on the subject, said our nation was 'one' culturally so that Sardar Patel, the first home minister of India, could unify it whereas in Pakistan, there was no cultural unity; it was destroyed in the name of Islam. Historians like Romila Thapar said the Vedic civilization had come from Central Asia, but the archaeological findings show that the Harappan civilization itself was Vedic. Sri Rajaram made a scathing attack on the opponents who called the desired change in the history as 'the idea of saffronisation'. 'How is it called saffronisation, if we can go to hundreds of years old history, and bring the facts out?' he queried.

Sri K. I. Vasu viewed that correction of distortion should start from science (meaning to say instead of history). Calling Arabic numerals as 'Arabic numeral' was wrong; he corrected them as 'Hindu-Arabic' numerals. India had first found them out, he said. Circulation of blood was mentioned in Charaka Samhita and Sushruta Samhita before William Harvey put forward. There were many such distortions that needed correction.

Sri Negi said the river Saraswati was 4000 years old. The modern technology and global engineering proved that. All kinds of new technologies re-establish the fact of river Saraswati's presence.

Session III. Vedic Culture: Influence and Spread

A university professor presented a paper on the 'Origin of Chess', which she called an ancient war game. The birthplace of chess, i.e. Chaturanga, was in India. Dice with which one has to play were discovered in Mohenjo-daro. In those days, the representative challenge to gambling match was equal to battle. Chess depended on the principle of 'karma'; it depended on the player's will and choice.

'Vedic culture is interwoven in the Bharathiya culture like the threads in Kanchi silk saree. If you go into one aspect of culture so many other factors get unfolded', said the Bharatanatyam exponent Padma Subrahmaniam. She extolled Vedic culture that has given respect to women. Though the Vedas are four, from them there are upangas namely, dhanu (warfare), ayur (health), gandharva (music or dance), artha sastra (economic, politics). She said the Tamil culture is in fact totally Vedic. The original concepts to Thiruvalluvar (or Thirkural) were Vedic. The so-called Dravidian divide had nothing to do with truth. Indonesia, country as a whole, clings to Vedic and Hindu traditions. They claim Ram as their god and Ramayana a book most revered. Smt Padma Subrahmaniam urged to unite all the brothers and sisters spread over the world on Vedic point of view.

In session IV on 'The Aryan Myth: Dimensions and Ramifications', Sri Michel Danino, Coimbatore, who did considerable research on Dravidian culture by way of archaeological study and survey said, the slogans like 'Dravidians were the earliest inhabitants of India, their culture is different from Aryans or Hinduism relating to Aryan culture', were borne out of colonial heritage.

'India's Civilization is far, far ahead (all times) even when the world was more or less barbarian', viewed by Dr. B. G. Siddharth, director, Birla Planetarium.

Praising India's contribution to the world in the fields of mathematics, science, chess, yoga, Vedanta, astronomy, etc., he said the scientists of the world looked back for Indian systems due to the collapse of the Newtonian and Cartesian systems.

Elaborating India's service to the world from the centuries immemorial, he said plastic surgeries and cataract operations had been performed in Taxila. Zinc smelting was also done dating back 2000 years ago. Ridiculing the retreat of US cryogenic rocket technology for India, he said, rocket technology was not new to India; the modern rockets were used in eighteenth century at Guntur (Andhra Pradesh) by Hyder Ali against the British.

'Advanced West reached a plateau. They have exploited the third world by colonialism and extortion. The era of exploitation is coming to an end. The third world is waking up. India is waking up', Dr Siddharth stated.

CHAPTER 13

Hindu Philosophy: Globalising World

(A talk of 2001)

The purpose of arranging the talk was to address the following issues:

1. Which thoughts, world view, and philosophy are conducive to harmony and which are exclusivist and conflict promotive.
2. Historic evidence and India's role in the knowledge societies that humanity is evolving into.
3. What should be India's message and how do we deliver it

Prof Subhash Kak and Stephen Knapp (Nandanandana Das) deliberated the issues.

Subhash Kak was a leading historian of science and researcher on computers, information technology, and ancient Indian history, who was a professor at Louisiana State University, Baton Rouge. He received several awards.

While saying Hindu philosophy is conducive to the harmony of the world, Prof Subhash Kak said, yoga was the hottest pursuit in USA, 30–40 per cent of Americans had gone through Hatha yoga at one time or the other as it taught the union of body and mind in a harmonious fashion. The practice of yoga slowly transforms into '*dhyana*' (meditation) and other practices. All these practices had set in motion great change in the world view, he stated.

'There is a mind body connection based on stress level. So, one has to recognise a technique to be calm. Indian system (i.e *Patanjali Yoga Sastra*) has the best solution. As medical treatment is very costly in USA, this therapy is much needed for them. The Indian methods of *yogic* practices unclog arteries, leading to healthy circulation of blood in heart patients. In unfolding Vedic knowledge, we get scientific knowledge', he said. 'The heart of Vedas and Upanishads are "*mahavakyas*" (great sayings). They inculcate *Adi Boudhik* and *Adhyathmic* thinking', he added.

Stephen Knapp grew up in a Christian family, during which time he seriously studied the Bible to understand its teachings. In his late teenage years, however, he sought answers to questions not easily explained in Christian theology. Knapp continued his study of Vedic knowledge and spiritual practice under the guidance of a spiritual master.

Stephen had also been to India several times and travelled extensively throughout the country, visiting most of the major holy places and many minor ones. He had written The Eastern answers to the Mysteries of Life, a series.

Stephen Knapp, while delivering the lecture, said that the secular governments have caused damage to Hindus and Hindu culture in India. He said while the minorities in India were getting tax benefit for their places of worship, Hindu temples were taxed.

Indian culture is a million-dollar culture. 'Can you give up your million-dollar culture for somebody's ten-dollar culture?' he queried. The deepest, most traditional and oldest culture is Hindu culture. He called Hindu culture as universal-centred. He urged everyone to fight against the Western self-centred culture for want of universal Hindu culture. He called the Hindu-Vedic culture as flexible and accommodative.

****

'Emerging Planetary Consciousness: Role of India and Vedic Culture' (Lecture meeting of 2001). The main speaker was Mr. Duncan A. Campbell, the attorney, USA

Duncan Campbell is a graduate of Yale College and Harvard Law School, whose extensive experience in the last thirty years has included the fields of psychology, philosophy, spirituality, law, business, economics, politics, communications, and teaching. He has travelled widely, in both advanced and developing countries including indigenous cultures. So, he was invited to give a presentation on 'Emerging Planetary Consciousness: Role of India and Vedic Culture'.

Sri Campbell, at the outset of his speech, quoted the book of Matthew Fox, One River, Many Wells. He said, 'From many wells, we go to that source, "One Great River". Similarly, from many other cultures, we go to Hindu culture, which has tolerance and universality'.

Sri Duncan, in his speech, very interestingly related the feminine and the masculine energy that are working in the universe. He reminded that we are all bound by the feminine energy. The earth, the water, etc., have feminine energy because they are life-giving.

Basically, science, in the form of global consumerism, is destroying the feminine energy. Added to that TV channels over the sky were wiping all the cultures in the name of unity. He lamented on the state of highly activist culture that prevailed in the West, which lacked inner depth and led to chaotic energy, without any wisdom in it.

Duncan Campbell stated clearly the difference between a dialogue and discussion. A truth emerges without a concerted effort in a dialogue. He said, of all dialogues, Lord Krishna's dialogue with Arjuna in the Bhagawad Gita was the greatest. In Gita, Sri Krishna stated that he would manifest himself in the hearts of people but not externally. Similarly, there was a great shift of world's youth to spiritual consciousness. 'Sri Krishna, Buddha and Christ were already inside us; we just have to awaken them', he said.

Sri Campbell stated that people were migrating from the West to the East, and they were feeling as if they were coming home with resonance. He said he himself experienced profound feelings being in India.

****

India's Contribution to the World of Science' (A Seminar of 2002)

Para and Apara Vidya: Physical, Biological, and Cognitive Sciences

Here, Vedic knowledge in higher form is 'para' and at a lower form 'Apara'. '*Apara Vidya*' has name (*nama*) and form (*rupa*). '*Para Vidya*' is purely Vedantic.

Ma. Seshadri talked about the diversity in the universe that had to be protected. He said diversity helps beauty and growth. He said Hinduism has been protecting all diversities. Hinduism, when it was on zenith, did not go with sword in one hand and Bhagavad Gita in another hand to destroy other faiths. In fact, the sword of Islam tried to enforce uniformity in matters. He cautioned people against globalisation that might threaten the diversity of Indian culture, religion, language, and family system.

Dr David Frawley, in his speech, discussed as to how *Pancha Bhootha* (five basic things: air, water, fire, sky, and earth) work. He gave Upanishadic quotations to explain. '*Brahmavichar* is the ultimate principle of Hinduism. Science is the basis of *Brahma Vichar*', he said. *Vichar* meant a quest, to find out. That is the inner perception to go into another consciousness. Similarly, *Atma Vichar*, to know who you are. Vedanta shows the way, how to transcend the inner and outer forms and internalise them. This we can approach through *yoga*, said Dr Frawley.

****

Digitisation of Ancient Indian Wisdom, Especially Vedas

'Param'—India's Advances in Information Technology and Its Play in Global Markets (Dr. Vijay P. Bhatkar, Founder Executive Director, CDAC, Pune delivered a talk on the subject in 1998).

Father of India's supercomputer Vijay P Bhatkar said, 'The venerable ancient heritage of India and the profound wealth of traditions, languages, philosophy and other cultural elements contained therein must be re-discovered and retained, with the use of computer technology, as an adequate repository of knowledge for future generations'.

Recognising that India's enduring knowledge is found in the canonical principles of its rich heritage, Dr Bhatkar proposed that the greatest challenge before the Indian computer experts is the reproduction and preservation of the original scripts and phonics of the spiritual texts in the form of a 'digital library'.

In this direction, the proposed digital library being pursued, along with Veda Bharathi and Sanskrit Bharathi, would be an enduring contribution of the country to global community, he said. Terming the move as a belated one, he quipped, 'Many countries including United States of America which had no heritage till Columbus landed there, have digitised their heritage'.

Dr Bhatkar placed emphasis on the necessity to devise ways to inculcate the values of the Vedic age in the present generation as he said, 'Man can never understand the true nature of science or reality without an adequate comprehension of his evolution from adi boudhik (knowledge of the physical entity) to adi daivik (dependence on the Supreme Being) to adhyathmic (intellectual pursuit of real knowledge). The destruction of the planet and our inability to understand the very goal of human existence have been the results of the bankruptcy of our intellectualism'.

Terming religion and spiritualism as India's essential fabric, Vijay Bhatkar mooted the idea of painting a multi-media interpretation of the Bhagavad Gita on the Internet, apart from developing temple towns as religious knowledge places with data. While technology is a continuously changing phenomenon, knowledge remains the same. Thus there needs to be a strengthening of this knowledge which is applicable to any time period.

On science as a contributing factor in development, he claimed that it was the equations of scientists and mathematicians such as Einstein, Newton, and Bernoulli that changed the course of mankind and not wars or political leaders.

*****

Earlier, a centre for study of science, society, and culture was inaugurated by Sri Seshadriji, Sarsanghchalak, the senior most RSS functionary (of Delhi) in Hyderabad in 2003. The centre was essentially meant for bringing to the fore the intermingling of science, society, and culture in Bharath.

'Science' is as a word or concept that dates back to only 600 years in the Western lexicon, whereas in our country, it has been existing and flourishing for the past 5000 years, said an eminent scientist in that function. He wanted this centre to fill the gap between the ancient science, society, and culture and the present by making a thorough research to link-up both. He also wished for the promotion of Ayurvedic medicine to cater to the medical needs of the rural poor.

Sri C. S. R. Prabhu, director of National Informatics Centre stated as a matter of fact, that the entire Sanskrit literature did not deal with the high technology involved in making the '*Vimanas*' and '*Brahmastras*' (that were used in wars). They just made a mention of them and left, he said. He wanted the empirical evidence of the technologies used by our ancients. He was satisfied, however, with the advancement made in the fields of metallurgy and alloys by the ancient Indians. 'The only Science of our country, that works now is Ayurveda', he said and wanted research in that field of medicine.

All the scientists present aired their views. Mananeeya Sri Seshadriji made a concluding speech, after having heard the scientists speak their mind. He said science was all about finding 'truth' in material aspect with an objective world view. Sri Seshadriji wanted the members of the centre (CSC) to have a missionary zeal to work and to unearth the facts of our ancient Indian science to bring to the fore. He also wished the institution to flower into national stature.

CHAPTER 14

Protection of Vedas and Culture: My Thoughts

I was a homemaker for a long time and then joined job and got some amount of exposure. Thereafter the association with the organisation led me to many realisations. My initial reaction to some of those meetings at the beginning was, what happened to the Vedas? Why these meetings? What is the importance of river Saraswati now, at this age?

Certainly, Hindus have a great regard for the Vedas. My upbringing was with those values. But I never thought that there was an imminent threat to them so that they should be protected. After seeing and listening to all these intellectual speakers, I thought, perhaps, mine was a frog-in-the-well type of attitude. Barring the RSS, I had not seen any organisation trying to protect the Vedas, let alone promoting them.

Of course, there are Veda Patasalas (schools where the Vedas are taught to become Hindus priests in temples) by Hindu Devasthanams, though very less in number. They teach only theological aspects of the Vedas. However, as far as my knowledge goes, they never go deep into the perspectives of the threat to that culture and protection of the Hindu culture from secular onslaught. Here, I am not out rightly supporting to teach political aspects of the country. At least the students should be made aware of Euro-centric imperialist theories and some amount of knowledge to counter them in scholastic or academic discourses with supporting evidence. The research on the

Vedic civilization should also be done extensively by Indian as is done with other academics and theology.

Before being exposed to the organisation meetings, I was naïve and thought how does it matter if Aryans were original inhabitants of this country or invaders in the present-day context. This naivety I find in many educated Indians even now. For long after leaving school, they forget much of the history taught. In any case, they remember certain things like 'Aryans' invaded India in ancient times without knowing the implications of the theory of 'Aryan invasion', which is still disputable. European scholarship was so powerful that it drilled this idea of 'Aryan invasion' into the psyche of Indian national leaders. For them, they had nothing to counter the theory as they themselves did not delve deep into their ancestry.

'Aryan invasion theory' was lapped up by the leftists and secularists of India as a convenient tool to bait Hindus with. This theory suits their whim to puncture the Hindu pride of being the first and foremost native inhabitants of this country. These so-called progressives were trying to neutralise the native Hindu theory by citing that like the Muslim invaders and the British that came from outside, so also the Aryan invaders, i.e native Hindus, came from outside.

Their plan was to bring some kind of Aryan and Dravidian divide. And also a kind of 'composite culture', by saying, 'Since you all were migrants from elsewhere into this vacant land of Bharat or India, it belongs to all with a combined culture'. However, they never oppose personal laws of the minorities. They never voice for a uniform civil code for this country!

I personally do not agree with 'Aryan invasion' theory, which is, of course, highly speculative. With or without that theory, Hindus in India think that they are the dwellers of this land from the time immemorial or, for that matter, right from the time the earth came into existence. The minorities in India are also part of this heritage as they, ethnically, belong to this region and have been converted to other religions in midway.

As of now, the Aryans and Dravidians worship the same gods, visit same temples throughout the length and breadth of India. The wedge that the schemers of history wanted to create has not been successful. There are organisation backed by the RSS that have been doing immense research on this front by exposing the fallacious arguments.

They have made excavations at the Harappan sites and found out that the skulls unearthed at the site reveal the racial composition that was more or less as the same with the Indians of now. Apart from 'anthropological expose', they have found other archaeological evidences also.

The deeper reason behind the Aryan invasion theory is to bring in 'composite culture' wherein Hindus are only a component of the composite whole. In fact, 'Hindutva', what the RSS says is, also inclusive. Here I present some of the arguments:

Once, way back in 1995, we had a debate with this 'composite culture' grouping in Pragna Bharati. The proponents of composite culture include Muslim culture generously and Hindu culture in a subtle and insignificant way and espouse the cause of secularism at the expense of Hinduism to a large extent.

Late Sri Vakati Panduranga Rao, an eminent journalist and the ex-vice chairman of Pragna Bharati, defended Hindutva in his lecture to be inclusive in all the ways of Indian culture, and there was no need for any other 'composite culture theory' to be in place, artificially inseminated. Composite culture is otherwise known as Hindustani.

In Late Sri Vakati Panduranga Rao's words:

Hindutva is a culture of thousands of years old. It is this robust culture that made India survive so long. Hindutva has the salient feature of Sanatana Dharma, which equips people to meet their material and spiritual needs. It serves the vast people of our country deservingly. It is a commitment to values and ethics and aspirations of this country. The mantra "Om Shanti" is for the internal and external peace of man as well as the entire creation. Upanishadic sayings yearn for peace. They say that "peace be to Mother Earth, peace be to water, peace be to air", so on and so forth. People who laugh at such invocations should know, by now, how essential their safety is for the mankind after the puncture of ozone layer and pollution of industrialisation. Our sages and rishis had a great insight.

Social practices change, from time to time according to the conditions prevailing in the country. But the basic values (what the sages had taught) remain permanent. Hindu society is always bent on reforms and welcomes them with open arms. The Hindu idea of dharma means the duties that the different units of society owe to each other.

Most of the Hindus do not make fetish of their religion. No Hindu believes that temples are the be all and end all of life. So also, Hindutva. It does not have an attachment to any particular form of worship or any particular ritual. For Hindus, gurus are the light that show the path. A guru does not tell that he credits with intelligence. Changes are advocated in the Hindu society from time to time. The opposition had not come even from Shankaracharya. He was also for opening to questioning and change.

The test to science is inherent in Santana Dharma. Science and Santana Dharma are co-existent.

We have this type of discussion on Hindutva vs. Composite culture, only in this land of ours; nowhere else. No other country allows majority to be told by the minority. Because of it, partition of the country on the basis of religion took place. Vote bank politics still feeds the poison of separatism.

An average Hindu feels insecure in their own land because of bullying and coaxing of vote bank politics. Hindutva is a reaction (though it is an undercurrent of the society all the time) to the teasing and bullying of Marxists and other religions. One should judge how good a religion is by that religion's attitude towards the other religions. Can the Bible or the Koran be debated as we do the Gita and Upanishads?

A society is a culture which absorbs latest changes. Hindutva is the eternal thread of the country and at times a reaction to the situation also. If at all, Hinduism and Islam can live together, it is the great message to the world. But how can one live with a culture of the minority, which says no to debate?'

The proponents of composite culture say,

> To the so-called progressive secularists who vouch for composite culture have a feeling that to recognise Dravidians and Aryans as settlers or natives and to treat the Muslims and Britishers as invaders is something atrocious. They feel the Muslims who settled gave the best to the country in matters of administration, architecture, and culture.

They query as to why anything done to improve the Muslims was called 'appeasement'? They wish the history to be rewritten glorifying

Aurangzeb and Tipu Sultan to be most secular. They rejected the common civil code as a burden on minorities and also a complex issue. They stress the need for setting up a large number of minority educational institutions to improve their lot instead of studying along with general public of India.

The counter-argument was

The so-called secular progressives always wanted the Hindu community to subordinate themselves for the unity of the country. To assuage the feelings of the injury caused to minorities, they would like to re-write history.

If we think dispassionately, there is no validity and rationale in their arguments. The Aryan-Dravidian controversy they put forth is artificial. It had been cleverly concocted by the then power-seekers, the British. However, Aryans and Dravidians are same in their customs and beliefs and the way they follow dharma.

It is the misconception of the religious minorities to think that Hindutva treats them in the same way as the Semitic religions did with others. Religious-based discrimination has never been done by Hindus in any sphere of life. Hindutva as culture is required to hold or bind the people of the country into 'one' and make the country distinct in the world.

To get true spirit for the integration of the country, one should cease to talk or think in the lines of minorities and majorities. Religion is one's private thing. As far as the worldly things are concerned all the people of the country should be abided by *one law* or common code.

Sri Atal Bihari Vajpayee, ex–prime minister had said that Hindutva and Hinduism to be the same in his speech in Hyderabad. Here I would like to present Sri Atal Bihari Vajpayee's view on *Hindutva and Hinduism* in 1997:

Sri Atal Bihari Vajpayee delivered the twelfth Sri Ramakrishna Dhoot Memorial lecture organised by Rajasthani Graduates Association in Hyderabad. Recalling an instance wherein some party leaders sought clarification over the words *Hinduism* and *Hindutva* during the party's national meeting in Bombay, Sri Vajpayee said both meant the same but were pronounced in different languages.

Hindutva is not offering prayers or organising people but it reflects the nationality. It has geological and cultural importance. It is a symbol of our ancestors who lived on the banks of Sindhu to develop a rich culture and of those who shared joy and sorrows equally.

He said Indian culture joined the country from end to end and should not be viewed as a religious one. One should follow the dharma of his country and decide on what is the right path by asking the inner self. If you are born in this great country, follow the Indian dharma. However, people started the other way around after they started learning English, he said.

The word *secularism*, incorporated in the Indian Constitution during the emergency, never found a place when the Constitution was being written by the earlier leaders.

Dr Babasaheb Ambedkar never considered it fit to think over the word *secularism* in including it in the Constitution. But people started twisting the real meaning of the word, thus leading to a controversy.

Moreover, this word should not have come after the partition of the country as we rejected the proposal to make a nation based on religion, he pointed out.

Coming down heavily on those advocating a 'composite culture' like in Lucknow, Sri Vajpayee said every culture is composite in nature and composite in character. The Indian culture is one which united the people and never differed because wheat is consumed in the north and people in the south eat rice. Earlier, he said, the flight by which he was to travel to Hyderabad was delayed as the weather had changed in the country's capital. That is to say, the country's weather is different from place to place, there are different terrains in the country.

CHAPTER 15

Contemporary Issues of Relevance

On Terrorism, Insurgency, and Human Rights, 1994

The one and only speaker invited to speak on the subject was Justice Ranganath Mishra, former chief justice, Supreme Court of India; chairman, National Human Rights Commission. By the time I attended the lecture on said topics, my knowledge on them was minimal. I heard about 'human rights', but I did not know what it included thoroughly. This report is based on my noting of minutes. The former Chief Justice Ranganath Mishra was so soft-spoken. At the outset, he said, 'After the World Trade Centre blast, it took only one year for the US government to get the culprits booked and brought to justice. Whereas India, being a soft state, with weak justice, could not do anything for Bombay blasts', said Justice Ranganath Mishra.

Humanity had been stabbed in the name of civilization in the World War II. First article in the human rights says that '*all human beings are born free and equal in dignity and rights. They are endowed with reason and conscience and should act towards one another in a spirit of brotherhood*'.

'The General Assembly of UNO declared thirty articles on human rights, out of which twenty-three and half articles were part of our Indian Constitution. They transformed India into egalitarian society. The cream of the UNO draft's concepts was engrossed and incorporated in the Indian Constitution almost forty-four years ago', he said.

'Human rights are a part of Indian way of life and philosophy,' the justice said and gave examples of how our forefathers knew that plants had life (before Jagadish Chandra Bose discovered) and did not allow to pinch or pluck them unless to offer to the feet of the Lord. Animals were sacrificed to the deity otherwise they were not touched (five to six thousand years ago). Indians had 'respect for life and certainly at a higher stage', he said.

'You have no right to touch, if you have no right to create,' was Gandhiji's philosophy. This philosophy in which India had been built, nourished, and elevated, and it had become a concept. The foreigners who had come as 'friends' and 'invaders' had been respected in this country. Since our country is economically ill, more advanced countries had turned into judges in Human Rights', the learned justice lamented.

'Good living' is dharma. In a family, each member, i.e. husband, wife, children, have to follow their dharma. Children's dharma is to live up to the expectations of parents. A raja's (a king's, e.g. Rama of Ramayana) dharma was to sacrifice personal things. And praja (people) also had a dharma, i.e. set of rules to be followed. We should propagate the motto of human rights: 'Treat everyone equally with no distinction.' It is also the cream of Indian philosophy. A civilized society gives permission to all those who were born here and living in this homeland the dignity of life and human rights. 'Today there is a lot of violation, quarrelling in the name of religion, caste and creed. So, regeneration of traditional values is needed. People should re-cultivate the Indian way of life our fore-fathers had said', he emphasized.

Ours is a country that is deeply rooted in the philosophy of 'I give, never take'. Now it has changed and started to be only a 'take' society. Individuals and society are healthy if the position of hand changes from 'taking to giving'.

All the well-placed people in the society should restore human rights though it is a big task. Even gods, when they took human shape, had problems. Rama and Krishna also had to face problems. For the mind to develop and come out, reasonable amount of problems is needed. One should take a resolution to 'restore a smile to every human being'. This would give a sense of satisfaction.

After listening to the learned Justice Ranganath Mishra's lecture on human rights, some of the young people asked questions, which were very pointed:

Q1: 'The relevance of terrorism in the context of human rights are not being made a topic in the speech. Are the insurgents alone prone to human rights or not the affected?

Ans: Indian Constitution part 3, fundamental rights, Article 51, part IV said that 'rights and duties are two sides of the coin. If duties are performed, rights are automatically followed. Right to question follows the hearing of answer patiently and calmly. Terrorists and Naxalites are outside the rule of law. Law is not able to touch them. A terrorist does not accept human rights. So how can we accept his theory? It is a good question to be posed, but life requires balancing everywhere. A society should be balanced. A terrorist must accept, he must not violate human rights,' said the former chief justice.

Q2: 'Does practising untouchability come under violation of human rights'?

Ans: 'Yes, according to civil rights, Art-17 is about untouchability. Even after thirty years of incorporation of it in civil rights, untouchability still rules. Laws remain in statute books. Law is not a regulator. Human rights we profess in one way and practice in another way', he said.

Q3: 'If demolition of Babri structure is assumed as violation of law, what about the hundreds of temples demolished'?

Ans: The chief justice said, 'Violation is not an answer to violation'.

Q4: 'What's your view on the abolition of capital punishment'?

Ans: The learned justice quipped, 'It depends on the state of society. There are many countries who accept abolition of capital punishment'.

****

Kashmir: Is Time Ripe for Holding Elections?
In Jammu and Kashmir, 1995

> *Background: Jawaharlal Nehru, the former first prime minister of India could not defend India against China's aggression in 1962 war. We had lost a part of India. Another ex-prime minister, Pandit Nehru's daughter, by agreeing to Shimla Pact with Zulfiqral Ali Bhutto which seemed to many people as a triumph, was a damp squib finally yielding Pakistan-occupied Kashmir (POK) to Pakistan, though it was never recognised before. She wished to buy peace with the pact. But it resulted in wars. Pandit Nehru and Lal Bahadur Sastry never admitted or accepted the legitimacy of Pakistan-occupied Kashmir (POK) as was done by Smt Indira Gandhi.*

The Kashmir cauldron is still boiling. So, I would like take you back to '95 and how it was thought of at that time to hold elections in the state of Jammu and Kashmir.

Dr Murli Manohar Joshi, eminent politician and political thinker, was the principal speaker. Before dealing with the subject—elections, conducting them ripe or wrong—Sri Murli Manohar Joshi clarified some of the important things. Among them first he said, there was no condition of Article 370 in the Instrument of Accession signed by the Maharaja Hari Singh. He also said how Lord Mountbatten, the then governor-general prevailed upon Jawaharlal Nehru to stop fighting the battle in Kashmir when Indian soldiers were about to throw out Pakistani soldiers. That led us to the worst state of condition to take the Kashmir issue to UNO with the promise of plebiscite.

Shimla pact was not done in the interest of the nation, said Sri Joshi. We, the Jana Sangh, opposed the pact. Mrs Gandhi should have forced Mr Bhutto to vacate the occupied Kashmir and should not have compromised on the Line of Control (LoC), he said.

In the days of Sheik Abdulla, Kashmir had a prime minister of the state, separate Constitution, and had an independent flag and the election commission had no access to the state. In 1953, when there was hobnobbing with the idea of 'independent Kashmir', Shyama Prasad Mukherjee sacrificed his life, leading to Sheikh Abdullah's arrest and extension of some parts of Indian Constitution to that state.

International interest in Kashmir is deep-rooted. The reason for introducing the Article 370 was to keep the relationship in ambivalence. The BJP had been demanding for the removal of the article to the state to be the real part of India.

The two forces working in Kashmir were, one, to secede from India to Pakistan, the other that wanted 'azadi'. The latter (Azad Kashmir) was serving the international forces, whose operation was successful in Afghanistan were diverted to Kashmir. CIA was also involved in that, he said.

The loyal Indians in Kashmir were driven out, he said, and others were asked to surrender their arms by police and were never given back to fight with the terrorists.

Sri Joshi also referred to his 'Ekta Yatra' for the integration of the nation. 'Slowly, slowly, Indian territories were eaten away by our neighbours, if we allowed Kashmir to go by, the same story would be repeated elsewhere in borders.'

As a conclusion, Sri Joshi said, 'By bungling the Shimla pact of 1971, the government wanted to hold elections under the pretext of "International Pressure"', he said. 'To conduct free, fair and fearless elections, he stated that the administration in the state should be strong and should wipe out the militants from every inch of Kashmir. Otherwise, elections would open Pandora's box again for international interference. We must also have a firm stand to get back the occupied Kashmir', he said amidst applause.

(Pragna Bharati Yearbook, 1995, pp. 98–99)

CHAPTER 16

The Supreme Court Ruling on Hindutva

Background: The judgement on 'Hindutva,' by the Honourable Supreme Court in 1995 was in Manohar Joshi's (Member of Parliament, Shiv Sena) and other connected cases, holding that the Hinduism or Hindutva is not a religion but a way of life, and therefore an appeal to the voters to vote for Hindutva or Hinduism by itself does not amount to corrupt practice under People's Representative Act.

Eminent political commentators and columnists' Sri Mohit Sen and Sri Arun Shourie spoke on the occasion (1996).

I am presenting a great dialogue on the topic by Arun Shourie with an eminent Marxist Mohit Sen to show the difference between the views of the two Political commentators. In between Sri Rama Jois, senior advocate's judicial perspective and quotations on Hindutva in various cases come into picture. I did not mention the case histories presented by him in his paper, for this book is not an academic treatise.

Arun Shourie, the noted columnist, had said, the Supreme Court judgement on the concept of Hindutva was not quite a full step but welcomed the judgement as a step in the right direction. Participating in a dialogue along with another political commentator, Mr Mohit Sen, Mr Shourie strongly condemned the hue and cry raised by the so-called secularists against the judgement.

Shourie said the Supreme Court had merely reiterated what the law itself says and what the Supreme Court had itself held on the previous occasions. 'What then accounts for the fury of the secularists?' he queried.

One after the other, Sri Shourie provided certain reasons that caused secularists' fury on the judgement. He said, 'The first feature which has offended them is precise that the court has treated candidates at par! On the reasoning of the secularists, when a Muslim candidate said, or when a candidate from among "the forces of social-change" said, "Islam is in danger, get together", there was nothing wrong as it is but natural for a minority to feel insecure; but when a Hindu candidate said, "Get together, Hinduism is in danger", why that was terrible, he was being communal, he was indulging in a corrupt electoral practice, his election ought to be struck down. When a Muslim candidate said, "Get together and bend this government to concede x, y, z", in the reckoning of secularists, he was just asking for amelioration; but when a Hindu candidate said, "Get together so that governments do not bend to these communalists and concede x, y, z", he was being communal and fomenting religious bigotry. The Supreme Court puts the two at par: as asking for something—say, a bank only for non-Hindus of the kind the government has set up—is not a corrupt electoral practice, opposing it is not a corrupt electoral practice either, as saying that Islam is in danger is not a corrupt practice, saying Hinduism is in danger is not a corrupt practice. That seems obvious enough. But just as obviously the secularists are not able to stomach it: for a fundamental premise of their verbal assault has been that there has to be an imbalance in favour of non-Hindus, of Muslims in particular.

'The second sin of the judgement for them arises from the fact that the Court has accepted, indeed adopted in toto the definition of "Hindu" of "Hindutva" which the RSS and the BJP have been maintaining is what they have meant whenever they have used these expressions . . . that is anathema in itself. But as repugnant if not more so is the fact that in doing so the court has adopted a description which is complimentary to Hinduism. "Hindutva", "Hindu" these words signify a culture of tolerance and universalism . . . But I confess to feeling just about half satisfied. The court says that the words "Hindu", "Hindutva" etc. refer to a culture, to a territorial region . . . It declares that the words are not to be taken to refer to a religion in the conventional sense . . . in a word everything except words that refer to the religion you and I, the vast majority of our country men practice.'[1] These are only some of the excerpts from Sri Arun Shourie's speech published in the organisation's yearbook of 1995, which I compiled and edited.

I would also present a few thoughts on the Supreme Court's Hindutva judgement of Late Sri Mohit Sen at that point of time in the meeting. The earlier speaker, Justice Sri M. Rama Jois, who presented a paper on the occasion, cited many important quotes on Sanatana dharma or Hinduism based on which some judgements were delivered.

Justice Sri M. Rama Jois said that Hindutva was a way of life and not a religion. The excerpts of his paper are the following:

'The judgement of the Hon'ble Supreme Court of India in Manohar Joshi's case and other connected cases, holding that the Hinduism or Hindutva is no religion, to vote for Hindutva or Hinduism by itself does not amount to corrupt practice under Section 123 of the R.P. Act, has received mixed reactions as it has always happened in respect of every important judgement delivered by the Apex Court. It is widely welcomed by those who stand for Hinduism or Hindutva and greatly criticised by those secularists who regard Hinduism or Hindutva as religion.'

In support of the submission that Hinduism or Dharma was no religion, but it was only a way of life or culture and secularism was a part of Hinduism, reliance was placed on various authorities and voluminous literature, stated Sri Jois and mentioned the most important as the following:

1. 'It is an interesting fact of history that India was forged into a nation neither on account of a common language nor on account of the continued existence of a single political regime over its territories but on account of a common culture evolved over the centuries. It is cultural unity—something more fundamental and enduring than any other bond which may unite the people of a country together—which has welded this country into a nation.' It was submitted that it was this culture which had forged the people of India into a Nation, which is now called Hinduism.

2. 'Thus, a philosophical and ethnological composite is provided by ancient Indian thought for developing Sarva Dharma

Samabhava or secular thought and outlook. The enlightenment is the true nucleus of what is now known as Hinduism.'

3. 'When we think of the Hindu religion, we find it difficult, if not impossible, to define Hindu religion or even adequately describe it. Unlike other religions in the world, the Hindu religion does not claim any one prophet; it does not worship any one God; it does not subscribe to any one dogma; it does not believe in any one philosophic religious rites or performances; in fact, it does not appear to satisfy the narrow traditional features of any religion or creed. It may broadly be described as a way of life and nothing more.'

4. 'Let us now turn to the practical side of Hinduism. Hinduism is more a way of life than form of thought . . . Hinduism insists not on religious conformity but on a spiritual and ethical outlook in life. The performer of the good and not the believer in this or that view can never get into an evil state . . . into fellowship all who feel themselves bound to the claim which the moral law makes upon them. Hinduism is not a sect but a fellowship of all who accept the law of right and earnestly seek for the truth.'

5. 'The term Hindu was first used by the medieval Muslim invaders to describe the dwellers of the Indus valley. But the culture we now know as Hinduism and which the Indians call Sanatana dharma—eternal law—predates that label by thousands of years. It is more than religion in the doctrinal sense that the west understands religion. One can believe in any god or no god and still be Hindu. It is a way of life, a state of mind.'

The Honourable Supreme Court on consideration of the above and other materials produced, followed the earliest Constitution bench decision and held that Hinduism or Hindutva was a way of life and was not a religion and therefore an appeal to vote for Hinduism or Hindutva, by itself cannot be considered as an appeal on the ground of religion. Therefore, the meaning of dharma/Hinduism/Hindutva, Bharathiya Samskriti is one and the same. It is no religion. This is also evident from the slogan 'Yato Dharmastato Jayaha' inscribed on the emblem of the Supreme Court.

'Hindutva is a dharma and its translation into religion has disastrous effects. Hindu dharma is the only antidote for all social, political, and economic problems being faced by the country',[2] he said.

Noted political commentator and columnist Sri Mohit Sen said, 'The judgement on Hindutva literally says "nothing", yet it says "too much"'. That is my considered view with all due reverence to the judges, who imparted the judgement. The learned exposition that Sri Rama Jois has given about the judgement tells that the judges have come to the conclusion that 'Hindutva' or 'Hinduism' is not a religion. That is not something that the judges should say! In fact, courts are not attending to the matters they ought to . . . lakhs of cases pending.

When it is said that the Supreme Court is saying 'too much', it is because it has given an *obeter dicta* if one propagates Hindutva one is not violating the Constitution. Now, if anyone propagates Hindutva in the manner in which our learned Justice Rama Jois has done, then certainly that is not the violation of the Constitution. It is upholding of the constitution. But is that the only way in which those who profess the Hindutva propagate when they go to the huntings.

The Supreme Court's saying that Hinduism is not a religion is not a point of excitement. The SC is quite as fallible as any other institution run by human beings. Therefore, one should directly discuss the question of Hindutva itself. What is wrong with Hindutva? Nothing wrong! What is right? Everything. Indians are certainly proud as our country has produced such a religion and also such culture.

As a matter of fact, Hinduism is a religion. Why should one be ashamed of calling it a religion? It is a great religion. It is very much a religion. It forms perhaps a very crucial element of a culture which is Indian. That is the distinction one can make. There is absolutely no reason to try and disguise the fact that Hinduism is religion and go about saying that it won't disagree with that or this. Then what is specific about Hinduism? Why should you be a Hindu? Hinduism is something specific. In that specificity, there is an enormous amount of greatness and enormous number of things which have gone thoroughly and terribly wrong. It is the duty of those who are proud to be Hindus to fight and struggle against that which is also taken to be Hinduism. It is also taken to be Hinduism because it is the practised Hinduism.

Similarly, bigotry, fundamentalism is no doubt specifically an attribute to Communism and Islam, though lesser extent also to

Christianity. In that sense, Hinduism is much broader church religion. Much more tolerant, non-exclusive religion. But in the name of Hinduism, is not fundamentalism propagated and preached? In spite of all the very strong words and tremendous eloquent speeches of Swami Vivekananda and others, they continue . . . What is this Indian culture? It is Hinduism plus. All of us should acknowledge it.

There are some elements in Hinduism which are very rarely referred to but are extremely attractive. There is hardly any other religion in the world which has such pagan element in it. That is the greatness of Hinduism. It is highly ritualised. It is a matter of high philosophy. It is also rooted in the kind of paganism, the ebullience, the vigour, and the vitality of the common people. It is very much a folk religion. It is a religion of pagans just as much as it is a religion of *Upanishads* and *Manusmruthi* etc.

As a concluding remark of this discussion, we can say that the question of the livelihood of the people is more important than anything else in this country. As Gandhiji said for those who had not come to that stage of realising god, god comes to them in the form of bread and work. Neither bread nor work are freely available to millions of people . . . It is to this that we should pay our maximum attention.'[3]

Late Sri Mohit Sen concluded his speech on Hindutva judgement as that of a Communist and Socialist. Unlike, today's communists, he did not bait Hindu religion and the religious practices. He admitted, at least, some nobility in the Hindu religion which the secularists of this country fail to admit. Before the meeting, when Mohit Sen entered the venue of the meet, I met him hastily and introduced myself. I told him that I regularly read the newspaper. I also told him that I never miss to read Arun Shourie's columns. Immediately, I corrected myself for mere mention of Shourie's by saying I read his columns also whenever they appeared in the newspaper. He just laughed. With the smile still on his face, he queried, 'Are mine (his columns) working as an antidote?' I did not know how to answer. I just nodded my head in negative. But I still admire the way he asked.

Those were the days people used to respect the educated and erudite scholars of any dispensation and any point of view. The common people, like us, had a kind of awe at their knowledge and command over their writing. Now the scenario has changed. Every person is either a competitor or a challenger of the other, even with a less or no knowledge because of the availability of platforms, flow of information, and surcharged environment all over.

1. 'The Hindutva Judgement Not Quite a Full Stop', Arun Shourie: Pragna Bharati Yearbook, 1995, p. 10
2. 'Supreme Court Is Saying Too Much', Mohit Sen, Pragna Bharati Yearbook, 1995, p. 18, 21
3. Paper presentation on Hindutva Judgement, Pragna Bharati, Rama Jois excerpts

****

Sri Atal Bihari Vajpayee's defence of Hindutva

Sri Atal Bihari Vajpayee, honourable leader of the opposition, spoke in 1996 at the inauguration of Vivekananda Youth Convention

Text of Sri Atal Bihari Vajpayeeji's speech:

When the people of this country were living with blind faith in dogmatic rituals under drudgery and foreign rule, Swamy Vivekananda brought glory to the nation by re-establishing self-confidence and esteem among them said Sri Vajpayee addressing the two- day youth convention at Hyderabad on the eve of Swamy Vivekananda Birthday celebrations.

When Christian missionaries were openly criticising the people of this country and their religion and when even educated and intellectuals were feeling shy to disclose their religion, Swamy Vivekananda proclaimed that he was the proudest Hindu born in this country. When representatives of all religions were praising the greatness of their own religions in the world parliament of religions at Chicago and when they were trying to establish the supremacy of their religion over other religions. Swamy Vivekananda said that Hindu religion accepts the faith of other religions also as true thus bringing special recognition to this great religion and nation, Sri Atalji added.

In 1947, India just got new constitution, but it was not correct to call India a nation in the making, said Sri Vajpayee and ridiculed the believers and proponents of this theory. He said this country had thousands of years of history and a tradition of performing poojas to the motherland. He compared the year 1996 with 1947 and said that this year would mark the beginning of a new era. The need of the hour was self-reliance and self-respect which will strengthen the nation and help get glory to the nation, he stated.

Swamy Vivekananda's Chicago Parliament address became popular because he expounded the principles of Hindutva in his speech, said Sri Vajpayee. 'Unfortunately, today Hindutva is being considered as dogmatic religion and has become a taboo, when the fact and truth about Hindutva are otherwise. Hindutva is life blood of this nation and the country can progress by pursuing the path shown in it', said Sri Atalji in his address.[1]

A monk of Ramakrishna Mutt quoted what Mahatma Gandhi and Rabindranath Tagore said on Swamy Vivekananda.

Mahatma Gandhi, after reading Vivekananda's works, said, 'My love on the country has grown one thousand-fold.'

'If you want to know India, study Swami, in him everything is positive, nothing is negative', said Tagore.

Swamy Vivekananda wanted for youth a man-making education. Swami stressed on the trained and sincere men for the country. Our university education makes men mechanised and absolutely useless in day-to-day life. Swami, always emphasized more on action i.e. the deed. He loved India so much that he said once, 'It is only India that can be called holy in the world'. The life of Swami, itself is a great source of inspiration for the youth. Man-making and character-making are most important. Otherwise the person is more dead than alive, said the revered monk.

Endnotes

1. *Pragna Bharati Yearbook, 1995, p. 92*

CHAPTER 17

Article 44: Uniform Civil Code

Background: The judgement on uniform civil code for India was a landmark judgement. It was delivered on 10 May 1995 by a division bench of Supreme Court of India. The bench, in their separate but concurring judgement, in a case where a Hindu husband had misused the absence of uniform civil code to convert to Islam and marry a second wife without dissolving the first marriage. So, the Court indicated the steps to be taken and efforts to be made by the Union of India towards securing a 'uniform civil code' for the citizens in terms of the court judgement.

Here are Sri Arun Shourie's views on uniform civil code which are still relevant. However, it needs revision and re-look afresh for younger generation.

'In Europe and USA, there are no personal laws for Muslims or any other religious group. Why there must be here? A uniform civil code is one of the primary step for unity, I am for it', declared the eminent journalist Sri Arun Shourie, while addressing a meet on Article 44 of the Indian Constitution (uniform civil code) organised under the joint aegis of Pragna Bharati and Andhra Pradesh High Court Advocates Association.

Elaborating how Shariat came into existence in India, by a legislation, he delineated the role played by Mr Mohammad Ali

Jinnah, in 1937, in collusion with the British for their partisan ends and brought forth Shariat Act. 'Should it (the act done) hold the country at a full stop forever?' he queried. He also added that the act was a lollipop for the Muslim League then, there was no rational, legal, or constitutional ground on which the entire argument on sharia can be sustained, he opined.

But, Hindu law was codified in the secular matters of marriage, divorce, maintenance, etc., way back. But nothing was done to codify Sharia, though marriage was regarded as a civil contract (not as a sacrament) in Islam, he stated. Referring to *Ulemas'* commitment, way back in 1985 (after Shah Bano's case) that they would codify their personal law, he regretted that they had not done so far for the fear of losing the entire power of discretion.

Denouncing the status given to Shariat (in the present-day context) by the protagonists of Islam, he mentioned, even during Muslim rule, Sharia was not followed. Up to 1935, in the north-west of India, Muslims there followed the Hindu law, not Shariat, he pointed out.

He lauded the constitutional committees appointed by the government in Pakistan and Bangladesh, which scrapped the 'triple talaq'. He pointed out many obscurities that existed under Shariat and explained how various sects contradict each other in enforcing their law. If one got a decree from a Shafi, a Hanafi would not recognise it, he stated.

Challenging the claim by some that women have equal status with men in Islam, he quoted what the prophet had said, 'In the case of evidence, one man is equal to two women due to deficiency in their (women's) intellect'.

Sri Shourie also made a fervent plea to the Muslim liberals not to get upset for the delay made in enacting a common civil code, and appealed to them to use the time to educate and awaken the women in the community. And he also urged them to do away with the propaganda that the Hindu code was going to be enforced.

Sri Shourie ridiculed the prime minister, Sri P. V. Narasimha Rao for his announcement from the ramparts of the Red Fort that he was committed not to enact the uniform civil code, and questioned whether it was a hallmark of compassion, tolerance, and secularism!

He wanted the RSS, the BJP, and the Muslims to dissolve the contentious issues with reason.

After an hour-long speech, he answered questions put forth by the audience.

It was an interesting academic meet. Sri Shourie, as is his wont, was thorough with the subject and delivered the lecture to the satisfaction of the audience. Sri T Bali Reddy, president, AP High Court Advocates Association, presided over the meeting.

****

Dangers of Weapons of Mass Destruction

A speech by the former Director- Research Analysis Wing of India

WMD (weapons of mass destruction) and NBW (nuclear bomb weapons) in modern-era Iraq-American conflict: Implications on India (a meeting in 2003)

Sri Raman, member, National Security Council, and former director of RAW, spoke on the subject. At the outset, he said, 'There was nervousness in the international community about Islamic countries having weapons of mass destruction. Islamic world didn't hold a nuclear weapon as a "weapon of state" but a "weapon of religion". Like India they never stated that it was for deterrence. Zulfiqar Ali Bhutto wanted to get nuclear weapon out of the money he got from Islamic countries. In the case of nuclear weapons, Pakistan would make a religious argument. They never considered the bomb they had made to be Pakistan bomb, they would call it an Islamic or *Ummah* bomb'.

Questioning the morality of the US' action for 'regime change' in Iraq, Sri Raman said that if Iraq had dictatorial regime, so did Pakistan (with occasional spells of democracy). He added none of the Islamic countries had a democracy, whereas in the democracy of India and Western countries, people were sovereign. Further stating that more than the US, India was the sufferer of terrorism. He said that India had lost many lives because of cross-border terrorism sponsored by Pakistan, but Pakistan did not pay price for it. Hence, he suggested, 'The answer to proxy war is counter proxy war. We must exercise our active defence'.

Sri Raman, while questioning the wisdom of America raising war against Iraq, said the action was a wrong calculation and the timing (of war) was not conducive as there could be more and more sandstorms in that region in April and the visibility would become zero. He further said that except Syria, many big countries, namely, China, Germany, France and Russia, had accepted that if Iraq had weapons of mass destruction, they had to be removed. France stated that if Iraq happened to use them, it would join the war, Sri Raman added. However, the former director of RAW discarded the theory propagated by many that the motivating factor for the war was the 'oil wealth of Iraq'. He said the US depended on Venezuela for its oil.

Elaborating on the reasons for the war, Sri Raman said, 'Restructuring of the Islamic world became imminent for the US. The US Defence Policy Advisory Board chairman and advisor to Donald Rumsfeld is Richard Pearl, a Jewish person close to Israel. If there were no regime change in Iraq, there would be no peace in Palestinian region. Hamas and Hezbollah were funded by Saddam Hussein. So, Saddam became the target'. However, he condemned the US' action of demonising terrorist leaders like Osama Bin Laden and also Saddam Hussein and making them household names. Never did India demonize any terrorist leader as a matter of policy, though there had been terrorist activity in J&K and the rest of India, he observed.

Sri Raman, weighing pros and cons of the war, said, in case, if Iraq collapsed in the war, the entire Islamic world would emerge as 'one', thinking that the religion and their existence had a threat. If America lost the war, the Islamic fundamentalists and their groups, Al Qaida and International Islamic Front, would become stronger and more determined, he added. He inferred that the decision of the US to wage war against Iraq was unwise.*

*Report of Pragna Bharati House-Journal

CHAPTER 18

Feminism—the Bharathiya Perspective

Centre for Women's Studies, Pragna Bharati conducted state-level convention on the topic, Feminism: The Bharathiya Perspective in 1995.

Feminist Movement: Dos and don'ts for India

Theme paper for state-level seminar: This paper was prepared and presented by Sri Vakati Panduranga Rao, vice-chairman, Pragna Bharati in the seminar, held in December 1995.

As the only surviving culture for over six thousand years, India had to pass through many critical periods but has survived because of her innate resilience rooted in eternal values. In this *Punyabhoomi* which is also a *Karmabhoomi*, the divine and the human were united through enlightened action. The ancient *rishis* clearly saw the need for changing social laws even as they laid down unchanging laws for aspirants to a higher life. They did not deny the body or its compulsions. While man and woman could live together fulfilling all desires, they were enjoined to do so, keeping the larger ideals of the family, society. and the ultimate relationship of all creation with the unknown source called divinity, which interestingly was called as Shakti-a feminine term. The four aims of human existence were labelled as dharma, artha, kama, and moksha. While the first and the last operated as the two banks to control the stream of life, artha and kama formed the stream itself for humans to freely float and swim.

The body represents the animal and the mind represents the potential to evolve into a responsible human being first and then become one with the divine. This is the outstanding and unique concept that this land has gifted to the humanity first. The body is a reality that cannot be ignored but that alone does not provide any meaning to the human existence. So—the ancients decreed—satisfy it without damaging the ultimate purpose. Control the body gradually through the body itself and then evolve to a stage where you are pure mind with body as an encasement. For this purpose, the physical relationship between man and woman was recognised and given due importance. But this relationship produces progeny and carriers of the torch of creation and evolution. Hence those procreating had a duty towards the children born through them. For this purpose, the institution of marriage was evolved.

'Marriage, briefly, is the pledged union of a man and a woman who propose to tread together the path of dharma or spiritual culture leading to the realisation of the oneness of the self with the Brahman. The Vedic marriage ritual is only a symbolic representation of this high spiritual ideal of marriage and married life, which couple ought to cherish throughout their career as householders.' (Vedic marriage ritual pub, the Bharata Samaja, the Theosophical Society of India, Madras)

'Religion considers man and woman as equal. This finds expression in the symbolization of Shiva and Shakthi, the duality of spirit and nature from which originates all creation. Shiva and Shakthi merged into one as half man and half woman is Ardhanareeswara. Man and woman are mutually dependent and looked upon as equal partners. There seems no doubt that the educational level of women was far higher in Vedic times than in the later medieval times . . . Among those who composed the Vedic hymns were several women. The upanayana ceremony was earlier meant for girls as well . . .' (Religion as Knowledge, Janaki Abhisheki, Bombay)

'Nowhere were the property rights of a woman recognised so early as in India.' ('History of Dharma Sastra, Vol. II, P. V. Kane)

'All the dharmasastras condemn unequivocally making marriage a commercial venture . . . In India from the earliest times, women have provided both moral and physical support to the men. Women have played a valuable part in retaining tradition. If not, literate they were certainly educated. They could think originally and independently' (Janaki Abhisheki).

During the freedom struggle women, marched shoulder to shoulder with men. Indian history has glorious examples like Rudrama Devi, Manchala, Jhansi Lakshmi whose valour was equal to men. The post-independent India has seen a tremendous leap in equal opportunities for women in education, employment, and other areas.

We have had a woman prime minister, and this year we have had the proud privilege of a dozen brave young women becoming the pilots in Indian Air Force. Women have proven their worth in every field as equal to men.

But does this mean that all is well with women in India? Definitely not.

Subtle oppression of the emerging new woman conscious of her potential and individuality, forced marriages, torture and violence by husbands, burning of brides for dowry, ridicule and rape, as well as many other atrocities are being committed, and unfortunately, they seem to be increasing by the day.

How do we face and solve the question?

Is feminism—the movement that originated in the West about one and half centuries ago—the answer? To answer this question, we have to have a brief survey of this movement from the West and its various ramifications.

The feminist movement, which in its heyday equated burning bras with total rejection of male domination of any sort over the body and the mind of woman, has now (according to Wendy Kaminer writing in the *Atlantic Monthly,* October 1993 in an article titled 'Feminism's Identity Crisis') assumed different sub-avatars.

'Vying for power today are post-structural feminists (dominant in academia in recent years), political feminists (office holders and lobbyists) different-voice feminists, separatist feminists (a small minority), pacifist feminists, lesbian feminists, careerist feminists, liberal feminists (who tend also to be political feminists), anti-porn feminists, eco-feminists and womanists.'

While Erica Jong has come to the conclusion after decades of changing male partners that no male seemed to be interested in her mind and that at the end of it all she was feeling lonely, Germaine Greer, another arch-feminist, has come to appreciate the virtues of maternity in her work *Sex and Destiny.*

The United Nations Organisation had to declare 1994 as the year of family and frantic appeals and efforts are on in the USA and the West to stop the breaking of the family, leading to parentless children who are threatening to destroy the fabric of the society.

While the overemphasis on rejecting the institution of marriage and the freedom of the body for the women is being regretted and reassessed, the other inequalities remain.

To quote the Human Development Report by the United Nations Development Programme at the recent Beijing Conference of Women,

- women do more than half of the work than men
- two-thirds of this work is unpaid
- whereas three-fourths of men's work is paid for
- women's share in parliamentary seats is 10% (7.3% in India) and cabinets 6%. So gender injustice in political and economic areas leaves much to be desired.

For this the very same report has suggested

- restructuring social and institutional norms: more equal sharing of responsibilities at home between men and women.
- encouraging men to take part in family care.
- the concept of paternity leave to supplement maternity leave.
- making work schedule flexible.
- initiating specific measures to move towards 30% as the minimum share of decision-making positions held by women at the national level in order to reach the ultimate 50% level.
- implementing key programmes for universal female education, improved reproductive health, and more financial credit.
- developing countries should earmark at least 20% of their budgets for human priority concerns including basic education, primary health care, safe drinking water, family planning and nutrition programmes.
- choice in spacing and number of children to be given to women.

These eight recommendations can be put into practice in India without any reservation and with the utmost urgency.

However social attitudes have to be changed through a stick-and-carrot policy. Children should be brought up in homes sharing all work without reference to gender. Any portrayal of women as weak or secondary citizens or objects of pleasure or ridicule over all the media in any manner should be strictly banned.

As Mrs Pramila Dandavate of Mahila Dakshata Samithi remarked, 'The struggle for women's emancipation is the struggle for human emancipation. And gender equality is meaningless unless the socio-economic system is purged of other inequalities based on caste, class or religion'.

The institution of marriage has to be defended at all costs and the family preserved while at the same time taking all remedial measures to ward off the evils that have crept in. Freedom of the body in the Western sense has no place in India, and any attempt to create a psychological divide between the sexes will be suicidal and should be resisted in full measure.

It should come as a matter of pleasant surprise to us that conservative housewives tired of watching passively from behind as men and feminists 'monopolise public debate-have met at Buenos Aires (Brazil) during October 1996 to come on to the centre stage on a global scale. Their slogan is 'Housewives—citizens of the world'. One of the 150 delegates from 14 countries, Ms Lita de Lazzari, president of Argentina's League of Housewives said, 'Feminists, lesbians, and homosexuals are all occupying the stage, so, why can't we? The recent United Nations Conference on women at Beijing is an example of feminists grabbing more than their fair share of limelight. The only thing (I say personally) that the feminists have done is to bring AIDS into the world, with free love, sexual liberty, and all that. Amen!'

Thus, does the ugly side of the Western model of feminist modes stand exposed and rejected.

India, with its age-old capacity for rejuvenation through reform, has to show the ideal path that ensures dignity and equality to women so that the family and the society emerge stronger to face the twenty-first century. It is easier said than done.[1]

****

My feelings now: Late Sri Vakati Panduranga Rao's lecture on 'Feminism—the Bharathiya Perspective' of 1995 has still resonance with the women of today. But the changes he envisaged in the paper have become a reality. Men sharing work with women in the families, men taking part in family care are to an extent a reality. However, I would give my perspective of the women of yore after listening to the lectures given in the organisation based on my noting them down.

I felt the women of ancient India to be strong and determined. Yet the feminists were repugnant at the mention of their names. The reasons were best known to them. Earlier, the criticism of feminists was only about not being able to honour family values. Feminists' inherent principle is individualism. The connotation in India for the word *feminism* is different from the West.

From the time immemorial, i.e. right from epic age, Indian women wanted their genuine wishes to be respected and for them to be treated on par with men intellectually. They have been feminists in India more or less all through the ages. If our epic characters are taken into consideration, there are ample evidences. Sita of Ramayana followed her husband Lord Rama to the dense forests, despite the plea made by him to remain in the place and not to take hardships, as she was not banished. She had a very determined and judgemental mentality. Hence, she accompanied him without paying heed to his words. Sita's strong will is shown in many instances of the epic.

Draupadi of Mahabharata was also bold, determined, courageous, and plucky. Shakuntala, Damayanti, Savithri, etc., were indomitable and could bear the rough shod of time. It is obvious from their life histories that a woman needs innate strength. But these women of epics are only revered by the traditional people of the country stuck to idealism. Feminists and also women-libbers have pathological hatred for these cultural figures and denounce their morals, saying that the figures of yore were husband- and family-oriented. Besides, they make no bones about dictating their own amoral values to ancient culture and religion and ignore the human nature. They like to rewrite history with their norms, which are injudicious.

Now since, the feminists have become a microscopic minority in India, to an extent, Indian culture remained intact. I am not contesting their theories of individuality, freedom of choice totally. An individual cannot grow to his or her full potential if he or she is bound by all sides, pressed hard, and suffocating. However, there are institutions like marriage that are to be respected for they have been established by our ancestors with their great wisdom.

Of course, I agree that there are certain traditions that have been coming from generations that have become redundant now. Any person, in the name of freedom of choice, should not exceed boundaries or limits of a society in which they dwell. All nonconformists are not geniuses and all geniuses are not nonconformists.

I, for one do not want those boundaries or that framework of the society to be fixed or to be hard or wooden. In any case, a flexible or elastic structure or framework has to be in place for a society. It should also be legally and ethically suitable to time.

****

A member of National Commission for Women from the BJP said in that state-level convention that it would not be proper to call 'feminism' a movement. But feminism gave scope for society to rethink itself in awarding proper status to women. This period of 'rethinking' could be called as 'transitional period'. At present, 'we are in transitional-era, an era of vacillation', she said.

The papers presented by the Indian women, in the Beijing Conference (World Women Meet), were accepted and applauded. That showed that the women in India were progressive!

The Indian society, especially the women, should not leave the moorings of Indian culture. If left, the society becomes like a rudderless boat. The so-called feminism of the West is irrelevant, improper, and unsuitable to the society.

'As our country is caught in cobwebs of caste, creed and religion, if the phenomenon of feminism is also introduced we would be inviting a new trouble. It literally brings a rift in the society. In a family system, a wife and a husband, a brother and a sister should co-operate with each other. A family's welfare depends both on husband and wife. We must caution and warn the west not to impose their system of rules on us. Geographically and culturally our country is different from theirs', she stated. When we think of women in India, we should think of women in other religions also. We must make efforts to bring Muslim women out of the clutches of 'Talaq', she added.[2]

******

Those meetings were of decades old. However, later, some of the meetings covered the other problems of women from time to time. The important meetings were on child marriages, how to prevent them or stop them altogether were on discussion extensively though not covered in this book. Frauds and failures of NRI marriages were also discussed in meetings because there were cases in North India mostly and elsewhere in the country where the NRI-based husbands duped their newlywed brides. No cases could be filed against them with the police as they were beyond the reach or purview of Indian law. How to deal with such situations where obviously the woman was the victim. These were some of the women aspects.

The other side of women issues, especially with regard to middle-class women who were pressed hard on both home and work fronts, was also pathetic. For many women opted for high pursuits and higher qualifications. They became professional and career-oriented.

Now the scenario changed for women in India:

The position of women has changed drastically after the liberalisation of economy and globalisation. They are much empowered now. Most of the women obtained the right they aspired for, for centuries. Indian women have become powerful and participatory in all spheres of life. Yet there is much needed to be done for their safety and security. Atrocities on women are still taking place without impunity.

Traditional families with mothers nurturing the children have changed. Now the idea of hegemonic masculine ideal, the man, has changed when both wife and husband are working (specially with the urban-employed). There is a sort equality prevailing in the educated sections between a husband and wife. Nuclear families have become a norm with most urbanites. However, these new trends have a flop side also. More and more ego clashes between modern wives and husbands leading to rampant divorces and, of course, re-marriages. Re-look, rethinking, cooling periods to settle the matters are lost.

Earlier, a father was hardworking, a sole breadwinner, and emotionally a distant figure to children. Time has changed. This change is because of influx of women in workforce. When both are employed, they are together bringing up their children. Now fathers are more open. They are more hands-on fathers. Frequently, young fathers seemed to be care-giving, nappy-changing, feeding, and bathing the child. Earlier, this was rare. Now a phenomenon! Despite the change, still the mother is a primary source of care-giving; none can replace her position.

Of course, in India, there are still many stay-at-home-mothers. Successive governments are taking mother-friendly policies, granting months of maternity leave and child-care leave. Now the Western countries also are giving importance to family system and family values. For Indian society family is the backbone. The main objective of the organisation is to protect Indian family system, especially the joint family where cooperation and coordination of the members have much use and that would lead to welfare of the family and welfare of the nation. This has picked up even in modern Western countries like the US where a child is sent out of the house at teenage to fend for himself. They realised the economic benefit and familial ties that strengthen human relations.

To show how the average Indian woman's psyche works, I would like to narrate a small clipping that I saw on a foreign channel on television. It was a documentary on Indian women and their condition. One can well imagine where they aim at. Generally, the foreign reporters shoot their films in rural villages.

India is so vast; there are some women who made giant strides on many developmental fronts. Yet Indian women's condition on foreign media is shown in poor light intentionally or otherwise.

The reporter asked the ordeals faced by the women of that area. Most of them had some trouble or the other because of their husbands. All said and done, rural India is patriarchal. So, as a solution (which is practised in the highly individualistic western countries), she (the foreign-correspondent) proposed to take one or two highly harassed women to the police station to lodge a complaint against their husbands. The women did not agree for it. They said instead of going to the police, they would not mind bearing the torture. The reason? Going to the police station and keeping their husbands behind bars would only add insult to injury for them. The other reason being they would lose their respect in the society where they live and will be looked down upon. The reporter was shocked; watching that, even I was shocked. Though their husbands have been violating the human rights, they have been silently suffering! Hence change in the attitude of men in the society has to be brought in with concerted effort.

The organisation Pragna Bharati, backed by the RSS, does not shun modernity. But emphasizes that modernity does not mean aping the West or Westernisation of Indians. Bharathiya specific living and values to have to be inculcated in the society. There is much leverage and flexibility in adaptation and adjustment to the changing aspirations of the country in the organisation's functioning. As girl-child is neglected in many states of India, the present BJP prime minister's slogan of 'Beti bachao, beti padav' is gaining momentum.

Endnotes

1.   Late V. Panduranga Rao, Feminist Movements: Dos and Don'ts for India, Vandemataram Newsletter, Dec '95–Jan'96, pp. 13–14
2.   Feminism: The Bharathiya Perspective, Pragna Bharati Yearbook, pp. 54–55

CHAPTER 19

Overall Impressions

Before concluding this part, let me put forth a few thoughts of mine on the organisations and its ideals. As far as the organisation is concerned, it differs from the Western world view of consumption and personal enjoyment at the cost of human and environmental exploitation. It negates hankering after sense gratification, which is the goal of the Western civilization and seeks for sense control whether in individual or group life, which is the essence of dharmic life.

The liberal thought of open-mindedness, individualism, liberty, equality, fraternity, human rights, and freedoms of all kinds, which are known to people as the Western concepts, are all Indian and Hindu too. Tolerance for different views has been in the tradition of this country. It is much needed now in this democracy. Basically, because of their philosophy, Indians are tolerant. That's why they could tolerate the Moghul and the British rulers. They do not have a revolting nature. Even Indian Independence Movement was by and large peaceful. Indians never try to punish whom they think went wrong. The kind of agony or agitation we find in the Western countries with highly activist nature on meaningless matters is not found in India.

It is the practice of the organisation to blend the ancient spiritualism with the mundane scientific things. For them, Bharathiya values are important. In fact, science analyses things with clinical precision; spiritualism connects and unifies. Yoga is one such spiritual experience! The West is embracing it wholeheartedly. They are fed up with materialistic outlook which they have been having for a long time. So, therefore, Indian intellectuals deriding Indian ethos, which is often found in our country, is absurd.

To preserve Hindu culture, Hinduism should survive in this land of birth. The RSS strives for cultural integration. Throughout the length and breadth India Hindu culture is pervading. From Kashmir to Kanya Kamari, there are centuries-old Hindu temples. Hindus believe them to be very powerful. Irrespective of caste and language, people travel to these places. For centuries, they have been journeying! Even during the days when there was no transport facility also, they went to these places on foot. They faced many ordeals. They went through forests where wild animals roamed around freely. They risked their lives to reach the temples. That shows their immeasurable faith! Hindus have physical, emotional, and spiritual attachment with this country.

Our ancestors from South India travelled to the north to have glimpse of Lord Viswanath in Varanasi. Those who go to Kasi, i.e. Varanasi, were considered as to going to *Kati* (in Telugu, a place of cremation) in those days. They used to think so because of the difficulty to reach the place going through thick forests with wild animals moving and posing danger. People at home were doubtful of these pilgrims coming back. Such was the difficulty! Coming back home, after the visit, was a miracle at that time!

This faith of Hinduism continued and survived the onslaught of many invaders. When I visited Varanasi recently, I felt nostalgic. For that was the place my ancestors longed to come; some of them took terrible pains to reach the place. More than god, i.e. the deity presents there, it is our forefathers' faith that moved me. I still remember my mother saying when she first visited Varanasi. She said the land where she walked in Varanasi seemed to be so pious to her. She thought, 'This is where Veda Vyas, the Maharishi walked once upon a time!' These revered sages have highest place still in our hearts. No secularism could ever take away our thoughts. Hence India was always 'one' country historically, because the majority of Hindus treated the full length and breadth of this country as a holy land to them for thousands of years.

Having scientific temper is good, but that should not berate ancient wisdom. They are not contradictory to each other. Often, science and spiritualism complement each other. This is what we find when herbal medicines are used as natural cures for certain diseases. Similarly, yoga asanas, in the same way meditation, often as calming-down technique for the mind in the stressful world. Science analyses things whereas (Indian) spiritualism synthesizes it. Indian spiritualism takes human mind to elevated heights. It's razor-sharp. But one has to have the mind to grasp it and orientation to perceive it.

Pragna Bharati has celebrated successfully the organisation's silver jubilee this year, 2017 and is still in the public service as forum for nationalist thinkers. When the very concept of nationalism is questioned today, Pragna Bharati's wings have been trying to make it understandable for younger generations.

Pragna Bharati has been promoting cultural and spiritual wings with renewed vigour on this year of completing twenty-fifth birthday. Bharat is emerging, and it should get its respectable place in the comity of nations. As eulogising the past will not take a person anywhere, Pragna Bharati is facilitating the new generation to collect the knowledge spread over the years, i.e. already existing knowledge, to re-interpret the values for modern times. That's how the organisation aims to make a modern, prosperous, and egalitarian life for the country's men and women.

Decolonisation of Indian minds:

One of the missions of the organisation is to decolonise Indian minds through education. Education, mainly at primary level, plays a vital role in shaping the children of the next generation. Traditional education in India was replaced by English education completely by Thomas Babington Macaulay through his education minute, 2 February 1835. His education minutes acclaimed fame for their notoriety. He had utter contempt for Indian education through Sanskrit and Arabic. There are many in India who contradict his views on traditional education system and the way he attacked and made snide remarks.

His aim to reform Indian education system was primarily, in his words (in paragraph 34), 'We must at present do our best to form a class who may be the interpreters between us and the millions whom we govern, a class of persons, Indians in blood and colour, but English in taste, in opinions, in morals and intellect'. (Minute by the Honourable T. B. Macaulay dated 2 February 1835, www.columbia.

edu>mealac>prichett) To serve the colonial masters, he wanted the English education to be imparted in India, not out of altruism. The colonial masters could not communicate with their language and accent to the natives. Hence, he wanted some intermediaries to serve them and the subjects they were ruling. The British expected from these collaborators, who were Indians but educated in English, to be more loyal to them by imbibing English values than their own country and its values. Unfortunately, the alienated Indians created by the foreign ruler still hold a sway on India's education system and cultural life. They are the controlling elite of the country.

So, most of the children who studied in English medium through convents developed disdain for Indian culture and values. For modern education system derived from the Western culture reflects dichotomy between science and religion. The Western system portrays science to be secular and religion to be dogmatic, which may be true of Western religions. In Indian case, it is different. The Vedic culture is scientific. Ancient India never dichotomized science and religion as two entities that contradict each other. They both synthesized and harmoniously blended for Indians from yore.

Thomas Babington Macaulay's diatribe on Indian system of education was no-holds-barred. Macaulay wrote, 'Who could deny that a single shelf of a good European library was worth the whole native literature of India and Arabia' (Paragraph 10, Minute by the Honourable T. B. Macaulay dated 2 February 1835 www.columbia. edu>mealac>prichett). He scorned at the native, innate worth of India. It is but natural to get annoyed at the callous way imperial rulers brushed aside the inherent pride the Indians have had.

So, there was a right anger at the highly rancorous words of Macaulay on Indian wisdom and the language Sanskrit. Primary education at the impressionable age that negates everything that is Indian has an impact on the child's mind. There are some group experts in the education system who argue, that the elementary education should be treated on par with the defence and internal security. For it forms the basis and opportunity for every person to develop. There should be a crusade for good quality elementary education to every child.

Macaulay showed his derision on Sanskrit when he wrote, 'It is, I believe, no exaggeration to say that all the historical information which has been collected from all the books which have been written in the Sanskrit language is less valuable than what may be found in most paltry abridgement used at preparatory schools in England' (Paragraph 11, Minute by the Honourable T. B. Macaulay dated 2 February 1835 www.columbia.edu>mealac>prichett).

After the independence, successive Congress governments, which ruled most of the time, continued the colonial dominant system. So, the frontal organisations of the RSS are inching towards decolonising the minds of people. They thought it to be an imperative. In the process, they are trying to turn the minds of people away from the Eurocentric ideas. India's culture and tradition, they would like to bring to the forefront. It is an intellectual battle.

It is very difficult to unlearn things learnt by people but it is not highly impossible to achieve the task. The reason being there are already convinced audiences and theorists prevailing for taking up the cause. Personally, I feel we cannot tick the clock back. Hence the changes should be in tune with the times we are in without leaving the essential Indian values of the past.

CHAPTER 20

Media's Question on Women Safety: Law and Order

English TV news channels, always try to emulate the Western channels in taking up issues and carrying out the debates. The problems of the West are different from that of India. For the West, free speech, immigration, LGBT rights are some of the issues paramount to them. For the people of India, the basics like the roads, electricity, and drinking water are still the problems. In this scenario, sophisticated discussions on free speech and university campus strikes, some candlelight marches, whether they being carried out with or without hitches in Delhi, do not come under high priority issues.

Europe is, as a continent, much smaller than Asia. India with more than 1.2 billion population is much higher than that of the entire Europe's population of 604 million. India exceeds one entire continent's population. Similarly, USA has very less population compared to India though it has fifty states. It's the fourth largest country, area-wise, after Russia, Canada, and China. But our media always compares us with the West in all aspects. Never bothers what the history of America is! Not even 400 years. Ours is 5000 years old. A young country with lesser population, more resources, well-entrenched infrastructure, strict law and order is anyway much ahead of us. Every person in Europe and America has an identity. If any, petty or big, crime is committed, it would be registered. Everyone has a Social Security number card. No job would be given to that person by any agency knowing his background history. So strict are the laws in developed countries. Criminals are punished stringently; once you are a criminal, you are a criminal for life.

The UK and USA are predominantly Christian countries that are adherents to Christian values! For them, confession is enough as an escape route from sins. Being secular in nature, their laws will not permit that. Once booked as a criminal, that's it. If they don't get a job, they will have no food. No one employs the person with crime record. To get livelihood, he resorts to crime again. In India, with more number of people, less identifiable laws (now the Aadhaar card has come into existence. But people don't carry it, can't remember the lengthy number either, under privacy laws, it cannot be disclosed for every purpose), yet our police is able to nab the criminals with the help of clues, and then they (criminals) languor in jails for years on end. Petty thieves are left on bail, after sometime, they might resort to crime again. Some type of rehabilitation is needed, but it is not on the top of the agenda of the government.

When did European countries become orderly? After the rivalries and tribal hatreds ignited two World Wars I and II. They all became united as European Union with a 'common market'. With the Brexit, the unity is not intact now. India as such has resilience. It did not participate in the World War directly to learn painful lessons.

Why I have compared the West with that of India, it means it is always the media who blames the government for not being sensitive to women's issues, vigilantism, gau rakshak, fights. Yes, the argument is agreed. There should also be law and order in the society at any cost. Police reforms are also needed, which are anyway in the offing. Again, if the policing is more, the liberals in the media cry hoarse, 'Oh, there is more policing in India'. If it is less, 'No law and order', they would say. However, there is also a necessity for public being cautious in averting danger to themselves and their family members. At least in some cases, like for, instance 31 December 2016 night, the incident of Bangalore bar or pub, misbehaviour of some boys with girls that caused an uproar in the media. These things are happening year after year. They have become annual rituals. I am not condoning the acts. They are totally condemnable. However, our English media, especially TV channels takes up all urban, sophisticated, English issues rather than grass-roots issue concerning ordinary people's lives.

For example, in South India, chain-snatching is rampant. Most of the women, elderly, when they walk on the road for a morning or evening walk, while going to work also, men on motorbike would come and snatch their chains frequently. The biker who drives would slow down, the other sitting behind as pillion rider, would pull the chain so forcefully sometimes it could cut the woman's neck to bleed, sometimes the lady would fall down by the force by which her chain is pulled and could be hit by a rock or some sharp object on the road (you can well imagine our roads with pebbles and potholes). When she falls down, she gets hurt or is even hospitalised. Some women succumb to injuries or shock and die. Our local media shows the visuals of chain-snatching and asks us to be careful because it is so common. Even the police advise us against the miscreants. Of course, they say they are also taking measures. This wearing of the gold chain as *Mangal sutra* is mandatory for married ladies in Andhra irrespective of caste and community. Except youngsters who opt it out.

One day when I was walking in the park, two police men in *mufti* came to the park and called all the women who were walking and informed about chain-snatchers roaming around the area. They apprised us in how many ways they hoodwink us to snatch. 'The chain-snatchers may ask you some address or door number of somebody in the locality, as an enquiry, as if they were strangers to the place. While you are engrossed in thinking, they pull your chain and go off on the bike, this is one way', they said.

'Or otherwise, the chain-snatchers themselves will tell you that some chain-snatchers are around, and to be careful of them. While talking, they may use several other gimmicks to rob you of your valuables. These are all diverting tactics, do not fall prey to them,' the police said.

They also warned, 'Cover your chains with your saree *paloo* to avoid snatching. The snatchers observe who comes daily for a walk into the park and when they leave. More than the gold chain, you lose your life, if you fall down at this age'.

When I spoke to a young boy of liberal attitude about how we, women, take precautionary measures by not giving chance to miscreants like chain-snatchers (without depending much on police), I asked, 'Why can't the girls who go late nights to parties in pubs take measures, what about their parents, why do they leave them knowing the condition outside?' One MLA from Karnataka was bashed for saying so at that time, when he said that it was also the duty of the family-members to take care of the girls.

The conversation I had with the young liberal boy, I am presenting here. I was, of course, by conviction, a conservative. When I stated the whole thing that was in my mind, after fully listening to what I had to say, our conversation followed as such:

> Liberal: How can you compare chain-snatching, a theft, a crime, with molestation? The basic premise of your argument is wrong.

> I: I was shocked, is going to pub in midnight for the girls, OK for you?

> Liberal: Yeah, OK.

> I: Why?

> Liberal: Because the Constitution of India guarantees that as freedom.

> I: It guarantees to me also the freedom to wear my gold chain and go out. Why should I take all precautions? Like how the media expects the police to take care of the girls, the same principle applies to my kind of women. 'I needn't put my saree *paloo* around my neck like a noose. The police should protect me'. If I think so, what would happen? Since I am taking care of myself, everything is going smoothly. Likewise, the girls or their parents should take adequate care of their girls.

> Liberal: Again, you are mixing two things. Molestation is a bigger issue. And a larger problem. In the case of Bangalore club, the law of the land was not enforced. Knowing there was a celebration, sufficient police personnel were to be deployed. That was not done. There are no proper women's safety measures in the country.

I: I heard one of the victimised girls in the club (in Bangalore) talking on a TV channel. She said to the anchor that she realised after a long time that somebody was groping on her. She said he did it for some time. It took time for her to realise what was happening to her, was her narration. Then she started slapping him, she said. The girl must have been drunk, otherwise, she would have known what was happening to her immediately. These girls who go to pubs and clubs, drink. 'Being in an inebriated condition and expecting nothing to happen to them and Police should take care of everything'. Is this way of thinking correct?

Liberal: What's your problem? She drinks. So? The Constitution of India guarantees the right to drink, eat, and speak what the people want to. It's not unlawful. There is no right for anyone on her body since she was drunk. In America, nothing happens to any girl who sits in a bar drinking throughout the night. If your problem is with girl drinking, you don't mind a boy drinking and being in the pub till midnight?

I: (I was slightly irritated at the gender-discrimination question hurled at me.) I don't like even boys drinking. But the world would not go by my way. I did not allow my sons to go out to pubs on 31 December midnight. Because on such days, youngsters make parties, booze, revel, in the end they lose their tempers. In their drunken state, the kind of talk, argument and the fights and fisticuffs, they hurt themselves. Some of them are booked by police and are held on remand. All this brings a blot to the boy and his family. So, I never allowed. Moreover, paedophiles would also be roaming around freely in the nights.

Liberal: Fine, that's your wish. You can bring up your children the way you want to. Nobody objects to what you do within the four walls of your house. That's your private life. As you said, to deal with so many cases, police reforms are needed. Many are voicing this concern in India.

I: (I was still lingering to drinking habit.) Don't you think people should be discouraged to drink? Like how they are educated not to smoke?

Liberal: It's not the job of the government. People make their own choices about what to eat or drink.

I: When you said that it is not the government's job to impose, what about total prohibition on drinking as imposed by some state governments like Gujarat?

Liberal: It is said that though there is total prohibition of liquor, it is available in that state. Those who are inclined to drink, they get from any quarter.

I: When I am asking whether drinking is good or bad, you are not answering the pointed question. You left it to individual choice. I agree Western countries are too cold. They have a reason to keep themselves warm by these drinks. But I don't find any reason to have to drink in India.

Liberal: People, they have to make their own choice. No amount of government's imposition would help. Even USA once tried this prohibition of liquor in their country and failed.

I: That means USA believed that it was wrong to drink!

Liberal: Yeah!

I: Drinking (any quantity) of liquor would not allow a person to have a normal sense of brain. The kind of talk people make in a drunken state is not balanced compared to the normal. I still can't understand why people voluntarily embrace a bad habit. I like Islam for this reason alone where it is heard that drinking is prohibited. There is nothing wrong in catching a good point from anywhere! Even in other religions also, drinking is not considered a virtuous thing. They further blame women for their behaviour if they are drunk.

Elsewhere in the world, some of the learned and educated advise others not to drink, specially they advise girls to remain sober when they go out to avoid crimes like molestation and rape. But they are bashed by liberals and feminists. One old woman judge advised young girls of her country while delivering a judgement, as a passing remark, not to consume alcohol and make themselves vulnerable for rape. This is not the first time a judge was saying so. Many had said earlier. But an avalanche of harsh words and criticism befell upon her. Her comment was seen as victim-blaming.

If any girl by listening to such advice remained sober, that means she was self-policing herself. Instead of facing the rape problem head-on, she was finding an escape route for herself. Her attitude is looked upon by some feminists, 'Choose somebody else, not me' kind.

Those who are advising the girls to self-police are at wrong side for these women activists. For, they are not addressing the problem of rape or molestation in entirety. They are choosing a shortcut, which is not a solution. Girls are the victims in all these cases. The women activists question persons who advise girls and call their attitude as, 'victim-blaming'. They expect the whole society to change rather than individual, girl-change.

If individually a girl's behaviour is modified by such advices by some elders, that would give more a fillip to perpetuate the stereotypes that strengthen rape culture. So according to some women activists, those who counsel girls or women not to be 'irresponsible or provocative in their dressing or uninhibited behaviour' are not doing much service to dismantle rape culture. Their appeal is instead of continuously judging a girl or woman for her behaviour, judge the society that blames women for rape. These arguments are fair, but the world seems to be different. On certain issues, one cannot change the whole world. So what is the easiest alternative? To be on safe side, instead of being a risk-taker. A rape is like an accident. It's an assault on woman. As per law, even a single woman should not be molested. But the ground reality is different. As a common individual in the country, I think why invite trouble and ask for recourse?

Equality between men and women in the world is easier said than done. It's a question of common sense in Indian society, to advise a girl more to take care of herself. Here I would like to provide a reference from a visual I had seen in the social media. Now, at this age of instant messaging of text, audio, and video, one video message was sent to me by many of my friends and relatives. They all seemed to have been terribly impressed by it. So, therefore shared it.

In that video one elderly woman was asked by a teenaged girl why her mother always objects to her going out in the night whereas allows her brother to go out. For that, as a reply, the woman asked that girl counter questions like 'Where does your mother keep her jewellery? Where does she place idols of god? Where does she keep her money and valuables?' The girl replied that the jewellery and valuables are always kept in a safe locker and idols in the *pooja mandir*.

Then the elderly woman said, 'You got your answer. To your mother, you are a precious jewel and like an idol of worship, so she is always protecting you. Any precious thing cannot be neglected or kept unsafe'. The girl was satisfied with the answer. Though girls in every generation question about equality with boys, they are lulled by these answers or somewhere nearing these.

With this kind of Indian psyche, what the feminists say falls on deaf ears. However, every section has every right to say or advise what suits them best for their girls. Freedom of speech!

CHAPTER 21

Indian Constitution: Liberal World View

The Constitution of India was drafted by highly esteemed eminent intellectuals. It reflects their vision for India. It has secular spirit. However, the words *secularism* and *socialism* were later introduced. About secularism in India, there was a small quibble, which I felt interesting, when I watched on television. Way back, when Ayodhya Temple Movement was at its height, one TV anchor of an English news channel asked mockingly the late Sri Acharya Giriraj Kishore of Vishwa Hindu Parishad (VHP) this way:

TV anchor: Acharya ji, why do you want to protect Hindu dharma? This dharma has been there earlier, now, and is going to be there in future (as per your calculations). What's the necessity for raising to keep it up now, that going to remain forever?

Acharya: Why do you want to protect secularism? It was there before you were born, it's there now, and it will remain so.

The anchor had no clue how to answer. I was amazed at the sharp reply given by the Acharya.

Those so-called secularists in the Congress and other parties preach Hindus to be cool, even if other religions provoke and convert Hindus under social justice garb. Sometimes it is said nothing happens to Hinduism and it has been existing for centuries. In the constitution of India, minorities could follow, preach and propagate their religion. So much for liberty! The same I would like to juxtapose and ask secularists, why are they so worried and concerned about the secular fabric of India? If it is viable, it will remain. There should be no effort to protect it.

In a most secular country like America, Christian evangelists preach other religious groups to convert. In India, only minorities are allowed to propagate. In the US, their First Amendment forbids Congress from both promoting one religion over the others and also restricting an individual's religious practice. It guarantees freedom of expression by prohibiting Congress from restricting the press or the rights of individuals to speak freely. It also guarantees the right of citizens to assemble peacefully and to petition on their government.

Indian liberals often question only the majorities in India. They know the majorities are fragmented by way of caste. This they exploit to the hilt. Their journalism does not seem to maintain balance. Mostly agenda driven. Some among them take journalism not as a profession but as activism. Activism tilted towards the ideals of their choice. It is better if they state which party they are supporters of. They copy the West in all matters, not in this regard alone. For the best of the journalism has arisen there.

In United States, the journalist (print and electronic) profess their allegiance to a party. Here, there is no such mention. Maybe because there are umpteen number of parties; like people, they are also confused. Of late, this question has been asked by one from among audience to a renowned TV anchor in a lecture followed by questions and answers, as to why journalists cannot come out in the open and take sides of a party like in USA (*New York Times*, CNN, Fox News have been taking sides). I was very keenly observing what he (the anchor) would say, but he evaded the question. There is no sense in not openly taking side by our journalists rather than having a 'holier than thou' attitude.

If they are really standing for people, people alone, they need to check the facts. For instance, K. Chandrasekhar Rao (known as KCR, chief minister of Telangana) donated jewellery (some crown and other ornaments of gold) worth more than five crores to Sri Venkateshwara Swamy (Balaji) temple in Tirumala (in March 2017). It was a kind of 'thanksgiving' for the formation of the Telangana State. Immediately, all the channels pounced on him. Covered the event as if they had the 'truth' with them. 'How can he utilise taxpayers' money this way for a religious purpose?' was their question. They were all melodramatic in their antics. Their anguish was that in a secular country, how could he do that act of donating that amount of money to a Hindu temple. KCR plays his cards well. He is not foolish or silly. He knew that he was accountable to the public if not to the anchors. He took the money out of 'common good fund' of Tirumala Tirupati Devasthanam (TTD) which was Hindu devotees' money.

The Hindu endowment money from all temples including Tirupati Devasthanam (Balaji Temple of Tirumala) is spent on secular purposes, scrutinised and audited from time to time by the state government. The same KCR donated from the government treasury huge sums of money to build churches and some Christian Bhavan in Hyderabad and increased salary of Imams and for building and repairing mosques and for an Islamic centre in Hyderabad. Are these acts secular for anchor journalists? Will these donations remove the poverty among minorities? Would they in any way educate them or give them food? But yet one should not touch the issues of minorities with a barge pole.

Most of the liberals in English media have left leaning. The left has no stand in the public. So, the left leans on the Congress, which is centrist, they call. The whole of the left and the Congress depends on the so-called minorities who are religious in nature. This appeasement politics has been taking place right from the days of independence and much before that.

Mahatma Gandhi's support for Caliphate in Turkey was one such move. Mahatma might have been under the impression by supporting Khilafat; he could gain the confidence of Muslims in India and they, in turn, strengthen the cause of independence struggle. Mahatma had gone to the extent of making Jinnah the prime minister for united India if he dropped the decision of having a separate country, the Pakistan. The height of pleasing did not work. For Jinnah, Hindus and Muslims living together was an impossible proposition.

Partition of the country on religious grounds was a big blow to India. The West had never faced this kind of a blow. Nobody asked them to carve a country on religious lines. Only 9/11 awakened America to a truth. Indian Liberals never ever counter the extremist elements in the minority Muslims. Even if they perceive such things in some incidents, they immediately come to their rescue by saying even Hindus do such extreme things and come out with a small list and try to neutralise the whole. Among the 80 per cent of Hindus, if suppose some miniscule had done something, that would be magnified and projected.

I know this kind of 'what abouting' (what about this or what about that) does not work in a democracy. It does not augur well. Anyway, the government of the day should deal with both categories of extremists. The imbalance is so high in India, one cannot help pointing out.

The UPA government (2004–2014) played a lot of politics in communalising crime. The Digvijay Singhs, Chidambarams, Sibals out rightly supported minorities at the expense of majority sentiments. Whatever credibility we had on Manmohan Singh, whatever good work he had done for India as a finance minister in PV Narasimha Rao's government, was all gone into abyss when he made the statement from Sharm El Sheikh that Muslim minorities have the first stake on India's resources. By saying so, he could divide the society effectively with such a divisive statement.

I do agree terrorism has no religion. As a religious group, Muslims are more assertive compared to Hindus in India and elsewhere in the world. Hindus being a loose conglomeration of castes, easily divisible. Being aware of this, the power-mongering majority politicians have been playing their sectarian minority cards. For them, it's a game. It's needless to blame Muslims in India. For they are also exploited by their leaders and vote-seeking Hindu politicians.

There should be no reason for so-called secularists to worry when the RSS wants to bring the Hindu community together. This is not to go against any minority community. It will strengthen weakly knit majority enfeebled by the wrong practice of so-called secularism in India. Let genuine secularism prevail! Let everybody be treated equally as envisaged in the Constitution!

If the left parties or the Congress or any regional party of renown thinks that they are right in their ideals, the people will definitely (now or later) embrace them. But the tragedy in India is the BJP (backed by the RSS) is the only ideological party. Others are bereft of ideology! The Congress of pre- and post-independence India has now become a marginal player. Because it is not changing with the time. Not knowing the pulse of the people.

USA and the UK (other European countries also), even if they call themselves secular, egalitarian, progressive, and developed, they are basically Christian countries. They follow Christian values. India is by its very nature a Hindu country. The inhabitants here were all once upon a time the followers of the same culture.

There is blend in customs of Christians and Hindus in South India. Christian women look like Hindu women, wear the same kind of dress, in marriages more or less the same kind of traditions (with *haldi, kumkum*) are followed. Same is the case with Muslims. The Muslim women barring in Hyderabad, rarely wear *burqas* here. Married Muslim women wear black beads and toe rings like any South Indian. Why I particularly mentioned about women means they represent the culture of the country more than men.

It may be wondering why I am writing about the secularism of the Congress, which was routed out in 2014 Parliamentary elections for its wrong pseudo-secular policies and of course corruption and other scandals. There is a section of media and the Congress, even now, they hold on to their same secular vision. For them it must be told that what they practised as secularism was not a true one. And needed to be corrected.

The Constitution of India: Incorporation of Liberal World View

When we hear liberals talk, it tends to be more rational and worldly. They never go by Indian culture. They go by Indian Constitution, which has many provisions that are borrowed from the West. To reiterate my point, I would present what Late Sri P. V. Narasimha Rao, the former prime minister had to say, in his address to the joint meeting of the US Congress on 18 May 1994, in Washington.

The former PM said,

> 'In his first inaugural address Thomas Jefferson spoke of "freedom of press, and freedom of person under the protection of habeas corpus, and trial by juries impartially selected". When India gained independence, we accepted these fundamental freedoms and looked to the Declaration of Independence and the Bill of Rights while formulating the Constitution of the world's largest democracy. Now, both countries are forever joined by the shared values of secularism, political pluralism, and the rule of law'.

In fact, we, Indians are following most part of the Constitution that was written during the British period. The West, especially the imperialist Germany, France, Portugal, Spain, UK, and other European countries had experienced a heavy loss of lives and material after the Second World War. Their realisation led to NATO, EU, and UNO. Human rights that includes all other rights, viz. free speech, free of expression, right to live with dignity have become part of it. These kinds of rights we find in Indian ethos. But not explicitly stated in those terms of vocabulary. Indian Constitution adopted them in toto. Our top leaders of independence movement in the Congress thought in their wisdom, they were better for India. For they (the fundamental rights) have a general appeal to humanity. The universal appeal of human race to be one irrespective of any race or any community.

Thus the above values we have been adopted in the Indian Constitution. However, people of India are unaware of them fully and most often go by culture, tradition, and practice. The Congress could rule the country so long because they could sell secularism to the people effectively in the beginning and willy-nilly later.

In beginning, soon after the independence of the country, they could show to the people of the country how far religious extremism could take, with the assassination of Gandhiji. Gandhiji's Khilafat movement to please Indian Muslims, his Satyagraha in Noukhali when Muslims died in communal riots. Gandhiji's fasting after independence to grant undue amount of money as share to Pakistan were irksome, in a minor way, to even the Congress. All Gandhiji did could be attributable to his broad-minded thinking, which had crossed all barriers! So, therefore, Gandhiji attained the status of Mahatma.

It's heartening to know Gandhiji's multifaceted personality. This has been enunciated by intellectuals like Arun Shourie and Ramchandra Guha many times. I reiterate what they said, and of course it is my firm view also that Gandhiji was the most intellectual among our intellectuals, a peasant among peasants, a labourer among labour, a child among children, an activist among activists, a simpleton among the flamboyant, an animal lover, an inspirer of women to spin the wheel to eke out livelihood. He encouraged women also to participate in their own way in independence struggle. The whole of the country and the Congress mourned his death.

Earlier to put spokes on the RSS work, the Congress said the RSS was involved in Gandhiji's assassination. The court cleared that there was no involvement by the organisation. Yet repeatedly, the Congress has been harping on the same string with no impunity. The court stated that there was no direct link to the organisation and the assassination. Of course, Nathuram Vinayak Godse belonged to Hindu Mahasabha and shared the ideology of Hindu Rastra. But what could he gain by eliminating a person?

One can argue and fight verbal battles with a living person. Nobody has got a right to take away the other person's life. No way in the case of Mahatma! The country fell right into the hands of faux secular politicians after the assassination. The truncated India after partition has been witnessing second bout of appeasement. It's appeasement-oriented politics of the Congress that led to divisions in the society.

Some of the feelings Godse had on the Congress are shared by many Hindus even now. He in his last statement says, 'When the Congress recognised the Muslim League as representing the Muslim community, viewed from the logical point of view it would not have been out of place to recognise the Hindu Mahasabha as representing the Hindus, or at least the Congress should openly have declared that it would look to the interest of Hindus. But the Congress never did this. As a result of this, in spite of existence of a very powerful body such as the Muslim League looking after the interest of the Muslims, a few Muslims who were still the members of the Congress also looked after the Muslim interest whereas there was none to look after the Hindu interest as such'.[1]

What Godse had said is still being continued in the present Congress. The Congress, even after independence gave recognition to the Indian Union Muslim League (IUML) in Kerala, All India Majlis-e-Ittehadul Muslimeen or AIMIM, once a Razakar Party of Qasim Rizvi, pre-independence. Not only recognising, but has had alliances with them in those states. Yet the Congress calls itself secular!

The assassination of Gandhiji, no less a Hindu by himself, muted all the Hindus for decades to come. The appeasement of Muslims has in no way abated. Some intellectuals among the Congress think that India has moved on; the travails of partition of the country are no longer an issue with the younger generation. True, time heals all wounds, but what about the scars left? They are the reminders of what trauma this country had gone through.

Endnotes

1. 'May It Please Your Honour' by Nathuram Godse, paragraph 109

CHAPTER 22

Liberalism in India

Karl Mannheim, in his classic work *Ideology and Utopia* argued that liberalism was a rationalist response to the religious fervour of the late Middle Ages. As a philosophy of social action, liberalism is future-oriented, seeking progress in human evolution. The kind of religious fervour found in late Middle Ages elsewhere was not found in India then and now. Scathing attack on Hindu values and appeasing minority religions and saying infallibility in their religious practices seems to be liberalism in India. Otherwise, liberals are not definitive in our country.

The Liberal media fully backs this pampering of minorities. It's no less in doing the same as secular parties. However, knowing the mood of the people, a section of the media started questioning the so-called secular practices of the country and why they are tilted towards one side.

The Europeans are very stern in their statements. 'We don't want any parallel societies', said the German Chancellor Angela Markel. She also said (on 7 December 2016), 'Our law takes precedence before tribal rules, codes of honour and Sharia'. She objected to the full-face veil also. 'The full-face veil must be banned wherever it is legally possible', she told. Merkel has been described as the guardian of Western democratic values!

When the German chancellor Angela Merkel proposed a ban on the burqa and niqab at a conference of her political party in

December 2016, she was following the lead of a number of countries in Europe, which already have such legislation in place. In France and Belgium, a woman wearing a full-face veil can be jailed for up to seven days.

In January 2017, there were also reports that Morocco had banned the production and sale of the burqa. Here, I am not arguing whether to wear a veil is correct or not. Many Hindus also in North India wear veil, maybe because of the influence of Mughal rule. People have the right to wear what they like. To practise the separate civil law, Shariah, was granted by the British to the Muslim community in 1937. It continued after independence because the founding fathers in their wisdom thought one-day, Muslim community would join the mainstream, leaving all apprehensions they have had in their minds after partition. Then they could codify the uniform civil code.

The Muslim leaders are always keeping the community at bay without allowing them join for the fear losing their special privileges. Which European country allows polygamy under law? It's injurious to public morals.

After years of oppression, it is good that some change is taking place within the Muslim community in India. The Muslim women are coming out against triple talaq. That itself may put an end to polygamy. It brings partially the UCC into effect. The liberal left, mouth shibboleths on everything but would not ask for scrapping triple talaq, Nikah halala, and for India to have a uniform civil code. Family planning is observed in a theocratic Islamic country like Pakistan, but not in India.

The liberal left never ever talks about the subsidy given to religious pilgrimage Haj in a secular country. Many people are not aware of the subsidy and laws like Sharia, courtesy of the British, continuation by the Congress after gifting a part of the country! The state has no control on Wakf properties. No liberal left questions.

There are minority educational institutions, there is minority finance commission. Yet they need reservation in other government institution! The 'minority' itself is questionable as far as Muslims are concerned in India as it being the second-largest Muslim-populated country in the world after Indonesia.

'Liberal democracy' and 'human rights' are the positive political concepts for any democracy. But political concepts can only succeed in transmitting a positive message when there is a consensus as to what constitutes a positive social outcome. For instance, students of JNU shouting of '*Afzal Guru, aapki khatil zinda hai, Kashmir ki azadi thak jung ladae ge, jung ladegi*' (Afzal Guru, your killer is alive, till Kashmir gets freedom, we will continue our fight). Is this freedom of speech merely for the sake of freedom of speech? Or does it bring any positive social outcome?

Liberalism merely encompasses an awkward choice between different kinds of freedom that most Indians do not identify with. For instance, one such is freedom of food versus cow protection. People often ignore what their neighbours or friends eat at their houses. It never becomes a topic outside unless they are celebrating a festival. When the unfortunate 'Aklaq incident' happened, all the liberals aired their culinary instinct of eating beef. How they eat and how much they like it.

Eating a particular thing at home is freedom of choice. Talking of eating a tabooed food for many Indians is crossing the limit. You can't expect you can hurt somebody's sentiment and the other person has to keep quiet. The trolls (some of them) in the social media, with their new-found freedom of airing their views started trolling against them. That may not be seen as an offence!

In a lighter vein, I quote from the recent book of Thomas L. Friedman, *Thank You for Being Late*, in which he writes on the inequality of freedom. He gives an argument by Dov Seidman, that all over the world we see people creating unprecedented levels of 'freedom from—freedom from dictators, freedom from micromanaging bosses, from networks forcing us to watch commercials, and freedom from the neighbourhood stores, freedom from the local banker, freedom from the hotel chains'.

'But when it comes to politics, the freedom people cherish most, he argues, is "freedom to"—the freedom to live the way they want because their freedom is anchored in consensual elections, a constitution, the rule of law, and a parliament . . . "Freedom from" happens quickly, violently, and dramatically', notes Seidman. 'Freedom to' takes time.[1]

Endnotes

1.   Tomas L Friedman, *Thank You for Being Late*, 2016, pp. 270–271

CHAPTER 23

Free Speech: Implications

The West, after the Second World War, realised that expansionism and imperialism was no good. After the carnage of millions of people, after presiding over their obituaries, they came to the realization. Had India been a part of that? No. I am for human rights. But freedom of speech should not be used as an excuse for slander or for intentionally maligning the opponents or for seceding some part of the country.

Talking about Jammu and Kashmir's freedom from Indian Republic would not come under free speech. It's a divisive speech. No liberal country on earth could accept that. The votaries of free speech—that is the United States of America—also would not agree to one of its states to go separate. Way back, President Abraham Lincoln, in his first inaugural address on the March 4, 1861 had said,

> I hold that, in contemplation of Universal Law of the constitution, the Union of these States is perpetual. Perpetuity is implied, if not expressed, in the fundamental law of all national governments. It is safe to assert that no government proper ever had a provision in its organic law for its own termination . . . physically speaking we cannot separate. We cannot remove our respective sections from each other, nor build an impassable wall between them. A husband and wife

may be divorced and go out of the presence and beyond the reach of each other, but the different parts of our country cannot do this. They cannot but remain face to face and intercourse, either amicable or hostile, must continue between them.

Abraham Lincoln's warning was so stern. All over the world, the governments would not tolerate secessionist tendencies.

In 1868, the US Supreme Court had to say, '*When Texas became one of the United States, she entered into an indissoluble relation . . . all the obligations of perpetual union and all the guarantees of Republican Government in the union, attached at once to the State . . . it was the incorporation of a new member into the political body. And it was complete and final . . .*'

So where is the question for J&K when we have given it so many autonomous powers and privileges? If we accede J&K, there are many other border states that become vulnerable. The liberals call India not a Hindu state. It is a multi-cultural, multi-ethnic and multi-religious republic. This way, it belongs to all, and it belongs none! By referring the J&K dispute to United Nations, unnecessarily Jawaharlal Nehru, the first prime minister had internationalised it.

USA, with only 300-odd years history, stood like a rock by making clear not to secede any of its states. Whereas India lost much of its land to carve out a country Pakistan. Liberals like Arundhati Roy make statements sympathizing separatist cause of J&K! On her the government of the day thought to be a fit case for a sedition charge!

The free speech of the left assumes that it has the right to decide whose speech is acceptable, whose is hate-mongering. I asked my liberal friend these questions:

I: It is said that sometime back, a baba, a yoga guru was not allowed to speak in Jawaharlal Nehru University in Delhi. Why was he not allowed? Do you think this is correct under 'free speech'?

Liberal: Do you allow a mullah to give speech in educational institutions? You know what they are expected to deliver.

I: You are only seeing his ochre robes. He is an entrepreneur also. He may speak on yoga. He may not be speaking on religion.

Liberal: If platform was given to one such person, a precedent would be established to give for another. Can you allow religious persons to speak in educational institutions?

I: I beg to differ with you. How can you curb a person's freedom to speak when freedom of speech is absolute in your opinion? I thought so-called progressives have more openness, tolerance, respect for the rule of law and yearn for a polite society.

Liberal: Freedom of speech is absolute for the person. The same kind of freedom to oppose the baba's speech is with the students who were protesting. Both have the right.

I: You say America is such a liberal country and stands for all freedoms. What happened in UC Berkley (in Feb 2017) was shameful. The Brietbart's deputy editor, Milo Yiannopoulos, had been no-platformed by students at UC Berkeley. The university, which traditionally had a reputation for free-speech activism, had just cancelled a campus address by the right-wing journalist after left-wing protesters mounted violent protests on campus. The left-wing protesters tore down barricades, lit fires, threw rocks and Roman candles at the windows, and breached the ground floor of the building. Why was Yiannopoulos not allowed to speak? Again, they are left-wing students. They could have silenced him by their argument.

Liberal: Do you know what that man stands for and what he writes?

I: I don't know, but I am for free speech, which is absolute in the US. Why were the left-wing students so absolutely terrified of free speech in the UC Berkley and tried to literally shut it down?

Liberal: That man's speech is very divisive, it is hate-speech, no-platforming of such people is the correct procedure.

I: Who will decide whose speech is divisive, whose is not? Whose is sectarian and whose is non-sectarian? These can be used conveniently.

Liberal: I can say certainly Yiannopolous by his writings an extremely right-wing bigot. He should not be supplied a platform in a prestigious institution like UC Berkley. President Donald Trump though condemned the action of the students, their action was correct in my view.

I: President, a Republican, ideologically right not only supported Yiannopolous but also in a tweet, he threatened to cut Berkeley's funding. The whole farce has actually made Trump right.

Trump's tweet has further troubled the waters in America's ongoing free-speech debates. The First Amendment is written into the American DNA—but for many who view free speech as a tool of social awareness and activism, to be on the same side as Trump and the alt-right seems revolting.

Liberal: That kind of free speech is not in the interest of the unity of the country.

I: The other side says the same. When activists emphasize that they are protesting in the name of the powerless, but end up handing victory to the people in power. They need to rethink their plans to fight. I'm not saying the students should be silent. They could be vocal. The problem lies with the aim with which they protest. The students and some of the professors of the JNU and its ilk were not simply trying to put forth the right message. Their goal was to censor the wrong message.

Liberal: If platforms are given, they are misused. These people become powerful. Their innuendoes and insidious talk should be curbed.

I: That is the very reason people ought to be invited. If students are unable to turn up and ask challenging questions, what on earth do they think they're accomplishing for the world and the things they believe to be right?

Liberal: Don't blame always the left. There are some right-wing groups that did not allow left leaning ideologists to talk. This triggered the left to pay back in the same coin.

I: Here we're talking about free speech. Universities should allow critical scrutiny of ideas. It could be of the left or the right.

Most people in India have come to regard liberalism as a repressive ideology imposed from outside and to be resisted at all costs. That's what the trolls in social media are doing albeit in a rough manner. Indian liberals who take a cue from European liberals should realize, today, Europeans have given up on liberal democracy as a guarantor of social security and upward mobility. They want to follow non-Western democracies, seeing the merit in them. So, all over the world, liberals are under delusion. Hence it is better not to ape the West. India, with its hoary wisdom of ages, has always been liberal— that is to be understood.

India offers a solid system of values that compensate the European wealth and material prosperity. India opened up its economy in early 1990s. Now we are enjoying the fruits of liberalisation. We have opened up our economy, not our borders. We have been isolationist because we have hostile neighbours.

A liberal, Western-educated and once an aspirant for the highest post in United Nations Organisation desired Pakistani people to come to India and do the jobs and make permanent homes! This is again aping the Western ideology. The Western democracies have reason to welcome immigrants. Their huge problem is that their population is getting older and therefore needed more workers to serve them— low birth rates dictate that these workforces have to come from other countries. That question would not arise in India. Of course, people to people contact would dispel many misunderstandings. But the point is the people of Pakistan have no say in their country. Their army dictates terms as to how the country should be run. Moreover, there is a trust deficit with Pakistan Muslims after the partition of the country.

Pakistani Liberal Pervez Hoodbhoy writes about liberals world over. According to him, 'Broadly speaking, liberals are a diffuse bunch wanting a freer world for themselves and others, both personally and politically. Some are faithfully religious, others indifferent, still others atheistic. Some drink, others don't. Liberals value choice and freedom of expression saying you have the right to dress and wear the clothes as you wish. Covering a woman's face or head should be optional. She can have a job if she wants, or stay at home if she wants.

'Extended into the public sphere, liberalism is about the intrinsic equality of men and women from all races and religions, religious tolerance, and the protection of political and civil liberties. Liberalism is admittedly a Western project dating to the Age of Enlightenment. Nevertheless, its many premises—such as the rejection of hereditary privilege and absolute monarchy—have won universal acceptance. Illiberalism is far stronger in Muslim countries'.[1]

Endnotes

1. Pervez Hoodbhoy: article in *Dawn*, Pakistan

CHAPTER 24

Threats to Free speech

Ramachandra Guha writes and mentions in one of his articles and the same published in his book *Democrats and Dissenters* at length on eight threats to freedom of expression in India. The first and foremost being sedition law, which he says is a colonial legacy. It should be scrapped and completely eliminated. Everybody should have a right for free speech. He quotes Gandhiji writing to the government of the time (the British) his explanation against sedition. That is as Gandhiji says, '*In my humble opinion every man has a right to hold any opinion he chooses, and to give effect to it also, so long as, in doing so, he does not use physical violence against anybody*'.

Guha clarifies that Gandhiji might have meant by 'use' to 'advocate'. With clarification, it means, 'Every man or woman has the right to hold any opinion she or he chooses and to give effect to it also, so long as, in doing so, she or he does not use or advocate physical violence against anybody'.[1]

The famous quote, 'misuse of the law cannot be an excuse for making a law' applies here also. The law is already in place. In the seventy years of Independent India, only a few were booked. Among them were JNU students, activists such as Hardik Patel and Binayak Sen, authors such as Arundhati Roy, cartoonist such as Aseem Trivedi, or the villagers of Idinthakarai in Tamil Nadu protesting against the Kudankulam Nuclear Power Plant. Are these examples demonstrative of the misuse of the provision? It is a debatable issue.

The law is clear that mere sloganeering is not enough and has to be accompanied by a call for violence. Since no violence had taken place after their divisive calls and revolutionary statements, that they should not be booked under the provision is an intellectual argument. But the kind of damage their statements do to the fabric of the country is not taken into account.

Left to themselves without slapping sedition law, they make more and more, their fellow travellers continue to carry them, the whole atmosphere in the country becomes vicious. People argue that there are many laws under Indian Penal Code to take care of. In that case the intellectuals (award-wapsi kind) should make a movement to scrap the sedition law. For it cannot be a grass-root movement in India. No ordinary person cares to bother what this sedition law meant or what the culprits booked under the law had done. Delhi cannot be equated to India. What the elite of Delhi know the rest of India are not aware of.

'Sedition charges are easily slapped, but seldom stick, but cause immense harassment in the process' is the argument put forth by Sri Guha. Nobody questions the statements made or acts done in the name of free speech. Those who make statements in the name free speech should have some tongue in cheek. Free speech for whom? Only for the elite? Cine actors, again, come under elite of the elite. Irresponsible statements to encourage secession should not be made under the garb of free speech. At present, all over the world, parts of the people in the countries are asking for separate nations for themselves. The recent examples being in secession-wary Europe, Catalan lawmakers voted on to declare independence from Spain, and Kurdistan sought separation from Iraq through a referendum.

People of the country need clarification on what is free speech:

The votaries of free speech should clarify us, teachers, whether the students in the schools need to be groomed with certain good values (patriotism, nationalism, respecting elders, talking politely, making their point clear without hurting others) or not. Or else, the teacher should leave them for their creative brains to bloom on their own.

Even in Western societies, children are expected to behave in a certain way, decent and civilized. They do not support unruly behaviour or talk. The iconic JNU students for free speech is a research student, not a small child. To him, the BJP's ideology is inimical. That's understandable. The way he criticized Bharatmata, revered by many, was atrocious. Sarcasm has limits. He was speaking from a public forum, not a private talk to the glee of his ideological mentors.

Time and again, it is proving in India that something sacred to any religion, especially the images that are worshipped, should not be touched. However, the practices of religions could be freely and openly discussed. As per the Constitution of India, freedom of speech is guaranteed. In the minds of people, there is a demarcation- 'This far and no further'. Unlike earlier days, people's awareness now has become manifold because of media and smartphones.

It is true of our national newspapers and TV channels to think their subscribers to be dumb and try to force their opinion, their freedom of speech, and their simplifying of things to us, the dumbos. If they wanted to convey the best knowledge, best ideas of this time, there is a way to do it. They need to be gentle and humane in conveying the message. This is culture. Opposite culture was anarchy or chaos.

Indian Parliamentary discussions on free speech—some excerpts:

'It is said by Dr Ambedkar in his introductory speech on behalf of the Drafting committee that fundamental rights are not absolute'.

'The right to free speech is one of our most treasured Fundamental Rights. It has been called the key-stone of rights, because without it we cannot even draw attention to the trampling upon of other rights. It is enshrined in Article 19 (1) of our Constitution', writes Sri Arun Shourie in his *Free Speech: How It Came About.*[2]

'The right to free speech, like other rights of the kind fell in the ambit of the Constituent Assembly's Sub-Committee on Fundamental Rights . . . It chose to procced with K. M. Munshi's draft as its working document.

According to the draft, 'Every citizen within the limits of the law of the Union and in accordance therewith', his draft provided, 'has: (a) the right of free expression of opinion.' The draft made a separate mention of the freedom of the press providing, 'The press shall be free subject to restrictions imposed by the law of the Union as in its opinion may be necessary in the interest of public order and morality.

'There was vigorous discussion in the sub-committee: By the time the clause was finalised by the sub-committee it became . . . (a) The right of every citizen to freedom of speech and expression. The publication or utterance of seditious, obscene, slanderous, libellous or defamatory matter shall be actionable or punishable in accordance with law.

'In 1962 October, the country was administered a devastating shock by China. There was a renewed concern about the unity and integrity of the country. Groups had not been wanting in India who had once again chosen to espouse the cause of the adversary, and to question the territorial integrity of the country. Moreover, a number of secessionist movements had reared their heads. The National Integration Council constituted a committee on National Integration and Regionalism. This Committee recommended, among other things, that Article 19(2) be amended to include 'the sovereignty and integrity of India' as one of the grounds in the interest of which speech and expression could be restricted. The proviso was accordingly amended in 1963 by the 14th amendment to the Constitution.' The factual data that led to Article 19(2) Freedom of Speech clause after the extensive Constituent Assembly debates.[3]

That was the description as to how the sedition law came into existence and the debates of constituent assembly and the curbs on freedom of speech and Press have into existence. The explanation given by Sri Ramachandra Guha was similar.

He writes, 'Tragically, after India became Independent in August 1947, instead of doing away with Section 124A and the like, we have retained and even strengthened them . . . But two events soon after Independence added to the insecurities of the Indian state. The first was the murder of Gandhiji . . . Six weeks later, at a secret conclave in Calcutta, the Communist Party of India (CPI) called for an armed war against the Indian state'.

Article 19(2) of the Constitution, as originally drafted and passed, had stated that the state could make laws restricting freedom of expression where the exercise of such freedom 'offends against decency or morality or which undermines the security of, or tends to overthrow, the State'. This first amendment expanded the areas where the state could intervene to restrict freedom of expression.

Nehru, Patel, and Ambedkar were acting under great duress, taking extraordinary measures at a time when the very survival of the Independent India was at stake. Yet that first amendment was not, in retrospect, conducive to the freedom of expression in India. For it reintroduced the power of the colonial laws which the Constitution had tried to remove or supersede. The amendment allowed the government of Independent India much leeway in supressing dissent and criticism, but the courts little leeway in protecting it'[3] (*Democrats and Dissenters,* p. 28).

However, I feel, the situation of ideologies and political parties is no different even now. The situation has not changed drastically. So much of plurality could drag country anywhere. Whichever government comes to power at the Centre should keep in view the unity and integrity of the country. It has to have a powerful law or tools at its disposal to control the unruly, disgruntled, anti-national forces.

In India, anything could flare up at any time. If people are let loose without any curbs on freedom of speech, any disaster can happen. However, there is a reason to get worried about because to curtail fundamental rights using the clause would rest with the legislature that in effect meant the government of the day.

The same adversary groups who could question the territorial integrity and secessionist movements in the country are still present. The JNU movement on Afzal Guru hanging and shouting slogans against India is a living example in the present-day memory. India's situation is volatile and has faced bouts of violence many times. There are fissiparous tendencies at work always. Some strict law sedition or otherwise is required.

Free speech- Hindu bashing by liberals:

Liberals in India appear to think that it is their birth right to bash the Hindus. Liberalism only entails criticising the majorities not to touch minorities remotely. It goes without saying that Indian minorities, most of them, were Hindus once upon a time. All of them were not from Turkey or elsewhere. Once a Hindu gets converted, he becomes a minority. Whatever special privileges the minorities have will apply to them! The minorities have their personal laws, educational institutions, rights to promote, and propagate their religion, to uplift their language, to keep up their identity. The other countries recognise minorities on ethnicity.

The Hindus who live in USA and the UK assimilate so well in the ways of their dressing, speaking, and celebrating festivals Christmas and Thanksgiving (as the majorities do there) so that they feel one with their culture and would not be discriminated.

Attacking majorities in India is easier than anywhere in the world. For the successive governments of the Congress have weakened and made them emasculated and incapable of intellectually defending themselves. The baiting of Hindu majorities of India is continually being done in other Western countries also by our Indian diehard leftists, extreme secularists, and the academic fringe to the amusement of the intellectuals of those countries. The type of calumny they have been doing against Hindus, no civilized person on earth could ever do. About them, the less said, the better!

However, in India Hinduism still persists in its pristine form for two reasons. One, basically Indians are religious, and the other, an organisation like the RSS works for the cause. There is one caution—some media groups have been consistently trying to bring all and sundry so-called Hindu groups into one umbrella and whatever havoc they cause on Hindu name, they are covering the rot with a nomenclature of Hindu or 'saffron terror'. They are promoting a dubious brand name, in all these cases. In any case, the miscreants should be booked as per the law of the land and punished. When terrorism has no religion, so also the criminality.

In this scenario of bad portrayal of country men, the efforts of the Honourable PM, Sri Narendra Modi, to bring about unity among the Indians within the country and outside in the non-resident Indians and to promote Indian culture, tradition, and values of life are laudable.

The Indian prime minister's outreach to the Indian diaspora in the foreign soil and the enthusiasm it created in the NRI Indians to attach themselves with this holy land and serve were recognised even by the Congress party. Precisely for that reason, to attract Indians of the US, Sri Rahul Gandhi, vice-president of the Congress party then along with Sri Sam Pitroda toured US (in 2017) to impress upon the policies of their party.

Endnotes

1. R. Guha, *Democrats and Dissenters*, 2016, p. 25
2. Arun Shourie's Column on Free Speech on 12 January 1997 in *Deccan Chronicle*, Hyderabad
3. Arun Shourie's Column on Free Speech on 19 January 1997 in *Deccan Chronicle*, Hyderabad

CHAPTER 25

On Nationalism

'A parochial, selfish, narrow minded nationalism has caused so much misfortune and misery to the world. A mad and exaggerated form of this cult of nationalism is today running rampant . . .' This statement made by M. N. Roy, as far back as 1942, may resonate with many even today, particularly in these times we live in, stated Justice A. P. Shah in M. N. Roy's memorial lecture (on 20 April 2017).[1]

'The more I read this lecture by Justice AP Shah, I ask myself, why did such an outstanding judge never adorn the SC', tweeted a celebrated anchor of a TV channel.[2]

The reason for liking his speech could be, due to the convergence of their ideas about the situation prevailing in India, in the NDA government's rule under Narendra Modi's prime ministership. That was purely his ideological perception, not entirely the reality. It cannot be called 'truth' in purity.

M. N. Roy was a Communist and therefore an internationalist. It's an open secret how repressive Communists' government have been in dealing with human rights and free speech. In 1944, M. N. Roy drafted a 'Constitution of Free India', where he included a chapter on 'Declaration of Fundamental Rights', which clearly stated that a 'right to revolt against tyranny and oppression is sacred'.

This thought was there in the Indian epic *Mahabharata* where Pandavas lived in the tyranny and oppression of Kauvravas and revolted at the end.

The author Henry David Thoreau was influenced by early Indian philosophy and thought, from which he drew his inspiration for the essay, 'Duty of Civil Disobedience'. Thoreau wrote, 'If the law is of such a nature that it requires you to be an agent of injustice to another, then I say break the law, let your life be a counter friction to stop the machine'.

Thoreau's essay influenced Mahatma Gandhi tremendously while he was in South Africa and in fact gave him the inspiration for the great non-violent civil disobedience he was to practise in the subsequent years so effectively.[3]

It was all before the Independence of India. Both M. N. Roy and Mahatma Gandhi found the British rule tyrannical. The principle they held was laudable. But to equate it to the present is a bit absurd. The present issues are blown out of proportion by some of the eminent because ideologically, the ruling dispensation is an anathema to them. The following paragraph raises the things that much avowed to the liberals and so-called seculars.

Justice Shah said, 'Today we are living in a world where we are forced to stand for the national anthem at a movie theatre, we are told what we can and cannot eat, what we can and cannot see, and what we can and cannot speak about. Dissent, especially in the university space, is being curbed, and sloganeering and flag raising have become tests for nationalism. We have a twenty-one-year old university student who is subject to severe online hate, abuse, and threats, only because she dared express her views'.[4]

Now one could easily understand why that particular anchor queried himself, 'Why did such an outstanding judge never adorn the SC'! The justice stood for what he has been asking for on daily basis in news debates. These opinionated anchors always stand by their views. They appear to have monopoly on truth.

On all these issues, I do not mind what the panellists say and what the anchors say, because the comments are free. But the anchors should shun the temptation to the monopoly of truth as their first duty.

People watching the television news channels should not be treated as fools. They have their wisdom. Way back, Raymond Williams said that Mathew Arnold, in his book, *Culture and Anarchy*, criticised the manipulation of opinion, by politicians and newspapers: a minority talking down, simplifying, sloganeering, to people they thought of as 'the masses'. He criticised the abstraction of 'freedom'; it was not only a question of being free to speak but a kind of national life in which culture, he argued, were those who had a passion for diffusing, for making prevail, for carrying from one end of the society to the other, the best knowledge, the best ideas of their time . . . to humanize it, to make it efficient outside the clique of the cultivated and learned, yet still remaining the best knowledge and thought of the time.[5]

In the Arnold's criticism of 'the manipulation of opinion, by politicians and newspapers: a minority talking down, simplifying, sloganeering, to people they thought of as "the masses"' appealed to me. For the opinionated journalists generally treat the audiences as 'the masses'. They expect them to gulp what they infer as news.

According to the ruling dispensation, people have their thoughts and opinions on repression and oppression. If the ruling class is suitable to them and their ideals, things are smooth, otherwise problematic. I had felt the same situation to be under the Congress rule before the advent of social media. Though I do not write anything under hashtag or never follow what trolls write, I feel happy that many in the society have got a voice.

Those who were marginalised once are now surpassing and going ahead of the mainstream media. Some twenty years back, it was so difficult to get a letter published in the newspaper in the Letters to the Editor column. We used to struggle a lot. If somebody said something supportive of Hinduism, immediately they were branded communalists. The real secularism lay in appeasing minorities. The learned justice did not raise voice at that time. He did not raise voice on uniform civil code. He did not raise voice on triple talaq, which is not in the interest of Muslim women. Of course, those were not his chosen topics for the memorial lecture.

Yes, I felt bad when cow vigilantism was rampant. In this part of India, i.e. South India where I live, there were no such incidents, and there seemed to be no such law of protecting cow. Personally, I do not like anyone taking law into their hands. But if the law of cow protection was not in place, many healthy cows would have been killed. The country would be left with little or no cattle. After all, livestock industry is also, like any industry, could go overboard. Have the gau-rakshaks not had volunteered, many would have taken that as an advantage and killed many a cow for commercial purposes, leaving cow an endangered species. Like how the contractors overcut (cut beyond their permit) the trees in the forests, like how the mines are dug beyond limit and resources looted, the fate of cows would have been the same. Since cows have no voice, someone should speak for them as they are revered in this country.

The twenty-one-year-old girl whose free speech was curtailed was lamented by the justice because of trolls and their threats. Of course, it was a sorry state of affairs. However, it was the same media that gave her the focus also with her friendly trolls!

I condemn the threats on her in no uncertain terms, but there is no doubt in my mind that she was driven by an ideology. Perhaps that ideology was tutored. With that ideology, she said, 'Pakistan did not kill my father, war did'.

The cricketers, actors, and politicians who commented, commented on the efficacy of the ideology, not on the girl per se. They have not criticised her, they mimicked by drawing parallels. The votaries of free speech should take cognisance of others' freedom. There are many twenty-one-years-olds in the South India, who are intelligent, studious, and creative. But they have confined to their academics and have not deviated to get attention. Their work speaks louder! Sundar Pichai, Satya Nadella seemed not to have spoken vociferously about their political views in the university campuses, but they are unquestionably creative.

'Standing up', for national anthem was made a big issue! This, respecting of the national flag, national anthem, and our country per se, have all been ingrained in us, through our culture and nurture in educational institutions, especially, from primary school level. Now the liberals question this very concept of respecting! Their argument is, it should not be forced on anyone. It is not the question of forcing. It is the question of grooming the society in a certain desirable manner useful to the nation. There is a need for the government to inculcate certain values to the people at large. They cannot leave them as an amorphous bunch. Top-down measures are necessary in imparting values among children and youth.

I remember one day when I was doing some work sitting on a sofa, my children who were small then were sitting beside me. They heard national anthem *Jana gana mana* from a neighbourhood school. That day there was school day celebration in that school. My children, they stood up immediately though they were at home and asked me to stand up. I was a bit reluctant to stand as some things were on my lap. Yet I stood up along with them till the end. They were very sincere in giving respect to the song as they were taught so in the school. Without their force, I do not know how I would have behaved. It would look quite odd to stand in the house. But we never used to leave the cinema hall till the end of the anthem. In our childhood days, the cinemas used to end with the national anthem. I still remember the flag fluttering during the song. Instead of some people standing, some leaving the hall while the song was still going on, I think the government removed it later to save disgrace.

When I say nationalism, to an extent, and patriotism are needed, I give another instance I faced as a teacher. One day I was talking about some general things in the class. Sometimes we engage students to talk about the things they like or dislike. Mainly to know how they express or communicate their feelings in English, as it was the subject I was teaching. Teachers do this activity at periods of leisure. This way the students open up and say what is on their mind.

As there was some cricket match going on at that time, one of the students in my class from Muslim minority community, who was very active in a way hyperactive, said laughingly while I was talking to them, 'Madam, I like Pakistan, even in cricket, I like Pakistan to win'. I did not know what to say. I was in a dilemma. Whether to rebuke or reprimand him or leave him without taking any such action. I was silent because I could not ask him forcibly to be patriotic. It should come from within, I thought. But as a teacher, it was also my responsibility to inculcate.

The students were young, if not guided now, when? was the question. A teacher needs articulation to convince the student to have devotion towards the country. The boy was already enamoured by Pakistan. How could I drag him out from that fixation? So, I smiled silently and kept quiet. But inside, I could not contain my guilt of not correcting him and putting him in a right track by giving him a true perspective.

After all, in the formative years of child, teachers are supposed to sow the seeds of patriotism and other core values of the country. Our secular liberal thinkers may say, what is wrong in thinking so? He being a small boy could be given some allowance to think. But would any Pakistani teacher tolerate their minority Hindu boy liking India better than Pakistan and stating it openly in front of her? Would she ask for loyalty towards the country where he lives? I do not think such a situation would arise there. I do not think minorities exist in that country. I do not think Hindus, even if they existed as a microscopic minority, would not have a voice to raise.

When I met my friend, the Telugu teacher, I told her what all happened in my class. And also my dilemma. She asked me as to what I had done at that time. I said, I did nothing. She said, 'Why did you allow him to have his say with no correction?' I said I had no clue how to mend him. As far as my friend, the Telugu teacher was concerned; she was gutsy and straightforward. She was a fearless fighter and would not spare anyone when it comes to certain basic principles. She had been working in the same place for a long time. She knew the students well.

She called the boy in the recess and asked him, 'Tell me, why do you like Pakistan when you eat the food grown here, breathe the air, and drink the water of India?'

Then he said, 'I like it because my uncle lives there'. That was the case with many Muslims in India. She became very angry. She said, 'If your uncle lives in Pakistan, let him live. If you like Pakistan so much, go and stay with him. When you are here, when this country is giving everything to you, you should like this country. How can you say that you like Pakistan?'

That boy had no answer. He just giggled and went away. He did not bother much about what she said. Love for the country should come from within. It can't be imposed externally, I thought.

It was a long time ago. During that time, we thought what we had done was correct. Now I have no clue how the liberals in India would have reacted to a similar situation. Teachers are by their very nature authoritarian and dictatorial. We could not mend him more subtly and more decently. Anyway, the boy did not budge. He was stuck to his view. That I could gather from his behaviour. Allegiance to outside nations because of extraneous factors like religion, causes a kind of a suspicion, especially with Pakistan, which is hell-bent on harming India. I think that was what the RSS would have meant! As of today, Indian Muslims are Indian. They pronounce their Indian identity more, which is a good sign.

By and large Indians are argumentative in nature. People may question, 'What's wrong in the boy loving Pakistan?' Even I thought so in that boy's case. He was a small boy; whatever his feeling was, he said it openly. I did not take it seriously. Children learn as they grow. Often grown-ups are flippant in making statements. They loosely say they like so-and-so country even if they belong to India. Does that mean they are less patriotic? Somehow, in the case of Pakistan, we take things more seriously. If a Muslim says he likes Pakistan, that's it. But always in the minds of Indians, there is a trust deficit as far as Pakistan is concerned. In this backdrop, the statement of the boy liking Pakistan was not taken well. An Amir Khan in India needed to say that he likes India, not an Amitabh Bacchan! To an average Muslim, there is no difference between India and Pakistan on religious lines. To an average Indian Hindu, it has a lot.

Indians are cynical and suspicious of Pakistani connection. India was divided on communal lines is a fact. After all, we fought the independence struggle together. At the end, when we were about to have our fruits of struggle, i.e. independence, Muslims asked for a separate country, Pakistan. Which was a clear betrayal at the fag end of the fight against the British. Those who were desirous of a separate nation had gone to Pakistan. The other Muslims who remained in India were all crestfallen with their community people betraying them and their country. Hence, they were given special rights and privileges to keep their identity until they themselves would come to mainstream. In due course, the founding fathers of the Constitution thought that they would get assimilated and ask for scrapping the temporary measures. The Indian NRIs from the majority community, who live abroad assimilate with the people in the host countries they live. Initially, after partition of the country, many film actors from the minority Muslim community changed their name to suit the audience who were mainly from the majority community. It was a kind of an adjustment.

As far as somebody liking Pakistan more than India means somebody liking the enemy of their motherland. Otherwise, why did the Parliament pass 'Enemy property bill' in 2016, which denies inheritance rights to heirs of individuals who left the country for Pakistan and China? The Pakistanis stabbed their mother India by vivisecting the country is a plain truth. Still they want to inflict wounds! One should understand that country's ploys, not loving it blindly.

The youth of this country, especially, should know what most of the so-called progressive say, about India. They say India is not a nation. Their view is, 'India is just a geographical expression. It is only the British who united it. We aren't even one nation—for a nation must have one language, one religion, one race' (Ref: Arun Shourie's article 6 June 1993).

But they call Pakistan a nation. Though it has no common language or history or common religion. It has Urdu, Pushto, Baluchi, Sindhi, Punjabi as languages. It has no common religion as they are divided into Sunnis, Shias, and Ahmadis. It has no history of its own.

About India's cultural oneness and cultural nationalism Arun Shourie writes (in 1993), 'Our cultural oneness is manifest, that unity has evolved over and been manifest for thousands of years. But for our ruling classes (the Congress and other secular-parties) to own, to talk about, to propagate the elements which constitute that unity has become anathema.[6]

Sri Shourie was strong supporter of nationalism but wanted it in moderation. When our neighbours are very nationalistic, he writes, 'To dilute it in our case while the others, especially our immediate neighbours such as China and Pakistan, are as nationalistic as can be, when they are in fact pugilistic would be to open ourselves to be torn up again'[7].

Shourie also said knowing about our tradition is not a regressive step. In fact, he advises, 'The object of getting to know our traditions and history is not to hurl ourselves back into the past of a thousand years ago. It is quite the opposite: the object is to contend better with the problems which bedevil us today, it is to prepare ourselves to better deal with the future. Similarly, the object of nationalism is not to cut India off from the world: it is to equip ourselves to deal with the world: it is to equip ourselves to deal with the world, to consort with others as equals.

'The bad repute that nationalism has among our intellectuals is derived from two inspirations: the writings of British "internationalists" and those of communist "internationalists". The British who ruled us were naturally very happy to have us imbibe "One World" notions:

these were a good solvent for the nationalism that Aurobindo and Tilak and Gandhi were stoking up.

'Going international is therefore one thing we would do well in which to trail others. As other countries in the world—in particular, our neighbours like China and Pakistan—shed nationalism, we may do so. But not more than them. Nor sooner than them . . .

'It is entirely true of course that nationalism can become xenophobia, that under Hitler what started as nationalism became racism, and eventually genocide. But on the other hand, it is nationalism—for instance the national fervour and determination which Churchill mobilised and came to personify, and the nationalism which Stalin the Internationalist, mobilised—which helped roll Hitler back. Moreover, what cannot become excessive?

'An excess of food can be fatal? Do we for that reason abjure food? Therefore, precautions are in order, not abjuration. And precautions are: that we endow our nationalism with a positive content; that to be focused always on the future; that we remain a democracy; that we remain, in particular, an open society . . . Without that leaven (nationalism), the country itself will not survive, and when it does not, nor will democracy, the open society and the rest.[8]'

How I felt and my analysis: I was terribly impressed by the analysis of Sri Shourie and thought what a sane way of analysis! It not only applies to nationalism, it equates to secularism also in India. Our secular leaders took the concept to such a level by tilting the balance towards minorities, thus making it appeasement-oriented in the eyes of the majorities.

Coming to nationalism, compare Arun Shourie's analysis with that of Justice A. P. Shah. Justice Shah went by the internationalists in describing nationalism to be a dangerous portent. Shourie, while supporting that nationalism is required for the country to survive, had put forth riders not to exceed. Those are nationalism with (1) positive content, (2) always focused on the future, (3) makes us remain a democracy, (4) helps us remain an open society.

If analysed and applied to the present situation in the country the first two conditions, i.e the positive content about the nation and the focus on future are thriving and are very much in force. The third one, to remain as democracy is guaranteed as per the Constitution as democratic values are enshrined in it and we are, by our elections, from time to time, following it very much. I have no doubt in my mind that the country cannot be otherwise. India will remain an open society. With the social media in place. It has remained more open. When it was less open, the elite had a say as to how others should behave, now everybody has a say. No sermonizing, no dictation, no hierarchy.

'The controllers of discourse and our rulers (the Congress and other so-called secular parties) have tilted it too long and too far on the side of the dread of possible excess'. These words of Shourie have a resonance even now. Bubbling with their international spirit, the kind of utterances these celebrities make enrages a common man. When so many soldiers have been losing lives at the border, the peaceniks mouthing shibboleths on having people-to-people contact and appreciating talents from enemy country (Pakistan) when our country itself has enough talent pool. When you praise your neighbour so much, people at home surely would mock at you by saying to go to that neighbour's house where you feel heavenly. These peaceniks often tend to demean their own country people in their love for the neighbouring country. If love is a universal phenomenon, 'love all!'

Nationalism knows no boundaries:

Now, nationalism has crossed all barriers without breaking physical walls and boundaries. With information technology, reaching far and wide, in a fraction of a second, ideals are transferred and promoted. The non-resident Indians, elsewhere in the world, are articulating their nationalism of their native country through globalised technology and electronic communication.

Within India, Indians are getting united and standing up for the cause of nationalism as they are becoming conscious of it through television channels. For the country's integrity and perpetuity, nationalism is needed. However, how much is too much has to be decided in this age of excessive texting and messaging.

Endnotes

1. Justice A. P. Shah in M. N. Roy's memorial lecture (on 20 April 2017).
2. https____t.co_c8sxVIfECZ_.html" Twitter-Rajdeep Saradesai

3. Bhavan's Journal 31 May 1994, p. 18, India Preparing for the next century—Text of address of PM P. V. Narasimha Rao, to the joint meeting of the US Congress on 18 May1994, in Washington. www.vlib.us/amdocs/texts/19linc/htm

4. Justice A. P. Shah in M. N. Roy's memorial lecture (on 20 April 2017).

5. Raymond Williams talked about 'Problems in Materialism and Culture' (London: Verso,1980). He commemorated 'A Hundred Years of Culture and Anarchy' of Matthew Arnold's *Culture and Anarchy* (a compilation of lectures and articles by Matthew Arnold)

6. Arun Shourie: On Nationalism, *Deccan Chronicle*, Hyderabad on 18 July 1993

7. Arun Shourie: On Nationalism, *Deccan Chronicle*, Hyderabad on 18 July 1993

8. Arun Shourie: On Nationalism, *Deccan Chronicle*, Hyderabad on 18 July 1993

CHAPTER 26

Truth: Many Facets

There is a saying in Sanskrit, '*Satyam brooyath, Priyam brooyath*'. That means one has to say truth, and it has to be pleasing to the person who hears it and should be beneficial to him. Truth should not be mixed with journalistic facts. A fact is fact. It has to be told. What is within our limits is to speak about the facts dispassionately. By doing so, you are giving value to the other human. All the religions preach not to hurt a person physically and also mentally.

Here I would like to mention one renowned liberal editor of repute and a staunch champion of press freedom to buttress my point. Charles Prestwich Scott, the editor of *Manchester Guardian* newspaper, had written a piece on the newspaper's centenary celebrations on 5 May 1921, the principles of which, apply to the present-day television editors also. He did not brush aside the commercial side of the newspaper. He said, like any other business, this newspaper business, has to pay in material sense in order to live. However, he said, '*At the peril of its (newspaper's) soul it must see that the supply is not tainted. Neither in what it gives, nor in what it does not give, nor in the mode of presentation must the unclouded face of truth suffer wrong. Comment is free, but facts are sacred . . .* comment also is justly subject to a self-imposed restraint. It is well to be frank; it is even better to be fair'.[1]

Some people by their irresponsible talk hurt others. Speaking truth does not mean speaking unthinkingly on each and everything. What you say is important, how you say it is also equally important. It is easy to become regressive, pedantic, and strident in your argument; however, truth expressed in a pleasant and understanding manner will touch the heart of the other person, and it will also lead to open up for a conversation. Truth is more important for a democracy to survive. In this post-truth era, truth in purity has much to say.

Political correctness and how it matters

I would like to share an incident from my experience. Every year we celebrate in schools Independence Day (15 August) and Republic Day (26 January). Attending school on those two days is almost mandatory for government schoolteachers. In the assembly, all the students stand up in their well-dressed uniforms with shoes on. They do march past, principal hoists the flag, students and teachers and other office and contingent staff salute the flag. These routine things happen throughout India. Specially in our school near the flag on a small dais, i.e. on a platform, Mahatma Gandhi, Jawaharlal Nehru's photos are kept. Those photos are decorated with flowers and are marked with tilak, a coconut, and lamps and sandal sticks to light are kept ready. For many days, I could not understand why both leaders were worshipped like gods. Of course, I have a lot of reverence for our freedom fighters who fought for the liberation of the country in true spirit.

Once it so happened that we have had a principal from a minority community in our school. Whenever this coconut breaking phenomenon had come, she would escape by saying somebody to do that. For her it seemed to be wrong according to the tradition she belongs to. So, one of the staff members broke the coconut and kept the pieces on either side of the photos, then flag was hoisted singing two, three patriotic songs, all the teachers spoke on the importance of the day. 'Why we celebrate it? What the country stands for? How the leaders struggled to get independence? What's our duty now? What the students supposed to do to make the flag fly high' were elaborated in those speeches. For years, together, the teachers give speeches. Each language teacher should give in the language she teaches. In the end, after all the speeches of teachers and some prominent students, the principal would deliver her speech.

That year, our principal, that day from the podium started praising the British. She said they contributed some good things to us. Because of their rule people got decent culture like English education and eating on the dining table, so on so forth, as if Indians were barbaric before their advent. When she was praising the British, we did not know what to do. We thought those were her personal opinions, which she shouldn't be airing from a forum that was meant to celebrate the end of a foreign rule. After the meet, when she was in her chamber we all (teachers) went to her room and asked whether it was appropriate for her to talk the way she did. She said she spoke nothing wrong. That was how, she said, she felt. We argued with her against her speech. One among us said it (the matter) could be taken to police for denigrating India on Independence Day. She felt little jittery. She said she was as patriotic as anyone of us. It was not her intention to downplay the country. Then we left the matter there to rest.

Often, people who speak on public forums should be conscious of what they say. Here, more than free speech, political correctness matters. Political correctness demands inclusiveness. It shuns discrimination of people on caste, community, gender-sensitivity, in the case of India, sentiments of the people.

After the independence struggle, concerted effort should have been made by our tall leaders to unify India and Indian oneness. Of course, there is Indian Constitution and Indian law for Indians to follow and abide by. More than that, there is no emotional bondage to make the country 'one'.

Endnotes

1.   *Bhavan's Journal* 31 October 1994

CHAPTER 27

A thought to Alternative Viewpoint

I started reading other than the RSS ideological articles and books. For I do not want to be safe, ideologically. I wanted to be strong and see the perspective of others dispassionately. And also, to see properly. To know why they are saying what they are saying. What others wrote I felt sometimes balanced, at places dogmatic. I have read Ramchandra Guha's book before US presidential elections and analysed it after the elections were over.

I have a great respect for Guha's erudition and scholarship. He seemed to me to be very balanced in his book while analysing people. But he was so much anchored to his so-called liberal ideology, it became frustrating for me to read some parts of his book. However, as a sample of my inconvenience, I will make a mention of two or three places where I differed with him completely. However, I am no one to question his entitlement to freedom of expression.

At the outset, in the very first chapter Guha says, 'Despite its occasional disavowal at the Hindutva programme, the BJP is a party of Hindu majoritarian many of whose members tend to suspect and even demonize Muslims and Christians.'[1] Perhaps this may seem to be true to the liberal view, but not of all Indians.

India has been divided on communal lines is a fact. That led to the partition of the country. It is not centuries-old story to forget it. Guha knows this better than anyone as a historian. There was not much resistance from Nehru or the Congress! Had India been united, we would not have the difficulties that we are facing with Pakistan, Kashmir, and Bangladesh (to an extent). It's a fact the Congress as a movement was instrumental in obtaining the precious thing called 'freedom' to the country Bharath. It also divided the country on communal lines. If the Congress wants to take the credit, let them also take the blame of dividing the nation. Of course, we cannot deny the hand and ploy of the British in making the partition. The British appeased Jinnah, they appeased the Muslim community. The Congress followed suit in adhering to that policy of 'appeasement' later to the advantage of getting votes. Pandit Jawaharlal Nehru was no less! Election after election, he assured minorities that they were safe only in the Congress hands.

The very ideology of the RSS and its affiliates, as far as I know, is to strengthen the Hindu community. *Hindu* is a generic word. It encompasses all the religions in India. For the other religious people are not immigrants. They are the converts from Hinduism. By bringing them under one umbrella, the country will have its name. Is Hindu such a taboo word for liberals? Otherwise, why then they say that the Hindutva forces want to gobble up the other religious minorities? Could they not allow a different thought process to prevail! Nothing can be forced in India in any way.

Western countries are sparsely populated. They welcome immigrants with open arms. They believe in cultural plurality. These multi-cultural countries would not mind getting divided. Look at the counties in Europe, they are so puny. The Europeans sit across the table and draw boundaries and divide without any bloodbath. Indians, by and large, want their country to be intact.

The majority of Indians have an affinity towards the country and its integrity. Though a poor country for too long, in patriotism (the feeling that this country's well-being and togetherness), we are rich. That's what we pledge every day in the schools. That's what is taught on all Independence and Republic days. I always used to tell my students in my Independence Day speech, 'You exist because of this country, your identity is this country. If this country won't survive, your culture, religion will not survive. If you study well and prove to be a worthy individual, you not only bring name to you, your parents and to school but also to our country.' Even in ancient scriptures, there is a sloka which says roughly, 'an individual can be sacrificed for a family, a family can be sacrificed for a village, a village can be sacrificed for a taluk, a taluk for a district, a district for a country'! Country is at any rate greater than all individuals in it.

To use the phrase 'demonising minorities' is unjust to those who oppose appeasement policy. Because the very philosophy of the RSS and the BJP is for unifying the country. They are for 'equality to all and appeasement to none'!

The development of the country depends on all, so the fruits of labour should also be for all! As a matter of fact, minority religious groupings are more organised in India than the majorities. Majorities don't have proper public relations (PR) like the minorities. Like in the West, they are not a solid monolith. They don't have intellectuals of their own to support them barring a few from the RSS. As a matter of fact, the Congress and other opposition parties 'demonise the RSS' to consolidate their minority votes. By now, the minorities of India would have realised that the BJP is not a pariah.

Guha also writes, 'The first years of Indian Independence were very fraught indeed. Had there been lesser men and women at the helm, or lesser party than the Congress . . . India could have come under military rule, or broken up into several different parts, or been subject to mass scarcity and famine.'[2] The Congress of then was different from the Congress of now. The Congress then inducted the best of brains into their movement. They were revivalist in their nationalism to get independence to the country.

To use 'lesser men and women' and 'lesser party than the Congress' is, in a way, a little uncharitable to other national leaders other than the Congress. They may be different in their world-view and ideology but how could one decisively say that they could break up the country? The Congress, even in its worst form, is better than any other party for them!

Guha's sympathetic overtones to Sonia Gandhi seemed to be a bit absurd. He writes, 'Sonia ran counter to the currents of culture and geography as well. Not even a Bollywood writer could script such a tale of a woman born in a modest home in a small town in post-war Italy, becoming, for a full ten years, the most powerful person in the world's largest democracy'.[3]

Though Sonia Gandhi was from a modest background, she had entered into a most politically influential prime minister's family in India. There is no surprise or bewilderment in Sonia Gandhi becoming powerful with the kind of background she has had. In 2004 elections, the Congress as party got only four seats more than the BJP party. The other parties came to its rescue in the name of secularism. Similarly, in 2009, the Congress fared a bit I better, but could not form on its own. Now they say the BJP, though it got absolute majority, its vote share is only 31 per cent. Both on 2004 and 2009 Congress' share was much less than that but it ruled for ten long years, making Sonia Gandhi the powerful lady. Many have not voted for it, but it gobbled up power and stayed to rule the country!

Guha admits the dominance of Hans in China by writing, 'In China . . . national identity has been massively defined by a single ethnicity and a single language. In numbers, economic power and political and military influence, the Han dominate China. If one is not a Han, the slog to the top most-if not all -professions is much harder. . . Mandarin, has become a pre-condition for membership of the nation community. Different dialects are spoken in different parts of China, but the official school and college system, and state-controlled media, all emphasize a single standard (or standardized) language, the knowledge of which is key to the professional success and political conformity'.[4] To me, Hans' dominance in China is agreeable, in India, Hindu assertiveness should also be viewed so.

The BJP and the RSS are not in any way against the diversity and plurality in the society. Embracing diversity is more important today than ever for creating resilience in the society of India.

Here is small mention of research findings on pluralism. Thomas Friedman, the foreign affairs columnist, The New York Times, writes in his book that, 'Pluralism is not diversity alone, but the energetic engagement with diversity', explains the Pluralism Project at Harvard on its website, 'mere diversity without real encounter and relationship will yield increasing tensions in our societies'.[5]

A society being 'pluralistic' is a reality (see Syria and Iraq). A society with pluralism 'is an achievement' (see America). Pluralism, the Harvard Project also notes, 'does not require us to leave our identities and our commitment behind . . . It means holding our deepest differences, even our religious differences not in isolation, but in relationship with one another.' And it posits that real pluralism is built on 'dialogue' and 'give and take', criticism and self-criticism—and 'dialogue means both speaking and listening'.

Being able to embrace and nurture this kind of true pluralism is a huge asset for a society in the age of acceleration—and a huge liability, if you cannot, for a host of reasons.'[5]

While writing about Pakistan, Sri Guha never ever finds fault with country for following theocracy. Never even questions ill-treatment of their minority. Always praises the people. When it comes to India blaming Hindus for some kind of excesses done to the Muslim community etc.---Often I question myself, why these Liberals in India show love towards Pakistanis?

Liberals encourage pluralism, they encourage open-borders, stand for multi-culture. These principles are okay in the West. They have open-borders, they welcome immigrants...Now in the present-day world, they are facing the music. Now they realised their borders to be fenced. So, sticking to the theories like, 'I am a Liberal, these are the principles I stick to, they are only the correct ones', would not work. The intellectual liberal theories, individuals can have in a democracy, but cannot be imposed on the country as a whole. I also ask myself, when liberals in India are so large-hearted to embrace Pakistanis, why then they hate some people of their own country like the gau-rakshaks in India? They are their fellow citizens, even if assumed to be misguided.

Liberals in India seem to be not-so-free individuals. They seem to be an organised whole. They all have similar views on issues of free speech, free expression, freedom of choice. But in the end, they are prisoners of their own liberal ideology, which is again vague. Otherwise, after gau-rakshak episodes, how come most of the liberals started writing about Gandhiji and what he said about cow-slaughter? They say that Gandhiji did not ask for a ban on cow slaughter. Then in that case, should it be construed that he was for cow slaughter? He never ever would have supported it. This beef brigade also speaks of pollution and environment protection! I would like to point out how harmful it is to kill animals including, cow in abattoirs; livestock farming causes damage in more than one way. When we hear about the horrors of industrial livestock farming—the pollution, the waste, the miserable lives of billions of animals—it is hard not to feel a twinge of guilt and conclude that people should eat less meat.

My views on meat consumption and on other issues, viz. schoolchildren should have moral and ethical topics in the curriculum, support for construction of Ayodhya-Ram temple, for having uniform civil code, and abrogation of Article 370 (plain case of appeasement) are my convictions. Constitutionally I, am not wrong.

I support the cultural nationalism of India because there are very many good things in our culture like respecting parents and elders, a social framework of meeting friends and relatives, especially, on festivals, in a way these are stress-busters. There are many Hindu festivals in India which are meant to break the monotony in public life. In the West because of their isolationist, individual, independent lives, they are more prone to psychological problems. Worshipping trees, rivers, earth (while laying foundation stone for construction) are all meant to protect the environment. The spiritualism in India, that says we need not chase material objectives excessively, leading life by being good and doing good is enough to have peace of mind, and they are worthy concepts. Whatever the great sayings in the world are all said by our greatest saints in India. As Roger Scruton said in his book *How to Be a Conservative*, that 'good things are easily destroyed, but not easily created'. I believe in it.

As the eighteenth-century philosopher Edmund Burke 'made a case for a society shaped from below, by traditions that have grown from our natural need to associate', rather than from above, imposed by a powerful state and an all-knowing political elite, is true in India also. Most of the Indian common people are unaware of what the elite talk. Indian people are by and large stuck to their age-old norms and tradition, which are not wrong, as long as they are within the permissible limits of the law.

I also support one more point of Scruton: 'Unless and until people identify themselves with the country, its territory and its cultural inheritance—in something like the way people identify themselves with a family—the politics of compromise [necessary for democratic functioning] will not emerge.'[6]

That is what the RSS has been saying all along in my view. They wanted cultural nationalism. They believe in nation state. The Congress, all these years, tried to scuttle the idea. The Indian pluralism is good. But it has to be fixed with the glue of Hindu culturalism. Hindus cannot be relegated to one section of the larger whole and side-lined in the name of secularism. Hindus are not asking for Hindu name to this country or to make Hinduism an official religion. In the West, though the countries like the UK and USA have a secular society, they have their official religion, Christianity.

Arun Shourie had written reams of articles opposing pseudo-secularism practised in India and how Hindus should assert for their due recognition. He was instrumental in taking up the cause. His political ideas at present may be different.

Majority of the Indians felt happy at the rise of the BJP and ultimately coming to the power with full strength. It is needless to say that leaders are born, not made. Sri Narendra Modi, our prime minister, is one such, dyed-in-the wool ideologist and a leader. As a prime minister, he belongs to all the communities. As Gandhiji once said, being a Hindu means being a Muslim, Christian, Parsi, and a Jew. I have no doubt in my mind on Prime Minister Modi's vision to taking India to heights. This is the prime minister who dedicated his life for a cause, that cause is to see that India as whole progresses. People of this country believed him and took pains to queue up during demonetization. No Indian doubts his intent in demonetizing or GST.

India is an ocean. It is very difficult to navigate this country. There may be minor aberrations in the ruling. Majorities in India have had a sigh of relief after the BJP—led by the PM Sri Narendra Modi—government came to power with full strength. The people want to see the momentum to be continued with renewed vigour with every passing day with inclusiveness of all communities in the spirit of *sab ka sath sab ka vikas.*

Endnotes:

1. Ramachandra Guha: *Democrats and Dissenters*, 2016, p. 3
2. Ibid., p. 28
3. Ibid., p. 13
4. Ibid., p.53
5. Thomas L Friedman, *Thank You for Being Late*, 2016, p. 116
6. Ramachandra Guha, *Democrats and Dissenters*, 2016, p. 275

CONCLUSION

To start with, the thoughts I had at early '90s were to an extent different from now after seeing much of the world. With age, people mature but do not metamorphose. I still possess the feeling that the so-called secular parties in India have overdone the concept of secularism. Almost all of my life, I have been under either the Congress or the TDP (Telugu Desam Party) rule in the state. Both are Tweedledum and Tweedledee as far as minority appeasement is concerned. As far as politics of North India is concerned, I am just an observer from the south. I have not travelled to any of the northern states. People around me are more interested in local polity rather than the national due to proximity. Now, with information boom, the news is in their pockets. A finger is their mouse to navigate what they need. Beeps and alerts do come to them each moment to know what's happening around the world. Thanks to the information technology!

The whole point of my writing the book is to present, in a simplified form, how I felt at various stages of my life about the country and the polity. In Ram Janmabhoomi movement days, we rightly felt that Indian secularism has let us down. By seeing the debates on television, we used to wonder at the intransigent stand taken by the Muslim leaders. In our friends and colleagues' circles, we used to talk about them.

Let me put it to you first how a Hindu psyche is, from my own family members' statements made earlier; though the picture is a miniature, you can magnify and expand for all. By nature, because of their philosophy Hindus are on the defensive.

My mother-in-law's advice:

When I started writing letters to 'the editors of English newspapers' in '90s, which were of little significance in my opinion, and talk to friends on those issues of minorities, my mother-in-law advised me that it would not be good in my own interest. Those who think majorities threaten minorities, always the minorities are at the receiving end due to brute majoritarian force, etc., in India, should know that it is not the case. Most of the majorities are silent on minority issues because religion is a sensitive issue in India. The freedom of speech given in the Constitution is limited to statute books only!

My mother's caution:

One day I was talking to some of my relatives the things I had seen and experienced on curfew days and also on newspaper writings that were favourably biased towards minorities. My children were listening intently to what their mother was saying. They were gazing at me curiously when I was making the spirited talk. My mother could not resist herself. She cautioned me. She said, 'Why are you saying all that before small children, what kind of impression they get? What kind of thinking do they develop? They need to live with all religions, people of all hues in the outside world'.

True, traditionally, in most of the Indian families, we are taught not to talk negative portrayal of things before children. All of us bring children up with certain values, which are universally accepted by all humans. Anything other than that is their personal or experiential realization later, when they grow up in life. So, we try to keep children's minds as clean slates (*tabula rasa*).

In fact, secularism is not a concept to be imposed externally by the government of the day. It has to start from home, from the early childhood. Rightly in a democracy, majorities are asked to follow the principles so that the rest (minorities) can be managed. In any case, in Indian democracy, as somebody put it, it is not the dog that wags the tail, it is the other way around. Always the minorities call shots!

My sister's questioning:

After the Bombay bomb blasts in 1993, there were riots involving religious conflicts. My sister asked me whether I was for it. I did not know why that pinpointed question was hurled at me, a peace-loving person. Since I was pointing the defects in secularism and saying few things that seemed to me to be odd with minorities, branding me automatically as a person against the communities pained me.

My husband:

He said one day that there was a function in his office. Since all the other officers were coming along with their wives, he asked me to come along. Then he said in a lowered tone, 'Please don't raise minority issues. It won't look nice'. I was annoyed at his advice. That was the time I was young, I thought the realisations I got were gospel truth. Faithfully, I should convey to other people who were ignorant of them by word of mouth and by writing to newspapers, etc. In a multi-religious society where people are expected to live harmoniously, these talks about communities is definitely embarrassing.

But wherever I went to the gatherings and functions, I used to advise my relatives who confined to two children they could have one or two more and why confine to just two. So, I don't feel strange when some BJP leaders make the kind of statements they make.

My colleague's irritable statements (this was in early '90s):

A colleague of mine in school used to say, 'Madam, If the BJP came to power, there would be bomb blasts in the country because the minorities will not keep quiet'. I said, 'Sir, the BJP will not allow such havoc to happen. The Congress is trying to wipe out Hindu religion. It's not recognising our patriotism. We are taken for granted by the party. The BJP is a disciplined party. Moreover, it is saying that it will treat us equally. Instead of giving a chance to it, you are talking ill of it'. I was naïve and innocent at that young age. For me, the BJP was the panacea for all evils in the country.

In day-to-day business, the community feelings have no place. We move on. The problem comes when extra privileges are given in the name of minorities which are denied to the majorities since they have no collective voice.

The egalitarian culture, they have inculcated after enlightenment is slowly eroding in the West. Primordial loyalties are surfacing. World over the scenario is changing. China has become more and more expansionist. It has become another East India company now. With its investments, it's making other smaller nations in South Asia, East Europe, and Africa its clients. China is flexing muscles by stealthily occupying the land and sea. North Korea is posing a threat to the world with intercontinental ballistic missiles and hydrogen bomb. Kim Jong Un's no-holds-barred approach is threatening the world. In this scenario, India has to be cautious of its neighbours, China and Pakistan. For a country to progress and to do trade, internal peace is the prime requisite. The society should be unified, by bringing all communities together to live cohesively.

None of the Hindus per se are against any minority community. But for the appeasement, policy of the Congress, minorities are not the disavowed communities. India requires the minorities' co-operation and understanding for marching ahead. But for the Mahatma's assassination, Hindutva parties would have come to power long ago, i.e. soon after partition of the country. Who would have stopped them when the partition itself had taken place on Hindu-Muslim communal line? Godse was sent to gallows. Gandhiji's ideals (not all, only appeasement) continued with continual erosion of the society. With the initial setback, the Hindutva proponents, introspected within and built the Hindu Society and their political party, brick by brick. Shah Bano case and Ayodhya-temple issue were the boosters to project the pseudo-secularism.

Each successive Congress government tried to ride on appeasement-oriented secularism, nepotism, favouritism, and corruption. In these more than three years-term, I feel happy to see the government at the Centre, working hard for the country with no self-interest.

The government should be for everyone. Hinduism from which Hindutva sprouts is inclusive. I follow the Adwaitha school of thought, in which there are no two entities (i.e no duality). I believe, the other person is 'me' in another form. That is Ekatma bhava of Deendayal Upadhyay. A spiritual thought, of course. Even in mundane life all citizens in a country should be treated equally to get the stated feeling.